Childless
by
Marriage

Also by Sue Fagalde Lick

Shoes Full of Sand
Stories Grandma Never Told
Freelancing for Newspapers
Azorean Dreams
The Iberian Americans
Unleashed in Oregon
Up Beaver Creek
Love or Children?

Childless
by
Marriage

Sue Fagalde Lick

Blue Hydrangea Productions
South Beach, Oregon

ISBN: 978-1-7336852-3-8
Library of Congress Control Number: 2012910297
Classifications: Childlessness—Sue Fagalde Lick—memoir—second marriages—marriage without children—Catholicism—stepchildren—old age without children

Cover design by Erin Seaward-Hiatt
Author photo by Nancy Lynne

Information for resources, websites and email addresses was correct at press time, but may have changed by the time you read this. Visit https://www.childlessbymarriage.com for updated information.

"Alone at the Kitchen Sink" was previously published as "My Imaginary Daughter" in *Still Crazy*, January 2012.

Orders, inquiries and correspondence should be addressed to: Blue Hydrangea Productions, 281 SE 97th Ct., South Beach, OR 97366, (541) 867-4692, sufalick@gmail.com, www.suelick.com.

Dedicated to all those women
who never had children
but love and nurture just the same

Table of Contents

Introduction

Baby Emily is the belle of the baby shower, her coming-out ball with the Valley Chorale. After a concert, we gather in the living room at Sherry and Ken's house to meet the newcomer. The women all want to hold her. June squeals and has to see her "precious little toes." The altos sing "The Stripper" as she peels off Emily's booties.

Nancy, who has four kids of her own, holds the baby with well-practiced arms and smiles as she rocks her from side to side. "I had forgotten how small they are at this age."

Carol, childless like me, flops Emily around awkwardly but bravely. Sitting on the floor on the other side of the room, I'm grateful for my sprained left shoulder. Old enough to be a grandmother, I still don't know how to hold a baby properly. They always cry and try to squirm away.

When Sherry retires to the bedroom to nurse Emily, I join Ken in the dining room. We dated for a while when we were both between marriages. I'm thinking that if we had stayed together, I could be the mommy now. But we were never right for each other.

Although Jenny, his daughter from his first marriage, is about to start college, Ken is thrilled to be a father again.

Over chips and onion dip, we talk about how lucky we both were to find such wonderful second partners.

Lois, mother of two grown children, butts in. "Susie, didn't you want to have kids?"

Ah, the question again.

"Very much," I tell her. "But we can't."

"Why not?" she presses.

I explain how Fred is much older than I am, how he has already raised his children and doesn't want any more. Plus he's had a vasectomy.

Sue Fagalde Lick

Ken says he is 15 years older than Sherry, but he was happy to welcome more children, and he couldn't deny his second wife the chance to be a mother.

What can I say? I mumble about Fred *really* not wanting any more kids. I say God meant it to be this way so I could write and sing, that health problems might have made it hard for me to have a baby. All the while I'm thinking *I got cheated, I was robbed, I should have done something before it was too late.*

U sually when people get married, they produce babies. It's like one plus one equals . . . three. Man plus woman equals baby. But that's not how it worked for me.

Both men I married wanted me, but they didn't want babies. Dogs yes, babies no. Why did I let them make this essential decision for me? Only now that it's too late do I realize that at least half the fault is mine. Somehow children never made it to the top of my to-do list.

Childless by Marriage is about how it happens that a woman might want to be a mother but doesn't become one because her spouse or partner can't or won't give her children. This is not a sociological study, nor is it a how-to book for women struggling to deal with infertility. There are other books that cover those subjects. Call it a precautionary tale about how the lack of children colors every day of a childless woman's life. If only someone had told me these things before I said yes. If only I had known what would happen later.

I don't claim to be objective. Born in 1952, I'm the product of post-WWII suburbia. My father worked as an electrician; my mother was a housewife. Nearly every family on our street in San Jose, California consisted of a working dad, a stay-at-home mom and two kids. Most of us were Catholic. We learned our prayers and studied our catechism lessons every night, and we went to church every Sunday. The language of the church became as much a part of my vocabulary as the Spanish words that dropped naturally into our speech.

I came of age at the peak of the women's movement, devouring every issue of *Ms.* magazine, proudly telling people I was a feminist. From the time I could scribble, I knew I wanted to be a writer. I was a musician, too, singing in every choir, banging away at the piano and

Childless by Marriage

guitar every chance I got.

My parents had trained me to follow my mother's example. Yes, writing and music were fine, as long as they didn't interfere with a woman's primary job: taking care of her home, husband and children. *We're glad you're getting good grades in school, and it's nice that you got your poem published in the district newsletter, but can you bake a cake? Can you hem a skirt? Can you diaper a baby?* TV shows and movies from the 1950s and '60s formed me in the Doris Day mold. Whatever else I might want to do, I would get married and have children.

I assumed I would have my career *and* be a mother. I never dreamed I would get divorced and never doubted that I would have children. I was wrong on both counts.

My first husband didn't want children, but when the marriage ended after six years, I figured I still had time. Then I fell in love with Fred, who already had three children--and a vasectomy. Pushing 50, the last thing he wanted was another baby. But at least we'd have each other for as long as I could imagine. I was wrong about that, too. So here I am now, post-menopausal, alone, and childless.

I am not the only one. The number of American women without children has increased tremendously in the years since I came of age. In 1976, 10 percent of American women over 40 had never had children. By 2008, the U.S. Census Bureau reported that 20 percent of women in the 40 to 44 age group were childless. That means one out of five women now enters menopause without giving birth. More recent figures show that among college-educated women of the baby boomer generation, one-fourth do not have children, even though many of them had always planned to be mothers.

While some of these childless women are infertile and others consciously choose not to have children, growing numbers find themselves in the same position I did, married to men who are unable or unwilling to father their children. We're often second wives whose husbands already have all the children they want. Busy with our careers and thinking that sooner or later we'll find a way to be mothers, we suddenly discover it's too late. Our reproduce-by date has passed.

Or as is noted in Statistics New Zealand, the country's census, childlessness can be a non-decision that occurs as a consequence of

11

Formatted: Centered

Sue Fagalde Lick

other things going on in our lives. "Childlessness is what happens while they are making other plans."

A few years ago, I put out a request for childless women to contact me, and my in-box has been flooded ever since. They have written from all over the United States, as well as Canada, Ireland, France, Germany, New Zealand, India, and the Mariana Islands. They comment on my Childless by Marriage blog, sharing heartbreaking stories that sound all too familiar. I include some of their comments here under first names or pseudonyms to protect their privacy.

Many of these women are married to men who don't want children, and they don't know what to do. Should they leave their husbands or give up their dream of motherhood? It's an impossible choice. They grieve the loss of the children that they might have had and find themselves alone in a world full of mothers. I can only tell them that it's a choice they have to make, that they have to consciously think, pray, and discuss this with people they trust because it will be one of the biggest decisions of their lives. They should not slide into it unconsciously the way I did.

The baby boomer generation to which I belong is the first to choose childlessness in large numbers, due to the advent of reliable birth control, legal abortions, and women pursuing careers outside the home during their most fertile years. Our mothers and grandmothers had far fewer choices. If they could have babies, they did. Now the next generations of women are deciding whether or not to have children and wondering what to do when they want children but their partners don't. I want the world to understand how it is for us, how it happens and how it affects our lives.

Generations ago, it was assumed that lesbians and gay men could not be parents. Today, many gay couples adopt or have children using surrogates or donor sperm. No matter what one's gender or sexual preference, it still comes down to two people agreeing on whether or not to have children.

I don't necessarily see life the same way as other women, especially the post-boomer generations. My working-class Catholic upbringing by parents with old-fashioned European views colors everything. Most of the women I talked to are not religious. Some are gay. Many came from broken homes. I came from the Portuguese-

12

Childless by Marriage

French-German version of "Leave It to Beaver"—except Wally was a girl. But we all have this one thing in common: We have not given birth.

When mothers gather, I feel as if I speak a different language. I'm an alien from a barren planet. But it didn't start out that way. I was a dynamite mother to my Chatty Cathy and Tiny Tears dolls.

Would I have been a good mother? Do stepchildren count? Was I right to give up motherhood for Fred? If I am not a mother, how do I fit in this world? And whose fault is it that my reproductive organs turned out to be as useful as my tonsils? You decide.

All I know for sure is that I chose Fred.

Formatted: Centered

Part 1

He Doesn't Want Children

1
Babies No, Dogs Yes

Fred was the kind of man every parent hopes her daughter will marry--kind, loving, handsome and gainfully employed. My brother Mike, who had worked for him in the San Jose Recreation Department, introduced us. To me, after one failed marriage and several unsuccessful relationships, he seemed like a gift from heaven. It didn't matter that he had three grown children from his first marriage, that he wasn't Catholic, or that he was 15 years older than I was. I had sampled the marketplace and knew he was a keeper.

Our romance progressed quickly from a kitchen conversation at Mike's Christmas party to a romantic proposal in front of the fireplace at Fred's 1930s cottage in Willow Glen. We cooked together, shopped together, explored historic sites and hiked in the woods together. We both loved music, dogs and books, and we couldn't keep our hands off each other. Would I marry him? Of course. He was the nicest person I had ever met, and we fit together as if God had planned it this way.

Fred knew that I was only 31 and still hoping to become a mother. During most of the first year that we dated, he never said anything to discourage those hopes. I knew he had had a vasectomy immediately after his third child was born. I pressed for answers as to why he moved so quickly to have the surgery when it had taken him and his first wife 16 years to conceive. The two older kids were adopted. Was there some weird genetic defect that made him fear another pregnancy now that the tubes were warmed up? No, he said, they just felt that they had enough children.

Then I came along, still waiting for my chance to be a mother.

Sue Fagalde Lick

We talked to my gynecologist about trying to reverse the vasectomy or having artificial insemination. We started collecting information on adoption. Although we had not made any specific plans, children remained on the agenda. Then one night on a camping trip near Yosemite, Fred dropped the bomb.

We were walking along a pine-needle-covered path from our cabin to the amphitheater where some of the other campers were putting on a show. After a hot day, a soft breeze cooled the air. Stellar's jays squawked to each other overhead, and from far away we could hear the voices of children playing ball.

Fred had been quiet for a while. Now he cleared his throat. "I really don't want to have any more children," he said.

My throat went dry. "You don't?"

"Not really. I'm sorry."

I don't know why I didn't stop right there and say something like, "Hey, if you want me, you had better want my children," but I didn't. We just kept walking. Perhaps I had lived so long without kids, they never seemed real to me. Before I met Fred, I had given up on getting married again. As the nerd girl who didn't date until she was in college and then only the losers, perhaps I feared that if I didn't marry Fred, no one else would come along and I'd be alone forever. More likely, knowing that my first reaction to bad news is always denial, I simply assumed he would change his mind.

Still, the news tore a hole in the perfect bubble I had placed around our relationship. I don't remember much about the evening's songs and jokes. All I could think of that night was Fred's announcement. He wanted to be my husband but not the father of my children. Did I love him enough to accept his decision? Would he change his mind in a year or two?

The thing that really hurts is that I did it twice. Fred was not my first husband who didn't want children.

Throughout my six-year marriage to Jim, a Vietnam vet I met at West Valley College, we kept putting children off, wanting to finish school, get better jobs and buy a house before starting our family.

Jim and I were kids ourselves, kids surrounded by other kids. Although I was 22 and he was 25 when we got married, neither one of us was ready to be a parent. I was a late bloomer, an overweight geek

18

who had no social life in high school and was not allowed to stray beyond the boundaries of Fenley Avenue until I got my driver's license at 19. Yes, 19. I was full of book-learning but clueless when it came to real life. Now I was in college, with a new sexy body, long straight hair and mini-skirts, acting as if I knew all about dating, drugs and the world. But I didn't know anything. I pretty much thought I had to marry the first person with whom I had sex. Jim, a boy in a man's body, moseying through school with only a vague idea of what he wanted to do, never actually proposed. He needed to be pushed up every step to the altar, but he went along with it.

We met in our economics class, a horrid class taught by an eccentric German professor who ridiculed us and mispronounced our names. Dr. W. would ramble on about GDPs and ROIs as we sat glassy-eyed, watching our GPAs disintegrate. If a student raised his hand to ask a question, he'd order us to look it up in our textbook. Which he wrote.

After class, Jim and I would sit out on the grass behind the building and talk. We were classmates sharing war stories. Jim was slender, with soft brown hair and brown eyes, long fingers, and chiseled muscles under his cowboy shirts. Raised in Illinois with a father from Texas, he had a tinge of the South in his speech and a laugh like bubbles.

One April day when I needed a ride home, Jim rescued me in his faded blue VW bug. It had green-flowered cloth glued to the ceiling and sides and putted like a tractor.

That was the beginning. We seemed to never run out of things to say to each other, and when we kissed, I melted. I was a virgin then. On our first date, we were going to a party but stopped at his parents' house to pick up a bottle of wine. They weren't home, and we started making out. He kissed my face, my neck, the tops of my breasts above my bra. I could feel excitement building, but when his hand moved up under my skirt, I stopped him. "No. Don't."

"Why?"

"I never—"

"You've never—?"

"No. And I'm not ready."

"Okay. We'll wait as long as you want."

I was relieved, but Jim wasn't going to wait forever. He taught me well, gradually taking me from kissing to heavy petting, mostly in his car or his parents' Chevy Bel-Air with the big bench seat. We often drove up into the foothills above Saratoga to park and make out. The first time he pushed my pants down and kissed me all the way down my stomach to my crotch, I thought I would die of excitement. Neither one of us could wait much longer, and I knew I would lose him if I didn't give in soon.

We didn't go "all the way" at first. By summer, Jim was getting impatient. He kept maneuvering me into position. I kept pushing him away. Finally, on vacation in Southern California, I gave in. I had assured my mother that "nothing would happen." Then we did exactly what I had promised my mother we wouldn't do.

"Are we going to get married?" I pressed that Fourth of July as we cuddled in zipped-together sleeping bags on a friend's floor in Victorville, California.

"Sure. But don't tell anyone yet." That should have been a clue.

Drunk on red wine and believing him when he said I could not get pregnant because he had already ejaculated, I let him put his penis inside me. It hurt. I bled profusely. But I felt I was truly a woman now, and our relationship would last forever.

The next morning, I sneaked out early to buy sanitary napkins. Then Jim and I squeezed into his friend Ivan's truck for a bumpy ride into the desert to do some target-shooting. I was sore and bleeding, but I felt free and alive. Jim was mine.

I was ready to do anything he asked. When he put the heavy pistol in my hands, I squatted in the sand, squinted at the beer cans set up on a rock 50 yards away and fired. My bullet landed off to the right, kicking up a plume of sand. Jim took the gun back and shot down every can.

When I look at photographs of myself taken that next day, I don't see a woman. I see a girl wearing pigtails under a brown suede sombrero from Tijuana. I was just a baby.

It was sheer luck that I didn't conceive a child that night, the first and last time we would have intercourse without birth control before we got married. After that, we were constantly in each other's arms, on the sofa, in the car, on the grass between classes, in the bathroom at his cousin's retirement party. Sometimes we made love in front of the fireplace at his parents' house or in the mountains where we hiked. When we were together, nothing else mattered to me.

Childless by Marriage

While we were dating, Jim was so good with other people's children I assumed that when the time was right, he would make a great father. I should have suspected that he didn't want children by the way he whisked me off to the college birth-control clinic right after that first time. Unlike men I met later who were lackadaisical about birth control, Jim always made sure we used a condom or that I had taken my pill. When I switched to a diaphragm, he encouraged me to put it in. At the time, I thought he was simply protecting my reputation--or guarding himself against the wrath of my father.

Dad, a big man with a big voice, accepted no deviations from his standards of behavior. I had seen him in action too many times. How many other fathers browbeat their 19-year-old daughter's boyfriend, then prohibit him from ever seeing her again—just because she admitted she saw somebody smoking marijuana at a party they attended? In 1871, maybe. But in 1971? That boyfriend, Stan, raced out the door and never came back. Ditto for Antonio, whom I adored, but whom my parents sent away without telling me until much later, when I wondered why he had stopped calling me.

We had plenty of screaming matches where Dad said "No!" to whatever I wanted to do and I ran to my room, crying, "You don't understand!"

Now I know he understood pretty well. He was just being an overprotective parent watching out for his little girl. In a way, his methods worked. My best friend Sherri and I were the only girls on the block who didn't get pregnant in our teens—mostly because we had no social life.

But I was out in the world now. Lucky for both of us, Jim wasn't taking any chances.

That sleeping bag agreement to marriage was as close as we ever came to a formal proposal. It was six months before we announced our engagement, several more months before Jim gave me a ring, and then only because his father insisted the engagement wasn't official without a diamond.

To me, Jim was an older, more experienced man. Now I think: *He was 25. He was a child.* But he had served in Vietnam, had

21

Sue Fagalde Lick

flunked out of one college and enrolled in another, and had a long history of romantic relationships. He could also take apart an engine and put it back together in a couple of hours. He helped me buy my first car, another blue VW bug, and taught me how to drive a stick shift. He loved dogs and all animals. More important, he knew a lot about sex and birth control, and he had the hots for me in my hot pants. I had this green velvet pair of short shorts with a matching vest that gave my mother fits.

Jim's parents nagged him to get married, so he did. But he wasn't ready to settle down. A German Shepherd named Heidi was about all the responsibility he could handle. Actually, he didn't take much responsibility for the dog either. I seem to have been the one walking her, training her and picking up her poop.

The morning of the wedding, Jim had his head under the hood of somebody's car, and his cousin was summoned to drag him to St. Martin's Church. Meanwhile I was throwing up with nerves. Just before we walked down the aisle, I turned to my father. "Were you nervous on your wedding day?"

He looked at me. "No."

"I am."

Just the night before, I had wound up coming home from our rehearsal dinner with my friend Sherri because Jim had gotten too drunk to drive. How could he do this to me, I thought, sitting in the back seat of her car like a child.

Standing on the altar in my homemade wedding dress, everything blurry because I wasn't wearing my glasses, I stood next to Jim and tried not to faint. Neither one of us had been regular churchgoers since childhood, but we had gone through the required marriage preparation, and now a priest we had just met went through the vows and made wisecracks about the challenges of marriage. I paid for organ music, but I never heard it.

When we got married in June 1974, neither one of us had a job, but we stayed at the Hyatt Regency in San Francisco for two nights. We blew the rest of Jim's savings on our three-week honeymoon, riding my brother's VW van up through Oregon and Washington to the Calgary Stampede in Alberta, Canada and back through Glacier and Yellowstone National Parks, finally rolling into Reno to stay with one of Jim's sister's in-laws because we

22

Childless by Marriage

had no money left. We didn't care. We were newlyweds, cruising through the West in our bathing suits, making love in a blue plastic pup tent, chugging over the hills on three cylinders because we couldn't afford to get the van fixed. It was a white van, with "Just married. Honk in Sympathy" spray-painted in blue on the back. Lots of people honked.

After the honeymoon, we lived on my savings--about $1,000-- and Jim's $300 GI Bill checks for the next six months. I had just earned my degree in journalism, but the newspaper where I had expected to work had no openings. Jim was years away from his degree, delayed by the Navy and constantly changing majors. By Christmas, I was stocking shelves at JC Penney and grading high school English papers, thinking, "I went to college for this?" My uncle hired Jim to work as a night-shift security guard at a local shopping center. Jim loved the uniform and the badge and spent $300 on a gun he wasn't allowed to use. I lay awake worrying about him shooting someone.

We lived close to both sets of parents. I hauled the laundry home to Mom and Dad's every Saturday, and we had dinner with Jim's folks every Sunday night. His father often slipped me money, saying, "Don't tell Jim." We were definitely not ready to be parents. We still needed parenting ourselves.

Our home was a townhouse apartment in downtown San Jose, right over the chain link fence from the I-880 freeway, the main north-south thoroughfare between Oakland and Santa Cruz. Our dishes and houseplants rattled constantly with vibrations from the cars and trucks passing by. To the east lay the railroad yards, where trains crashed together day and night. Jets roared overhead every few minutes from the San Jose Airport a few blocks south.

Inside, we had a living room and kitchen downstairs, two bedrooms and a bathroom upstairs, all furnished with hand-me-downs and wedding presents. Everything was coated with dog fur from Heidi and cat fur from the cats Jim kept sneaking in. Our cars were always breaking down, and we could barely afford food. The air was foul, and bums and druggies lived in the apartments next door and across the street. In six years, our apartment and cars were burglarized four times. Living in constant survival mode, we rarely thought about having children. That would come later.

23

Sue Fagalde Lick

Our folks didn't pressure us, although I vaguely remember Jim's mother giving us a teddy bear she had bought for the grandchild she hoped to have someday. Still, rereading my old journals, children were always part of the plan—at least *my* plan. Over and over, I repeated it like a mantra: "I want to quit my job so I can have children and be a freelance writer." Interviewing for a position at the *Palo Alto Times* that first year, I sat there in my gray mini-dress and lied to the editor. When he asked, "What do you want to be doing in five years?" I said, "I want to be an editor on a good-sized publication, maybe a metro daily like the *Times*." I didn't dare tell him I planned to have babies and be a freelance writer.

It was always those two things together, freelancing and babies. Which did I want more, I wonder now. Two years into the marriage, I wrote a description of my dream house. It had a darkroom, office, deluxe master bedroom, a garden and a big yard for lots of pets, but there was no mention of a nursery or rooms for children.

Of course, not having children, I didn't realize how difficult it would be to write and take care of little people simultaneously, at least until they started going to school all day. I think I believed my writing would be like my mother's knitting. I could do a little before breakfast, in the afternoon between laundry and dinner, and at night while the family was watching TV. But writing doesn't work that way, and neither does parenting. If you're on deadline, it's hard to stop to take a child to the orthodontist. If the child gets the flu, you can't leave him to do an interview.

In other words, if you're knitting a sweater and hear your daughter vomiting, you don't finish the row; you throw down the knitting and run. Perhaps having a child would change me, but I have to be honest. I was always the sort of person who would not only want to finish the row but the whole sleeve and would resent being interrupted. In fact, some of the puppy pee stains on my carpet occurred because I kept telling the whining dog, "I'll be there in a minute" and continued to type for considerably more than a minute.

My only knowledge of motherhood came from books, TV shows and movies. Unlike many couples our age, we were not surrounded by friends and relatives having babies. We socialized mostly with my brother and his wife and Jim's sister and her husband, none of whom were talking about children. In fact, all three couples ended up divorcing before any of us got pregnant.

24

Childless by Marriage

A year after we got married, I joined a community choir called the Valley Chorale. Nobody had babies there either. Those few parents who joined soon found they couldn't keep up with the weekly rehearsals and concerts almost every weekend.

My mother and I gave a baby shower for my Aunt Suzanne, who was pregnant with my cousin Rob. I sat on the floor, making a list of all the gifts for her thank-you notes. As we reached the seventh gift, someone handed over the package I had just wrapped that afternoon, a crocheted onesie that would never fit a newborn. A cry rang out. "Susie's gift is the seventh one! She's going to have the next baby."

Everyone laughed and clapped as I sat mortified. "No, no," I said. "Not yet." Having only been married two and a half months, I wasn't even close to ready.

It was all like an extension of school. Jim and I were busy having fun with our friends and building our careers. I attended a few baby showers for pregnant cousins, but didn't worry much that I wasn't pregnant yet. We had forever ahead of us.

There weren't any rug-rats around when I was growing up. When my brother was a baby, I was still in diapers, too. Subsequently, I was the worst babysitter ever. My aunt let me take care of her son Rob once. He screamed the whole time, and she never asked me to babysit again.

The first night I cared for little Shawn and Annette down the street, I had to call my mother in to help. The little guy had cut his finger. Blood all over. Toddler screaming. His sister making it stereo. I couldn't tell whether he had cut his finger off or what. Plus he needed a diaper change, and I had no clue how to do it. My mother cleaned up the tiny cut on Shawn's finger, kissed it, bandaged it, took care of the diaper and soon had both kids calm and happy. Magic.

Then there was the great Jell-O explosion. I don't remember exactly what happened anymore. I think I was typing my homework at the kitchen table. The kids wanted Jell-O, so I said go ahead and help yourself, which you don't do with pre-kindergartners. Next thing I knew, there was red Jell-O on the dark green sofa, on the light green walls, on the beige carpet, on the curtains, on the kids and even on me.

"Oh my God," I gasped, looking around at the destruction. I sank

25

Sue Fagalde Lick

onto the Jell-O-stained carpet, horrified. A real mother would have
changed and bathed the kids and cleaned up the mess with appropriate
cleaners, but I had no idea what to do. Leaving the kids covered in red
goo, I dabbed at the Jell-O on the walls with paper towels, making the
stains worse than they had been. It's amazing that I still got my 75
cents an hour—and was invited back again, with strict instructions not
to give the little ones anything to eat. People assume that by the time
you're 16 you can babysit. Not true. Not if the only babies you have
ever been around were made by Mattel.

Nine months after I married Jim, I was hired by the *Gilroy
Dispatch* to write features and light news. After running
around all day doing stories and photos in the rural
communities of Gilroy and Morgan Hill, then wishing my rickety VW
bug back up the pot-holed highway they called Blood Alley, I was
exhausted. On top of work, I was also taking photography classes
(because I had lied and told them I knew what I was doing in the
darkroom), and I was still singing with the chorale. I had no energy
left for motherhood. Besides, I was sleeping alone.

Jim worked the graveyard shift on his security job. He was also
going to college on the nine-year bachelor's degree plan, flunking
classes, changing majors, and changing schools. For a long stretch, he
was unemployed, and all my relatives decided he was a bum. Then he
started applying for jobs—in the California desert and in Anchorage,
Alaska. By the time I accepted the possibility of moving, he had
changed his mind.

My six-month job at *The Dispatch* led to work at the *Northern
California Retailer*, the California School Employees Association,
and then to the *Milpitas Post*, one of a chain of weeklies where I had
interned. I re-enrolled at San Jose State, hoping to expand my job
possibilities with a second degree in creative arts. I resented the fact
that Jim was still in school when I was the one who was good at it. He
was never home anyway, so why shouldn't I take classes, too?

Two years into the marriage, sweltering in the *Campbell Press*
office where I had been transferred from Milpitas, I wrote, "Every
year I move back the date when I will stop working for other people
and start freelancing and having babies. Jim's college graduation date
moves, too." While I struggled along in the newspaper business, he
insisted that he couldn't work more than part-time, if at all, until he

Childless by Marriage

Childless by Marriage

graduated, and he kept extending his years as a student.

After three years of marriage, on Aug. 18, 1977, I complained, "At 25, I have my degree, but I'm stuck in a horrible job to pay the bills. I want desperately to have a baby and start freelancing, but I can't because Jim is still messing around."

A week later: "We've pretty much decided to wait another year for a baby. Jim wants to go to school another year. We need the time to get our act together anyway. We're beyond broke at this point, and this apartment is no place for a baby. Of course, if I somehow accidentally get pregnant, we'll accept the baby happily."

Working or not, Jim spent his time at home sleeping, stretched out naked on the bed while I took care of everything in our apartment: meals, laundry, cleaning, caring for our dog and cats. I juggled the bills and the budget. There was never enough money. I stretched Christmas cheese-and-sausage boxes for months, with cheese burritos, sausage omelets and zucchini with cheese. Half the time, Jim wasn't home for dinner anyway. Toward the end of the marriage, we took out a loan to pay bills and buy groceries. The money was gone in six weeks, leaving us facing a black hole, with nothing left for another month's rent.

One evening when I was on my way out the door to school, Jim insisted I get on the phone with his mother. "I want you to move in with us," she said. "That way you can save some money and get ahead."

What had Jim been telling her? I couldn't go live with his parents.

"No," I protested. "We have our own family and our own home." Okay, it was two adult humans and two animals, but I assumed children were coming in the near future.

As I hung up, Jim glared at me. "If you won't move to the folks' house, then you'd better get a job that pays a lot more. Otherwise, I'm going."

"You can't be serious." I glanced at the clock. "Oh Jesus, I don't have time for this."

"Figures. Go."

In shock, I grabbed my books, got into my VW Bug and drove to San Jose State. I slid into World Lit ten minutes late, taking the open seat next to a reporter friend. "I think my husband's going to leave

27

Sue Fagalde Lick

me," I whispered.

"God, I'm sorry," he whispered back before we turned our attention to *Oedipus Rex*.

But Jim didn't leave. We squeaked through another month and then another. Eventually he got a part-time job with the U.S. Geological Survey in Menlo Park which eased our finances a little, but between work and school, I rarely saw him anymore.

The marriage wasn't all bad. I have fond memories of hiking, swimming, exploring Death Valley, playing on the beach, and incredible lovemaking, times when it felt like us against the world. But I spent too many nights looking out the window waiting for him to come home, not always knowing where he was. Sometimes he would call after midnight to tell me he had had too much to drink and decided to sleep over. Or a friend needed him to help with something. Or he was just too tired. He did drink too much, but it took me six years to figure out he was also sleeping with other women.

It all felt as if we were playing house, and he wasn't playing it right.

Perhaps the baby showers got to me, or maybe my ovaries were feeling neglected, but I did start thinking more seriously about children. My cousin Marian, whose mother had just died, clasped my hand as she met me in the aisle after the funeral. She was finally pregnant after years of trying. "Susie, don't wait too long. Don't wait until your mother passes away to have a baby." I knew she was right.

But not yet, Jim always said. And indeed it did not seem like the right time. Wait until I have my degree and we have a house, he said. That made sense. When grandparents and nosy aunts wondered aloud when Susie was going to have children, my mother ran interference. "Oh, they're not ready yet." "Yes, of course she wants them." "They will." God bless my mother.

And God bless Jim's mother, who went to her grave without grandchildren. Much as she tried to micro-manage every other aspect of our marriage, she kept her mouth shut about babies.

In 1979, I started babysitting the next door neighbors' infant. Remembering my previous babysitting failures, I hesitated to take on this tiny diapered screaming machine, but I hoped Jim would help. Wrong. When I brought the crying baby back to our apartment, he instantly raised a fuss. "Shut her up. I can't stand that noise."

"I'm trying. She's just a baby. Maybe she's hungry."

28

"Well, I don't want her here." He sniffed. "God, she stinks." He lit a cigarette, grabbed his keys, and walked out the front door while I stared into the infant's red face. If he couldn't stand this one, who was only here for a couple of hours, how would he handle a baby of our own?

When they got home, I told the neighbors I was sorry but I didn't have time to take care of their baby anymore.

Shortly after that, I thought I might be pregnant: late period, fat belly, nausea, weariness, all the symptoms I had seen on TV. Jim was not happy. "If you're pregnant, I'm leaving," he said.

Surely he didn't mean it, I thought, but I'll never know because my period started a few days later. We continued to use the diaphragm. In the early years, we had occasionally used condoms on camping trips and wilderness outings, but now we rarely went anywhere together.

By 1980, it was over. After returning from a geology trip, Jim told me he wasn't sure he could stay married to me. It was January. I had spent most of the holidays alone. Now here he was in his red plaid shirt and faded jeans, smelling of cigarettes and campfires, his beard scratchy. I had waited by the window for hours and jumped up to greet him. But he was cool, setting his backpack by the door, hitting the fridge for a beer, seemingly unwilling to sit down.

"Well, how was it?" I asked.

He shrugged. "Fine."

"I missed you."

Silence. He swigged his beer, lit a cigarette and blew out the smoke, then cleared his throat. "I've been thinking a lot. I'm not sure I can stay in this marriage."

I was stunned. "What? Why?"

"I-I feel trapped."

As his words hit home, I began to cry. I became hysterical. I screamed and sobbed, not caring that it was late and the neighbors could hear. "I don't want a divorce," I said. We were both Catholic, but beyond that, I still loved him and wanted the marriage to last forever. "If we have to live apart, okay, but I want to stay married."

He comforted me until I quieted down, and we went to bed

together as usual, but he didn't take back what he had said.

We didn't break up right then. We went on, working, going to school, and visiting our parents or our siblings on weekends. Jim disappeared for days at a time. I went off on my own, too. I spent a week in Monterey without him, traveled weekends with the chorale and stayed up late covering city council or taking classes. Sometimes we were as friendly as ever. Other times we barely spoke to each other. Many nights I slept downstairs on the bony sofa bed with the dog and cat while Jim occupied the bedroom. On our last anniversary together, over burritos at La Paloma, we speculated about what it would be like if we split up. I could take a better job somewhere else. I could have my own apartment. Jim could go exploring wherever he wanted to . . .

Having never been on my own, the possibility appealed to me, especially with our marriage going sour. But to never have children? To be alone for the next 40, 50, or 60 years? That was hard to face.

Meanwhile I was ridiculously busy. Jim complained that I never had time for him, and he was right. I was writing poetry, going to school, singing in the Valley Chorale, working for the newspaper, and trying to take care of everything at home. "Busy, busy, busy," he chanted.

Finally, six years and two weeks after we were married, I figured out that Jim had a girlfriend. It was the Saturday of Fourth of July weekend. She was his carpool partner, but why was she calling now? Jim had finally graduated from Hayward State the month before, and he wasn't working that weekend. Then I heard something in his voice, that soft, teasing way people speak to their lovers, and I realized "Kate" was more than a carpool buddy.

When he hung up, I asked the question: "Are you sleeping with her?"

He shrugged and nodded.

"Does she know you're married?"

He cleared his throat. "No."

"Oh my God."

The pieces fell into place. He had dated other women, letting his college friends think he was single. He told them I was his sister. I had no idea.

We sat facing each other on the dog-torn and fur-covered sofa. "Well, that's it. We can't stay married," I said.

30

Childless by Marriage

"I guess not."

Finally we agreed on something. But we didn't have much time to talk about it. I was due downtown to cover the big holiday celebration for the *San Jose Sun*. I grabbed my notebook and camera and left. Busy, busy, busy.

I moved back to my parents' house. My brother and my friend Ken from the chorale moved my stuff out in Ken's van as the cat sat yowling in a cage back in the apartment. The bedroom furniture had come from my room at home, so I took it back, leaving Jim's clothes and a pile of blankets on the floor. Jim moved back to his parents' house two weeks later. We were so broke at that point that we could not have paid another month's rent.

My mother was sad, and my dad was ready to kill my soon-to-be ex. Jim's parents begged us to stay together, but Jim and I both knew the marriage was dead and probably should never have happened in the first place. Breaking up was the first thing we had felt good about doing together in a long time.

2
Finding Prince Charming

The girl who never dated in high school made up for lost time between marriages.

There were guys, there was sex, and there was always birth control. I fell into a three-year relationship with a man who was everything Jim was not. TJ was red-haired, bearded and big. He hated nature, but loved music, art and books. Frighteningly intelligent, he ran on high speed 24 hours a day, sometimes making me laugh, other times scaring me with his intensity.

Occasionally he was cruel, rough in bed, belittling in the things he said to me, but I convinced myself that this, not my ex-husband, was finally the love of my life.

Now working at a newspaper near San Francisco, I drove 50 miles down the 280 freeway most Friday nights to spend the weekends with TJ in his apartment. During the week, he called at all hours of the night and showed up at my office on deadline demanding my attention. He never got enough sex; I never got enough sleep. If I said "no," he told me I didn't love him enough and threatened to break up with me. Yes, I know I should have told him, "Fine, get lost," but I was "in love." Any woman who has loved an abusive man knows how tangled the ties between her and the man become, especially when her self-esteem has been ground down by a recent divorce.

We argued over birth control. Unlike Jim, who shied away from children, TJ already had two sons from his first marriage. Now, although technically he was still married, refusing to get a divorce for fear of the financial consequences, he pushed for a permanent relationship and urged me to stop using my diaphragm. In the middle of making love, he would whisper in my ear, his beard soft against my cheek, "Take that thing out. Let me fill you with my sperm" or "I think someday you're going to have my baby."

"I hope so," I would whisper.

I wanted it. I knew better, but because all too often he pinned me to the sheets and wouldn't let me sprint to the bathroom for my diaphragm, I bought a book on the Fertility Awareness Method (also known as the rhythm method) and started charting my temperature and vaginal discharges every morning. On those days when it seemed safe, I took a chance, then sweat through the days until my period started. TJ's voice was like the voice of the devil whispering in my ear: "I'll give you all the babies you want, but in exchange you will be completely mine."

If I were to become pregnant, I would lose my career, be drummed out of the church where I had started leading the congregational singing on Sunday mornings and devastate my parents, who had always made it clear that my life would be ruined if I got pregnant without being married. I would be trapped in that apartment with the baby and a Dr. Jekyll-Mr. Hyde partner who had no boundaries.

Where I couldn't save myself, circumstances—or God—saved me. On July 4th, (yes, again on the Fourth of July), TJ dumped me, saying I was too stubborn and selfish for him. His sons were visiting from Montana that weekend, two little blonde boys, ages 6 and 8, with huge blue eyes and freckles. We had gotten along wonderfully. The kids made me feel for the first time what it must be like to be a mother. It was easy to love them, to watch them playing and feel proud that they were so good-looking and bright, to see them with their father in a tender moment, to play my guitar and sing and catch them singing along in their tuneless little voices.

But it wasn't to be.

The fight began over a pie. I had bought an apple pie, but TJ wanted peach. Out of money, with a car that threatened to die at any minute, I refused to go buy another pie.

"You're selfish," he said. "You don't love me enough to buy me a peach pie."

33

"I thought you'd like apple. Everybody likes apple pie. I don't have any more money."

"You don't love me."

It was a song I had heard many times before. I stopped listening and cooked dinner for us and the kids. But I underestimated his anger this time.

As I headed for the coffee table with my plate, he grabbed it out of my hand and dumped it on the floor. I can still see the pieces of chicken, peas and rice embedded in the gold shag carpet.

"Go get me a peach pie!"

"No!" I began to cry as I got down on my knees to pick up the food.

"Leave it."

As their father and I screamed at each other, the boys sat side by side on the couch. The older one hollered, "Stop it. Please, stop it!"

TJ finally held the door open for me. "You'd better go."

I took one last tearful look at the boys who might have been my stepsons and stumbled out. The fireworks from the nearby Great America amusement park flashed overhead as I drove out of the apartment complex for the last time and headed for the freeway home, crying so hard I could barely control the car.

The breakup put me into such a funk that I couldn't work, couldn't eat, couldn't sleep. I drank too much and felt too sick that Monday morning to go to work. I asked to have my notes sent to my apartment so I could finish the stories that were due that day. But I just stared at them, unable to write a word. The editor put the paper together without my articles.

I struggled through the next few weeks, so down I feared I'd never smile again. Finally, I closed myself up in the file room and called San Mateo County Mental Health. "I need help," I told the person who answered the phone. "I'm so depressed I don't know what to do." She gave me an appointment for later that week.

Face to face with the sweet woman who did my initial interview, I saw clearly for the first time that I had been mistreated and didn't deserve it. Without taking time to deal with my divorce, I had jumped straight into an abusive relationship that destroyed my self-esteem.

Childless by Marriage

Meeting weekly with a kind psychologist who took the time to listen and help me make sense of the previous years, I began to accept my losses and move on.

I had other relationships, but none of them worked out. By the time I met Fred at a Christmas party at my brother's house, I had begun to think I should get used to being alone. I had come to the party with my parents. But there he was standing by the refrigerator in Mike's kitchen, kind, good-looking and interested. A supervisor in the San Jose Recreation Department, he had been Mike's boss, and they were good friends. It felt so easy to talk to him.

As we left that night, Fred asked if he could call me. "That would be nice," I said.

For years after, my mother would tell people she knew then that Fred was the guy for me.

On our first date, dinner followed by videos at Fred's house, we fell in love. Like Cinderella, I had found my handsome prince.

I joke sometimes that I finally got the cute football player. Fred played in high school and college. But it was more than that. He was warm and gentle, with kind brown eyes, a thick beard, woolly sweaters and corduroy pants. He was smart, funny and interesting, and he loved me. It would be six more months before he proposed, but we both knew from the beginning that we would eventually get married.

Fred already had three children. Michael was seven, about the age my child would have been if I'd had one with Jim. Gretchen and Ted were already teenagers, too old to be mine. Getting to know them would be more of an adventure than I ever imagined, but when Fred and I were dating, we rarely saw the kids. We focused all of our attention on each other.

Despite Fred's declaration in the woods, I honestly believed that somehow I would still have children. But how did I expect that to happen? Immaculate conception? One stubborn sperm that survived the vasectomy? I was 50 before I could say, "I am never going to be a mother" and mean it. I have asked dozens of childless women if they could say it out loud. Most had no problem with it. But just as I delude myself that I can lose weight while eating muffins for

35

breakfast every morning, I held on to the idea that I might still have a baby.

Looking back, I have to wonder why I wasn't more insistent on having a child. Was it that I felt lucky just to get Fred? Was I too insecure to speak up for my own needs? Was it, as my friend Carol suggests, that deep down I didn't really want children? Otherwise, why didn't I plant my size 9 feet firmly on the floor and say, "Hey, buddy, if you want me, we're going to have a baby"?

Here's another frightening thought. Perhaps I married myself a daddy so I could stay a perpetual child, responsible only for my own needs. As much as it makes me squirm, let's consider the possibility. I had been through some tough times: bad first marriage, bad relationships in-between, bad jobs, depression, never enough money, and parents who loved me but seemed to see my writing and music as wastes of time. Firm believers in the sink-or-swim method of parenting, they offered no help in those years when I couldn't pay my bills and found myself at the grocery store deciding between milk and crackers.

The Christmas I met Fred, I was once again in a financial fix. I had quit my newspaper job and given up my apartment two months earlier to sing with a traveling show that should have made me rich. Instead, the show went bankrupt; we never got out of California. Now I was doing temporary office work, singing a few gigs with an accordion-playing friend, and living with my parents again. Since the TJ breakup, I was also alone. In short, I was miserable.

Along came Fred, mature, successful, responsible, and huggy-bear handsome. He had recently separated from his first wife. He loved me, loved my music, loved that I was a writer. He bought me gifts, took me on expensive vacations, and treated me like a princess. In some ways, he was everything a girl wants in a father, plus I could have sex with him. God, did I just say that? Okay, it's a little bit true. I needed someone to take care of me, and I knew that he would. But it wasn't just that. I loved him, and in those early years when I was in my 30s and he was in his 40s, the age difference didn't matter.

Was I looking for a father for my children or a father for me? When Fred proposed as we lay on the braided rug in front of his fireplace, what did I say after I agreed to marry him, after I cried and got mascara all over his white shirt? Did I say, "Now we can raise a family?" No. As we were still holding each other in the afterglow of becoming engaged, I said, "Now I can freelance." With Jim, the dream had always been to stay home and work as a freelance writer while raising our children. This time, I didn't mention children.

Fred let go of me and stepped backward, a stricken look on his face. He had assumed I would keep working full-time and share the financial burdens. "Um, uh, I don't know," he responded.

At least he didn't take back his proposal. Instead, he grabbed some champagne and we went to tell my parents the good news. They were sitting in the patio when we arrived, bubbling with excitement. My parents not only approved; Dad cried.

That was June 22, which happened to be the anniversary of my wedding with Jim, not that Fred had any idea. In setting a date, we wanted some time to plan. We also needed to get past the holidays and tax season. Fred had been doing people's taxes for years to supplement his income from the city. We chose May 18.

It wasn't long before we moved in together. I had finally managed to get another newspaper job, at a trade paper called *Computer Systems News*. I rented an apartment in my parents' neighborhood, but I was barely making enough money to pay the rent. Meanwhile, Fred's landlord had decided to sell the house he lived in, and he had to move. We were already engaged; it made sense to live together. My father found the house for rent on Ardis Avenue, the next block over from where I grew up. The same age and style as my parents' house, it immediately felt like home. With our wedding preparations well underway, we U-Hauled our stuff to the house and settled in.

Having done the traditional nuptials with our exes, we refused to be bound by convention. Unable to find a Catholic priest who would marry us in the church, we asked Fred's retired Methodist minister friend Carl Stocking to perform the ceremony, and we sought places in the San Jose area that would be different from the usual wedding sites. San Jose State, where we had both gone to school at the same time but never met? The Rose Garden? Vasona Lake? One of the many wineries Fred frequented?

37

Sue Fagalde Lick

We wound up at Evergreen Community College, where our friends and family gathered in an amphitheater beside a pond on a warm sunny day. Refusing to be hot and uncomfortable in traditional garb, I wore an embroidered dress from Mexico and a crown of flowers on my short curly hair while Fred and his groomsmen, my brother Mike and our friend Dave, wore Mexican wedding shirts. My friends Sandy and Sherri wore short burgundy dresses they had made from cloth and patterns we picked out at House of Fabrics.

A cassette tape of our favorite songs played as we prepared to walk down the path to Pachelbel's cannon. Then, as ducks quacked from the nearby pond, Fred and I held hands and promised to love and honor each other for the rest of our lives. Unlike my first wedding, where I feared I would throw up or faint before the ceremony was over, I felt nothing but happiness flooding through me as we exchanged rings designed by an artist we had met at an art and wine festival.

I didn't realize it at the time, but this ceremony was missing one of the vows I had exchanged with Jim at St. Martin's. In the Catholic ceremony, couples promise to welcome children and raise them in the Catholic faith. At my first wedding, one of us might have been lying, but we both said we would. When Fred and I got married, our vows said nothing about children. But we were so happy it didn't feel like anything was missing.

We held the reception in our back yard. Fred and my brother had borrowed recreation department tables and chairs and put up rented blue plastic canopies. Fred had bought me a piano for a wedding present, and now we rolled it out to the patio, where local piano-bar favorite Scotty Wright played all afternoon. Our friend Pat Silva prepared a Portuguese feast of pork stew, sweet bread, salad, fresh strawberries and, of course, plenty of wine. The cake was chocolate.

What about Fred's children, one might ask. Some couples include their children from previous marriages in the wedding ceremony. We didn't. It honestly never occurred to us. Michael, Fred's youngest, was now living with his mother in Austin, Texas. Fred's teenagers, Gretchen and Ted, attended the wedding simply as guests. If they were quietly seething over the marriage or being left out, I never heard about it. We were too wrapped up in the joy of our

38

Childless by Marriage

do-it-yourself wedding.

There was no tossing of garters or bouquets, just a wonderful party at which we stayed until only the Silvas, my parents and my brother and his wife remained. As dusk settled over San Jose, Fred and I changed our clothes, loaded our suitcases into the car and headed to the coast for the first leg of our honeymoon. We were going to San Diego, with stops at Hearst Castle, Universal Studios, and his parents' house in Burbank.

Unlike Jim's and my romp through the west in a painted-up VW van, we traveled like grownups in an unmarked Honda Accord, staying in bed-and-breakfast inns and posh hotels, each stop carefully planned. When I left on the honeymoon with Jim, I was also leaving the home where I had lived my entire life with my parents. Everything was exciting and new. On our wedding day, Fred and I woke up together in the house we had shared for nine months, amid the remnants of our at-home ravioli rehearsal dinner. My period was raging, cramps and all. When we fell into bed hours later at an elegant B and B in Pacific Grove, we did not have sex. Exhausted, we simply went to sleep in each other's arms.

But the romance was there and never faltered. Twenty-five years later, when other couples seemed to do nothing but pick at each other, we were still holding hands like newlyweds. Did not having children together have anything to do with it? Maybe. I believe we shared the kind of love that few people find. The honeymoon never ended.

Despite our difference in ages, we had so much in common. We were both left-handed, came from working-class California families, loved to read, and loved music so much we often burst into song in the car or while cleaning house. We both cried over movies and loved to wander through antique stores. We also couldn't keep our hands off each other.

It wasn't perfect, but it was darned good.

The first two years of our marriage, I freelanced a little on the side while I bounced from one job to another. From *Computer Systems News*, I moved to The *Hayward Daily Review*, where I worked swing shift in a windowless basement as a copyeditor. When the paper was sold to a bigger company, I was among the 20

Sue Fagalde Lick

editorial employees who lost their jobs. I went to work at a trade paper called the *Corporate Times*, which folded after a few months. Then I became editor of the *Advocate Journal*, a newspaper sponsored by the Santa Clara County Bar Association, which was sold six months later to our competitors. I moved downtown to work for the new owners, but it was clear they were phasing my paper out of business.

Meanwhile, Fred and I had purchased a doublewide mobile home in southeast San Jose, confident that it would go up in value. It was located in an upscale park called Chateau La Salle, with a guard at the gate, manicured lawns and a clubhouse that looked like a castle. Fred had sacrificed his half of the house he owned with his first wife to keep his retirement. Under California law, she would otherwise have been entitled to half of his retirement income from the city. Now he was anxious to re-stabilize his finances and buy another house. We expected to sell the mobile home at a profit and buy a house in five years.

The newspaper business was never easy, and I still wanted to freelance. On our second anniversary, in May 1987, we were cruising on the Delta Queen steamboat as it docked under the arch at St. Louis, Missouri. Fred had grabbed a chance to lead a group of seniors from San Jose on a "Four Rivers" tour and bring me along as his assistant. The calliope was playing, I was floating on champagne from the farewell dinner, and I felt as if the world had been revealed to me during our week on the Mississippi River. It was time to quit my job and write. At that point, I had a contract to compile a guide for newcomers to San Jose. I also had regular article assignments for several newspapers. Fred's job supervising community centers and senior centers for the city of San Jose was solid. It made sense, even if I was tipsy when I made the decision. I went home and quit the *Advocate Journal.*

Having heard my constant complaints about the job, Fred approved. If he had qualms about my lack of a monthly paycheck, he didn't mention them.

Lacking money for tuition, I had had to drop out of school when Jim and I split. Now I re-enrolled, this time seeking a master's degree in English. As I continued to write freelance articles, I was also

40

singing, volunteering at the San Jose Historical Museum, and spending hours enjoying Chateau La Salle's pool, spa and gym. I didn't have children, but Michael visited during holidays and summer vacations, and we saw Fred's older kids occasionally. Busy as we were, that was enough.

F our years into our marriage, 11-year-old Michael hadn't even unpacked his suitcase when he asked the question that threw our lives into a tizzy. We were sitting at the dining room table after lunch, making plans to go cut down a Christmas tree. Behind his thick-lensed glasses, Michael's brown eyes were huge.

"I have to ask you guys something."

"Sure. What?" his father said.

"Can I come live with you?"

Gulp. While Fred sat speechless, studying the lace tablecloth, I jumped in. "Have you talked to your mother about this?" Surely, a quick call to Annette would end this discussion. What mother would let her son go?

"Yes, it's okay with her."

Sweet Lord.

We telephoned Austin and learned that Annette was in on the plan. Michael was about to enter middle school, and the institution he would be attending had a reputation for gang fights and ineffective teachers. She may also have wanted to defuse the conflicts between Michael and her boyfriend's kids, but the official reason was that he would be better off in San Jose.

I had watched Fred weep as we drove away from the airport every time we dropped his son off at the end of his visits. I had enjoyed having Michael around for holidays and summer vacations. He was cute, sweet, smart, funny, and good-hearted—a little Fred.

My friend Carol says she faced the same situation with her second husband. His 12-year-old son wanted to come live with them. "Sure, he can move in," she declared. "But I'll be moving out." The son stayed with his mother.

I never considered saying no.

"You're less selfish than me," Carol says.

Maybe. Or more selfish. Here was my chance to be a mother.

41

If Michael moved in, we couldn't stay in the mobile home. In those days, Chateau La Salle did not allow children. Plus, the nearby schools were every bit as bad as the ones he would have attended in Austin. So we had to move before Michael came back in September.

Contrary to our expectations, prices on mobile homes had gone down instead of up. It took months to get one offer, and the potential buyers found thousands of dollars worth of needed repairs: dry rot, substandard shower stalls, leaky windows, and more. We wound up borrowing money to get out of the mobile home. Instead of earning a down payment on a house, we lost $12,000.

We rented a house up against the south San Jose foothills. Moving into a suburban neighborhood full of young families, we paid our $1,200 a month and tried to save a little here and there. I was fully committed to freelancing, not even considering looking for a job, and now I had a live-in son. It seemed that I had finally realized my dream of being a stay-at-home mother-writer.

In January 1989, my book money ran out, and my two main article clients both went bust. Our expenses had gone up. Fred was the kind of guy who liked to stay out of debt and have a comfortable cash cushion in savings. A barely employed freelance writer wife did not add much to the bank account.

By March, Fred had begun suggesting that I get a job. I wanted to stay home and write books. Over the years, we have rarely fought, but I held my ground this time. I had been working as hard as I could to earn money with my writing, plus I was helping to raise his son without being able to have my own children. After many more years of the ups and downs of the writing business, including a couple more full-time jobs, the memory is blurry now. But back then I was very clear about it in my journal. "If I don't get babies, I'm damn well going to get books."

So I continued to freelance, and I did not have a baby with Fred. Michael was almost 12 and fairly independent when he moved in. I could work all day while he was at school. After the first bumpy months before he made new friends, he was usually busy with his buddies after school.

But I was the one who met with Michael's teachers, took him to the doctor, bought his school clothes, forced him to wear a helmet

42

when he rode his bike, made him try to eat vegetables and helped him carry his plaster of Paris model of Brazil to school.

Although it would have been much more difficult if I'd had a baby, it was still a challenge juggling work, grad school, and step-motherhood. Many nights, I'd be cooking and working at the same time, literally running back and forth between the stove and the computer, usually with a gaggle of teenage boys parading through, a fax coming in and a husband wondering when dinner would be ready.

In 1990, I dropped out of my master's degree program because I couldn't handle it all. But in some ways, parenting remained a sideline. At Michael's junior high graduation, I did double duty, rarely occupying my seat in the parents' section because I was taking pictures for the *South Valley Times*. I was also a regular contributor to *Bay Area Parent*, gleaning story ideas from my experiences with Michael. He won't eat vegetables? I did an article on it. He's color blind? Another article. I just didn't tell the people I interviewed that I had never had children of my own.

To be honest, I don't see how I could have fit babies into my life. I was perpetually busy writing, singing, going to school, and volunteering at church, the San Jose historical museum, and California Writers Club. I went off to music camps and writers' conferences, stayed up late covering city council, and spent hours practicing piano and guitar. I was still busy, busy, busy.

In 1990, my first real book, *The Iberian Americans*, came out. A slender hardbound title that described the experiences of Portuguese, Spanish and Basque immigrants, it bore my name in big letters on the front and on the spine.

My father opened the title page and read "Sue Fagalde."

"Lick," I added softly, reminding him that I was Mrs. Lick now.

Mom, who loved books, was overjoyed. I don't think a baby would have made her any happier. She planned to show the book to everyone she knew. Dad wanted to put a banner on his car and announce the news about my book over the CB radio. They crushed my earrings and glasses hugging me. They called me "author" and predicted I'd be famous any minute. It was all so sweet, like reaching the top of a mountain I'd been trying to climb for 38 years. It may be

43

that all I ever wanted was that total recognition from Mom and Dad.

You see, there's this status thing about having babies. The ultimate success. I had books instead. At least they both start with the letter B.

3
Beyond Happily Ever After

The time in which a woman can bear children is short compared to the full span of a long life. While physically able in our early teens, most of us wait until our 20s to even think about getting pregnant. By our 40s, our chances are quickly fading away. Yes, adoption and infertility treatments can expand the window a bit, but if your mate doesn't want to have children with you, the result is the same. You spend the rest of your life as a childless woman.

As we moved into the 1990s and my 40th birthday loomed, our lives had fallen into a pattern. Each morning, Fred went off to work at the recreation department, Michael went to school, and I went to my bedroom office. I was freelancing for several local newspapers, going out for interviews, coming home to write my stories. I had also started another book, this one about Portuguese-American women.

Still busy, busy, busy, I moved up the ranks of the California Writers Club to president of the Silicon Valley branch and a member of the state board. After a few years off between marriages, I was singing in the Valley Chorale again, with Fred as a beloved groupie. I was also doing some singer-songwriter gigs on my own, dragging Fred and Michael to various coffeehouses and festivals. Fred was my roadie and my biggest fan, carrying my gear, singing along from the audience, and telling everyone how great I was.

I volunteered at the San Jose Historical museum, where I put on white gloves and catalogued musty sheet music in the archives. Fred and I both donned costumes for the annual Victorian Christmas and Living History Days celebrations. I'd sit on a bench in the old firehouse singing and playing my guitar. The notes rang off the concrete floor as visitors inspected 100-year-old fire trucks and Fred passed out my business cards.

I had also joined the choir at St. Julie's church. Uncomfortable with the church's views on divorce and remarriage, I had been an off-and-on Catholic for several years. One Sunday, the sermon spoke to

Sue Fagalde Lick

me, and I felt Jesus calling me back. With Fred a non-practicing Protestant and Michael knowing no religion at all, I started going to Mass every week alone. I was the only adult in the choir who didn't have a spouse and children coming to Mass with them. The other singers absorbed me into their families.

After three years renting the house we had moved into so that Michael could live with us, we bought a three-bedroom house nearby on Safari Drive. It wasn't the best house in the world. The elderly owner had let it go for years. What wasn't broken was filthy or just plain ugly. Water had leaked under the bathroom floors so we had to replace them. Pink wallpaper clashed with puke-green linoleum in the kitchen, and brownish colonial-patterned wallpaper lined the hallways. Faded squares on the peach-colored living room walls showed where the previous owner had hung her pictures.

With Fred's blessing to do whatever I wanted, I threw my self into home decorating, tearing off the old, painting on the new. With each wall or door I painted, the house became more mine. TJ used to say that I had "straw in my teeth." He was right. I loved feathering my nest.

Our new home did have its good qualities. Someone had removed the wall between the master bedroom and the bedroom next to it, so we had a huge bedroom suite with space to lounge in. I painted the bedroom "pond lily" yellow. The carpet was turquoise. For my birthday, Fred took me to the outlet stores in Gilroy and we bought a flowered comforter that included both colors.

I made the master bathroom white with cornflower blue tile, and Michael's bathroom white with sea-green tile. I had fun prowling home-décor stores and climbing on top of our bathroom counters to putty and paint.

Michael's room turned into a dark nest, with the blinds usually closed, the bed unmade and clothes piled on the floor. It was his space to do what he wanted.

Fred converted the den into his office, setting up his rolltop desk, file cabinets, bookshelves, and copier just beyond the kitchen.

The tiny extra bedroom became my office. The day after we moved in, I was standing in the middle of my furniture and piles of boxes wondering how on earth I would make everything fit when the

46

phone rang. First I had to find the phone; then I had to find paper and a pen because an editor had an assignment for me. Could I do it right away? Oh sure, no problem, I said, so boxed in by file cabinets and desks I had to climb over a pile of boxes to get out of the room.

It all came together somehow, a cozy little home I could have lived in forever. My office looked out on the patio, where a slatted roof filtered the sunlight onto a worn barbecue table, a brick barbecue pit, and a riot of orange poppies. Beyond the patio, roses of all different shades of red, purple and pink ringed a lush lawn with a sturdy oak tree with a wooden swing.

Fred and I both loved roaming the aisles of antique stores. While still in the mobile home, we had purchased a 1920s table and chairs. Fred had already bought an old cabinet-style radio and a handsome mahogany nightstand.

Driving down Minnesota Avenue one Sunday, I noticed a yard sale outside an antique shop in an old mansion and pulled over. As I walked up the driveway, I immediately fixed on an odd-shaped chair.

"That's a Morris Chair," said the white-haired man who ran the shop. "They recline, like this." He pushed the back of the chair forward then let it fall back. "Have a seat," he said, pushing the seat back up.

I sat, feeling the cream-colored cushions embrace me, resting my hands on the smooth wooden arms.

"Nice, huh? I'll give it to you for $200."

"Hmm." I loved it, but I needed to get Fred's opinion. "Let me go get my husband and see what he thinks."

A half hour later, the old man followed us home with the chair in his rusty truck. Researching Morris chairs for a story later, I discovered $200 was a steal. But we would soon do even better.

One of Fred's tax clients was cleaning out her mother's house and had no more use for her old-fashioned china cabinet. She called us to her house one day to see it. Mahogany with three drawers and three glassed-in shelves, it was the perfect place to display my growing collection of ruby Depression glass, along with my grandmother's silver tea set and the bride and groom that had sat atop both my grandparents' and our own wedding cakes. She gave it to us for free, along with a 1940s loveseat.

47

Sue Fagalde Lick

As the house took shape, traffic whooshed by on Santa Teresa Boulevard just beyond the fence. Car brakes screeched at the nearby stoplight. The roar never ceased, and exhaust fumes soaked the air, especially on weekday mornings and afternoons when students and their parents arrived and left from the high school across the street. We often sat in our back yard, enjoying the sun, but it was hard to breathe and hard to hear. Again in the flight-path from San Jose's international airport, we had to pause in our conversations when planes flew over.

Still, it was home.

A family of gang members lived next door. The sons, who wore their jeans halfway off their butts, spent all day on their cell phones and were in and out all night. When the neighbors' Christmas decorations disappeared, they were traced to that house. When someone shattered my car window with a BB gun, I knew where to find the culprits.

Many fine families with limited means lived in the neighborhood, but dry weeds poked up everywhere, and every flat surface bore the marks of gang graffiti. You made sure you kept your doors locked

In addition to the roses and quirky décor, the house on Safari came with a new family member. The former owner, Georgia, was moving into a senior residence where she couldn't have pets, so she asked if we would take Lady, her aged calico cat. We were delighted to adopt this sweet, petite cat who was no trouble because her old knees wouldn't let her jump anywhere she wasn't supposed to go. She quickly accepted us as her family. Holding her, she felt like a baby in my arms.

Life was good. When I needed a break, I hiked in the nearby foothills, sitting high above the valley, letting my mind wander as I watched the tiny cars on distant Highway 101 and picked out the landmarks of our lives: our house, the church, Michael's school, Kaiser Hospital.

I was writing a lot, playing a lot of music, mothering Michael, and enjoying a growing circle of friends.

We traveled often. Each summer, flush with tax money, Fred and I would head to the mountain town of Murphys or venture farther to

48

spend a week in Fred's parents' timeshare in Waikiki while Michael
visited his mother. We started going to Oregon every few years,
usually to Bandon, sometimes a little farther up the coast. We loved
the quirky beach towns, the friendly people, and the lack of crowds.
Staying in the funky paneled rooms at the Sunset Motel or at a bed
and breakfast on the spit, we drove and walked for hours exploring.
We celebrated our anniversaries in white-tablecloth restaurants where
we promised to spend another year together, got tipsy on champagne
and fed each other bites of chocolate cake.

At an antique store in Bandon one Fourth of July, I was drawn to
a display on a table with a big ruby pitcher and seven ruby glasses.
The owner had arranged flags and red, white and blue balloons in the
pitcher and set it all on a blue scarf. I called Fred over to look,
assuming this was not something I could actually buy.

"Do you want it?" Fred asked.

"Well sure, but . . ."

"Then let's get it." As the woman took apart her display and
wrapped each piece in thick paper, I couldn't believe we were really
doing this. It was expensive, a luxury, nearly a hundred dollars.
Nobody in my life had ever bought anything just because they wanted
it. But that's the way Fred was: "Do you want it?"

It was like those Disney movies I watched as a kid. If you really
wanted something bad enough, you could have it (except for babies).
I had never experienced that before. Well, yes, I got a bicycle one
Christmas and I got dolls I really wanted. But with most of my
requests, my mom laughed and said, "Yeah and I'd like a Cadillac."
Dad would remind me that I was lucky I had shoes. This handsome
husband of mine did it so many times: piano, electronic keyboard,
ruby glass, paintings, jewelry. Do you want it . . .?

He did the same thing for himself, sometimes spending alarming
sums on new stereos, a bike or some other luxury, but never to the
point that it caused us any problems. I was so used to doing without,
but Fred believed in possibilities, not impossibilities. His cup was
always half full, and he could always get more.

49

Sue Fagalde Lick

As so many Californians did in the '80s and '90s, we dreamed of moving to the Oregon coast, to a life that was free of traffic, smog and crowds, where prices were so much lower we could afford to buy a house by the beach. But as long as Michael was in school, we weren't going anywhere. For the time being, we were thinking like parents.

In 1990, while Michael spent the summer with his mother, Fred took me to Portugal on a three-week tour that included the Azores islands my ancestors came from, as well as stops in Madeira and Lisbon. My new book was on Portuguese women, and I felt the need to continue my research in Portugal. Fred was game to go anywhere I wanted to go.

He endured hours in the sweltering Civil Registry as a clerk paged through thick handwritten volumes full of names and information about births, marriages and deaths, looking unsuccessfully for information about my great grandparents. He sat through countless folkloric concerts, fish stews, and bus tours along the edges of steep mountain cliffs and declared it all wonderful.

I was the youngest person on the tour by decades. As I climbed on and off the buses laden with camera gear, the others made fun of me. "*Vaca*," they'd point. "Another cow. Go take a picture." And I would. It was an expensive, romantic trip laden with castles, cobblestone streets, and the food and music of the old country.

If we'd had young children, we couldn't have gone to Portugal. In our partially childless life, we did lots of things full-time parents could not have done. If I had had children with either Jim or Fred, they would not have been old enough to leave behind, but Michael stayed with his mother, and his siblings were already on their own. We were free, and we had money to spare. For the moment.

50

4
Trouble in Paradise

Nobody's life stays perfect forever. In 1991, six years into our marriage, things happened that tested our resilience. In March, my step-grandmother, Rachel Fagalde, fainted in her bathroom and was taken to the hospital. The doctors found that she had advanced stomach cancer. She never recovered enough to go home. Meanwhile, my 94-year-old grandfather could not stay at their house by the beach in Seacliff alone. We knew he couldn't see well, and he seemed to fall a lot, but until he was on his own, none of us realized that he was suffering from dementia, the result of numerous small strokes. He wound up in a nursing home. Visiting him became a heartbreaking weekly ritual as he forgot our names, lost his ability to walk and generally deteriorated.

It was a scene I would relive 20 years later with another man I loved. Thank God we don't know the future.

That same year, we were watching TV when the phone rang.

It was Fred's father. "Don died." Then he said some things that didn't make sense. I turned off the TV, asked my father-in-law to wait a second, and handed the phone to Fred.

"Honey, it's your father. I think he said, 'Don died.' I don't know . . ."

I held Fred's free hand as he took the phone. His breathing grew fast and shallow as he heard the story.

Don, Fred's youngest brother, was a truck driver. He was working under one of his trucks when the jacks holding it up collapsed. He was crushed, dying instantly. Fred's father watched it happen.

As he hung up, Fred began to cry. I held him until his sobs eased, then helped him make plans to fly to Las Vegas. His brother had lived there for years. Just recently their parents had joined funds

Sue Fagalde Lick

with him to buy a house in Vegas together. The idea had been that Don would be able to help them in their old age.

I still smile at the memory of how I first met Don. One night while I was cooking dinner at the house on Ardis before we got married, I heard a rumbling outside. I hurried to the window. An 18-wheeler was parked out front, taking all the space between our driveway and the next. "What the heck?" I muttered.

A burly bearded man jumped out and hurried up the walk swinging a six-pack of beer in his hand.

He laughed at my puzzled expression and said, "Hi, I'm your brother-in-law. How about a hug?"

In five minutes we were friends. Now he was gone.

Also in 1991, doctors found a suspicious growth on Fred's thyroid, a tiny gland in his neck. Twice before, they had removed parts of his thyroid, each time fearing the growths were malignant. So far, they were benign, but they decided it was time to remove the rest of his thyroid. In addition to the fear of cancer, this surgery also held the risk of damaging Fred's beautiful black-coffee voice.

My mother and I sat in the waiting room at Kaiser Hospital for hours. I had started knitting a forest green cable-patterned sweater for Fred. My knitting needles clicked loudly in the heavy silence.

A TV flickered, muted, unwatched. A nurse at the door kept track of people coming in and out and quietly talked on the phone.

It was taking too long, I thought. They had said it would be only two hours, but now it was getting dark outside, and the nurse couldn't tell us anything. I knit until my hands ached but didn't know what else to do. The back of the sweater grew inch by inch in my lap. Michael would be home from school by now. I called to tell him I was still waiting and to make himself some macaroni and cheese.

Finally, the nurse beckoned to me. "They're bringing him to his room. You can wait there."

I glanced back at my mother.

She was putting on her coat. "I've got to go home and make your father some dinner," she said. "Call me later."

I hugged Mom good-bye and hurried to Fred's hospital room.

Childless by Marriage

Sitting in the hard chair by the empty bed, I couldn't keep my mind from wandering. What if Fred had cancer? What if he was dying? What if his voice was ruined?

When they rolled him in on a gurney, his appearance didn't ease my fears. He looked dead, so pale, blood oozing from the bandage around the front of his neck. As I gazed down at him, he opened his eyes. "Hi," he whispered and reached his hand out for mine.

It felt limp and cold. I clutched it tightly, rubbing warmth into his fingers.

As the orderlies receded, the doctor arrived. Everything was fine, he said. He found no signs of malignancy. Fred should be able to go home in a day or two. Tears slipping out of my eyes, I nodded, relieved but still scared by how weak my husband looked.

Ah, but Fred was strong. I often said he was bionic, like TV's six-million-dollar man. The next morning, I got a call that he was up and ready to go home. What? It seemed crazy, but I found him sitting in a chair, fully dressed and speaking normally. Blood still seeped from his wound, but he was well enough to leave, they said.

In another day, I was struggling to keep him down. Except for the stitches on his neck, no one would know he'd just come home from the hospital.

Other storms were brewing. The city of San Jose had run into financial trouble. Rumors surfaced about major cuts in the recreation department. Concerned about the future and wanting to accumulate more money, Fred took a part-time weekend job at Mirassou winery, a family-owned operation in the east foothills. He led tours and worked in the tasting room, serving up samples to a steady stream of visitors who came through the heavy wooden doors to linger by the warm fireplace, swirling their wine in heavy-bowled glasses.

For Fred, who loved wine and loved hanging out at Mirassou, it was more fun than work. I can picture him standing behind the counter, holding a glass of cabernet up to the light. "See that color?" He held the glass to his nose. "Ahh. Hints of oak and berry. Now swirl it. Look at those legs."

It was the same winery we had visited on our first date on the way to dinner. Fred was picking up Christmas gifts. I had never seen anyone spend so much money on wine. Now, with his employee discount, his collection at home steadily grew. We added monthly "cab nights" to our social calendar. In addition to his regular weekend hours, Fred volunteered for every holiday and special event. Sometimes I brought my guitar to entertain the customers. Although I had never cared much about wine, I enjoyed the ambience and being with Fred in a place where he was so happy.

F red's job with the recreation department was eliminated in 1992. He could have moved to a new job at the same level in another city department, but at 55, with 25 years working for the city of San Jose, he chose to take early retirement instead.

It wasn't the best time to retire. We were only one year into our mortgage on the Safari Drive house, with four years to a balloon payment, and Fred had just bought himself a Mazda pickup. Michael had three more years of high school. I was still freelancing, but my most lucrative clients had just run out of money.

Fred's pension was good, and he had income from his tax practice and his job at Mirassou, but I felt the need to contribute more to the family budget.

I wasn't looking for an actual job, but a series of circumstances led me into one. We had just returned from a trip to Oregon when a writer friend called. She had been hired as editor for one of the Metro community newspapers, a chain of weeklies that covered most of the cities in Santa Clara County. Would I like to do some freelancing for the *Los Gatos Weekly Times* home and garden section? Sure.

It was a great gig. I got to wander around some of the area's most wealthy estates, interviewing their owners and asking nosy questions about plants, furnishings and wall treatments, writing it all up in full-page articles for which I was well paid. Bliss.

A few months later, Metro had an opening for a part-time reporter at the *Saratoga News*. Was I interested? Well . . . Money was tight. Freelancing was getting harder. I took the job. After that, things changed quickly. The Saratoga editor got into trouble with management and was fired. Her boss knew that I had been an editor before and asked if I would take the job temporarily. Temporary turned into permanent. I started working full-time as editor of the *Saratoga News* in March 1993. It was a good job. I loved putting on my grownup suits and sitting in my glass-walled office, from which I commanded an ever-changing staff of reporters and interns. One of those interns took to calling me Mom. I lapped it up.

Writing, editing, laying out pages, and attending staff and management meetings, I was soon too busy to miss freelancing. Besides, as long as it had something to do with Saratoga, I was free to write whatever I wanted. My book didn't seem to be going anywhere; editors couldn't see a market for a volume about Portuguese Americans. So I set it aside and focused on my newspaper work.

As editor, I often received press releases from The Pet Network, a local dog and cat rescue agency. Remembering the close bond I had had with Heidi, the German Shepherd Jim and I shared, I decided I wanted another dog. Now that Fred and I had a house of our own, there was no reason we couldn't have a dog. We started going to animal adoption fairs, visiting rescue dogs displayed at various area shopping centers.

When we first met Sadie at a PetSmart store, her name was Snapple. A German Shepherd-yellow Lab mix, she had the same dark eyes as Heidi had, the same lush multi-layered fur, and the same plumed tail, with the sturdy body of a Lab. She was mostly the color of the Snapple iced-tea drink.

As I reached out to pet her, she wagged her tail. "Fred, look. What do you think about this one?"

"She seems nice."

The dog's tail wagged faster.

Snapple had a problem. The volunteers said she was so aggressive with other animals that she couldn't be boarded with any other dogs. Hmm. We had a cat, and we certainly didn't want a dog that was dangerous. We decided to keep looking.

Two weeks later, Snapple was still there. Now they called her Sadie, having decided her name was discouraging potential owners. She sure was pretty. As we leaned over to pet her, she licked our hands and wagged her tail. She didn't seem to have any problem with the other dogs nearby that day. We asked to take her out for a walk.

Sue Fagalde Lick

We strolled around the store, then sat on the warm pavement just outside the back door. This dog acted as if she was already part of the family.

"I like her," I said.

"Me too," Fred replied.

"You want to live with us?" I asked the dog.

Her dark eyes sparkled as if she understood.

We came back in, paid $100 for the dog, bought a leash, collar, bowl and food, and loaded her into the Honda.

Our cat wasn't too happy with the new addition. When Sadie came bounding into the back yard, Lady, sleeping on the lounge in the patio, flew at her with her teeth and claws extended. I grabbed her off the startled dog, and we started a life of dog in the back yard, cat in the front and never the twain should meet.

It wouldn't be for long. Lady had already been diagnosed with a rare form of skin cancer and would die a few months later, but things were tense for a while.

Michael was happy with the new dog. When we weren't around, he let her sleep in his bed. We started signing Christmas and birthday cards from Fred, Sue, Michael and Sadie, letting people wonder if we'd had a baby girl.

Our family complete, I was happy with my job while Fred had his part-time endeavors. It worked pretty well. For a while.

It started subtly. My eye makeup always seemed to end up near my eyebrows. Some days I felt as if I couldn't see as well I should. I told myself I needed better makeup and new glasses.

I was also gaining weight. One day at work I walked into the restroom, looked in the mirror, and saw my white slip showing through the torn sides of my red skirt. I had burst right through the seams. Too many Saratoga lunches, I thought.

But more symptoms followed. My nails kept breaking and clumps of hair came off in the shower. My periods had gotten shorter and less frequent. Menopause already? I was only 43.

It got worse. At a chorale concert in a church near Sacramento, we were barely into the third song when I started feeling faint. As I stood there in my long pink gown singing "Deep River," my hands tingled, my heart beat too fast, and the room began to spin. I kept my eyes on the director and struggled to keep singing. I fought for air, flexed my knees, told myself I could hang in there until intermission. But I couldn't. Things were starting to go dark. I bolted for an empty seat in the front pew and sat staring through giant black holes as the show went on without me.

What was wrong? I didn't know. I had taken an allergy pill before the concert. Maybe it was a reaction. All I knew was that after years of singing with the chorale, I was suddenly watching from the audience.

I returned after intermission, but after that day, each concert became a battle to stay on the risers and stay upright. One time, I sank onto the risers, hiding behind the pink dress in front of me. Another time, I walked straight off the risers and out of the room, sitting in a coat closet until the others came out.

Meanwhile, my eyes were getting worse. They ached, and I had trouble seeing the words on my computer and on the page proofs that I read every Monday.

I spent a lot of time at Kaiser Hospital. I saw dermatologists, optometrists, cardiologists, and psychologists. The latter gave me Xanax tablets which I carried around but rarely took. When I did take them, I never knew whether I would feel sleepy, drunk, calm or just as anxious as before. She also referred me to an anxiety group, where other women talked about panic attacks so bad they couldn't leave their homes and drugs that turned them into zombies. The more I heard, the more frightened I became, sure I was losing my mind.

Unable to get through a concert without feeling as I were going to faint, I took a leave of absence that would turn into permanent retirement from the chorale. I didn't tell them what was wrong; I just said I was too busy with my new job.

Finally, an ophthalmologist, a smart lady from India, took one look at me and told me to get my thyroid tested. She showed me in a mirror how my left eyelid had pulled back a measurable distance from my bulging eye—a typical sign of Graves' Disease, a hyperthyroid disorder.

I swallowed a small dose of radioactive iodine, went off to run errands then returned for an x-ray-like test. The tech sent me back to the waiting room while she processed the results. I was sitting there pretending to read in that crowded waiting room when she came out and told me loudly in front of everyone that I had Graves' Disease. My thyroid was out of control. And yes, it is ironic that Fred and I both suffered from thyroid problems. Another thing we had in common. Fred's brother, mother and grandmother all had thyroid disease. If we had had children, they probably would have had it, too.

Hormones produced by the thyroid affect all the systems in the body. If you have too much, everything runs too high, goes too fast. Thus my heart was doing the jitterbug all the time, and I was having panic attacks, my body overflowing with the adrenaline that powered the fight or flight response even when there was no threat. With Graves', fat builds up behind the eyes, making them bulge. People can become legally blind with this disease. There are other symptoms: falling hair, weak nails, achy joints, hot flashes, disrupted menstrual and digestive cycles. Patients gain or lose large amounts of weight in a hurry. Lucky me, I gained 20 pounds seemingly overnight.

My doctor put me on a strong medication called propylthiouracil, PTU for short. I took the vile-tasting pills four at a time three times a day. In later years, other doctors would call it chemotherapy. I just know I was miserable. My panic attacks increased. My heart beat fast, my ankles swelled, I struggled to see, and my moods varied from irritable to rage. At staff meetings, I would pretend to be organized and confident despite the swirling haze between me and whoever I was talking to.

It was a stressful job. I was always trying to do my own work while struggling to balance the needs of my staff and the community with the mandates of management. My staff had been reduced, and I never knew how much space I would have for stories. I would get my pages with the ads already filled in and start screaming over the phone to whatever poor soul at the main office got my call. I needed more space! How did they expect me to do this?

Meanwhile I developed holes in my memory. One afternoon on deadline, the mayor called, furious about a story we had run. I tried to defend my reporter and the newspaper's right to publish the facts, but he demanded to speak to my boss. Suddenly I couldn't remember the phone number that I called every day. Nor could I find it anywhere. I took a guess, but it was wrong and the mayor called back, even more enraged. I finally got the number from a reporter, assured the mayor this number was correct, then winced as he hung up in my ear. I covered my face with my hands.

How many years had I been meeting deadlines, doing the impossible in a ridiculously short period of time with not enough resources? And for what?

I finished that issue, filling what little space I had, then took my customary walk down the street to get a tall iced tea and a giant chocolate chip cookie. No wonder I was gaining weight.

Ultimately, my boss took me for coffee and quietly suggested that maybe I'd be happier in a less stressful position within the company, maybe copyediting or a writing job. It wasn't really optional.

I moved to the Los Gatos office and started writing columns and cover stories part time. It was actually a great job, and I started feeling better if not completely well, but I wasn't going to stay in that job very long.

It was 1996. I had just gotten my paycheck. I stared at the numbers in dismay. How could I work so hard for so little? Fred had gotten paid, too. He made more on his retirement than I made working at the newspaper. It wasn't fair.

Stomping into Fred's office to complain, not the first time, I found him studying a notice from the mortgage company. We had lived in our house for five years. The plan, touted by the mortgage broker, had been to make a lot of money with San Jose's ever-climbing housing prices, sell for big bucks and move to Oregon. But apparently we had a gift for losing money on real estate. Prices had stopped going up. And now, we had a massive balloon payment due. Unless we depleted our savings, we couldn't afford it.

"Do you still want to move to Oregon?" I asked.

Fred tossed the paper into the air. "Yes. Let's do it."

Michael had graduated and moved into an apartment with friends. My grandfather had died the previous January. Fred had retired, and I had grown weary of my job. In Oregon, I could freelance. It was time to go.

Sue Fagalde Lick

We called a real estate broker and started packing. We thought we'd have months to prepare, but our house sold the first week it was on the market. Suddenly we were flying up to Oregon to find a rental home, then flying back for a glut of good-bye parties. We gathered friends and relatives to pack the rented yellow Ryder truck Fred would drive to Oregon. I would follow him with the dog in the Honda.

With each good-bye party, I wondered more if we were doing the right thing. I had lived in the Bay Area all my life, never more than 50 minutes away from my parents. We had been working so hard to fix up the house for sale and then to pack that we had barely had time to think. That Fourth of July, Sadie and I sat up on the water district trail on a hill near our house with dozens of neighbors, watching fireworks flashing in all directions. I could see the displays from Great America to the north, from the county fairgrounds straight ahead, and from Morgan Hill to the South. What have we done, I asked myself. I had a good job, good friends, family nearby. Fred's kids all lived in the Bay Area. But it was too late. The house was sold. If I had kept my mouth shut, life would have gone on as it always had. As usual, I asked and Fred said yes.

I buried my face in Sadie's thick golden fur and cried amid the pops and whistles of fireworks and loud music from someone's boom box playing in the dark.

If we'd had children or been more attached to Fred's children, maybe we would never have left, but we had started building a dream of a more peaceful life on the Oregon Coast, a life with no traffic, no crowds, no balloon payments. Michael didn't need us anymore. The other kids were grown. Don's sudden death had shown us how short life could be. Fred would find another winery to work at. I would have time to sing and write. Maybe I could become a quilter. It was the life of retired people with no children left at home. I was only 44, but Fred was 59, ready to embark on the next phase of his life, which did not include children.

5
What Have I Done?

For the first few years of our marriage, I didn't complain much about not having children. Basking in the honeymoon glow, with work going well, a new house to take care of and my stepchildren giving me all the mothering opportunities I needed, I didn't have time to complain about never having given birth. But as I approached 40, my attitude changed. Suddenly everyone around me seemed to be having babies. I watched my brother and my best friend become parents. A friend with whom I used to go out drinking at El Torrito's, the one who had proclaimed, "Nobody is ever going to call me Mom," was about to have her second child. Holding their babies, I wanted one of my own so bad my heart hurt.

In September, 1990, as I was ripping out the hem on Michael's Boy Scout pants because he kept growing taller, I started to cry. Lately I had gotten nothing but rejections for my writing. The laundry, cooking and housework seemed overwhelming, and I had spent too much time looking at other people's children, knowing I would never have any of my own. I cried as I stitched, fighting to see the thick green cloth and avoid poking the needle through my finger. Fred put his arms around me, and I began to feel better, but I knew I would cry over this many more times.

At a women's retreat the night before my 40th birthday party, grief hit me hard. Sitting in a circle with 15 other women, we read the Bible story in which Mary and her cousin Elizabeth are both pregnant. That led us to thinking about the women in our lives. Our leader, Jeanine, asked us to light candles and name the women who been there for us in the dark times. Many of us teared up as one woman after another spoke about mothers, daughters and friends. But as I stood and lit my candle, naming my mother, my elderly writer friend Ethel, and Grandma Rachel, I completely lost control. I started sobbing and couldn't stop.

Jeanine hugged me and told me it was okay, I was in a safe place. I had never cried in front of other people like that. Why did I cry now? I'm not sure. But it was sparked by the exercise and the reading about the two pregnant women sharing something I would never share.

I suspect turning 40 had something to do with my weepiness. A TV special on daycare centers got to me late one summer night. I cried in the garage, where Fred couldn't hear me. In my journal, I wrote, "To never have a baby, to be 40 and see the door closing, to never cuddle a toddler and teach it everything—it kills me sometimes. The career is great, and it's fun to cuddle the cat, but nothing else fills that void."

I often dreamed that I was pregnant. The dreams were so real I'd wake up rubbing my belly, surprised to find it flat. Where was my baby?

Every Mother's Day was a misery. For weeks, the media yammered about gifts for "Mom," and mothers were singled out for flowers and special blessings at church. I never knew whether to stand and be honored or sit with the little girls.

My mother, God bless her, never complained about my not giving her a grandchild. In fact, one Mother's Day as I explained to my sister-in-law that I didn't get any presents because I wasn't a mother, Mom scolded me. "Don't ever say that." Another Mother's Day, she embraced me and told me I was a good mother. I was taking care of Michael, doing things that a mother would do, but in my heart, I didn't feel like one. Sometimes I felt a horrible sense of loss, for example when I saw my father playing with my cousin's dark-haired baby girl.

Over time, I became more philosophical. I told myself I had a wonderful home, terrific friends, work and hobbies that I loved and a fantastic husband. I had Michael and his siblings. The world was full of young people who could use my love and my help.

It took years for me to understand that it was not all Fred's fault—or Jim's either. When I got married and continued to use birth control, I chose to be childless. When I failed to say, "I want a baby now, not 10 years from now," I chose to be childless. When I married

Childless by Marriage

a man who had had a vasectomy and who had told me that he didn't want any more children, I chose to be childless. I could have held out for a husband who was eager to procreate—knowing he might never come along—or found a way to become a single parent by adopting or making a withdrawal from a sperm bank. But I didn't. I chose Fred. If my biological clock was ticking, it didn't tick loudly enough for me to hear it over the other demands of my life.

For a long time, I blamed everyone but myself for my failure to have children, but I'm the one with the baby-making equipment in my belly. I could have stopped using birth control any time I wanted. With my first husband, I could have insisted that we get pregnant, or I could have tricked him by just pretending to put in my diaphragm. Even if it led to divorce, at least I would have a child. But I didn't want to do it that way.

I could have told Fred that I wouldn't marry him unless he agreed to find a way to have children. That's what my friend Debra did when she married a man who, like Fred, was older and already had children. The marriage didn't last, but she has her daughter, whom she adores.

My friend Ken agreed to start a new family with his second wife, Sherry, because he could not deprive her of the chance to be a mother. I dated him first. He was sweet and dependable, but I didn't love him. Should I have married him anyway just so I could be a mother? Using a man that way seems like a worse sin than going to my grave with an unused uterus.

Another friend, John, who, like Fred, married a much younger woman, was 59, with two adult offspring, when Jasmine was born. I remember the day I saw John and Lizzy at a music festival in Toledo, Oregon. It was a perfect August day for a small-town winging with booths up and down Main Street, classic cars on display at one end and nonstop folk music at the other. Weary from strolling up and down the crowded street, I decided to join the folks sitting on orange folding chairs by the stage outside Bank of the West.

I didn't notice Lizzy's belly until they stood to move their chairs into the sun. Was it really rounded under her denim overalls or was I imagining it? No, she was definitely pregnant. It struck me like a blow. That he would do this for her showed so much love. "That he

63

would do this for her" echoed in my head like a mantra. A corresponding chant answered: "but my husband would not."

I was certain John did not want to start raising children again. Without anyone telling me, I could see the whole picture: Lizzy was young, she wanted a family, he loved her, and he could not deny her that part of life.

But I got it wrong. When I asked John about it later, he said he was the one who wanted another child. Lizzy didn't mind doing without, but he wanted a chance to do a better job than he had before. Now in his 60s, he sometimes complains that he can't retire because he has a little girl to raise and put through college, but he always says it with a smile.

Sometimes I'm jealous of Sherry and Lizzy because they had babies and I didn't, but it's at least half my fault. Not only did I never make having children a deal-breaker, but I never asked Fred what he would have done if I had. When I hit him with the question a few years ago, he sighed and answered, "I don't know. I might have been gallant and agreed to have children. Then we would have had to figure out how to do it." But he was quick to add, "I just didn't want a little kid." He said he would have married me if I had already had children, but he didn't want to deal with babies again.

Other husbands are more blunt about it. "I'd have been gone," one friend's husband said when she asked him how he would have reacted if she had gotten pregnant.

Some women are relieved to find men who don't want children. Mary, a music teacher and concert pianist, was delighted to acquire a readymade family when she married Roy. Between her stepchildren and her students, she says she has all the children she needs in her life and plenty of time for the work she loves.

Roy worried more about her lack of children than she did. "Are you sure?" he kept asking.

"It was fine. I just didn't want any. My sisters' kids have all been little problems," she says, adding, "I wouldn't have been a good mother until I was about 45, and then I was too old. I like it with other people's kids. I can get them all excited and then say, 'Go home to your parents.'"

Childless by Marriage

More and more women are opting out of motherhood, preferring the freedom to concentrate on their hobbies or careers rather than devote themselves to a vocation for which they feel no strong inclination. They are all too aware that most husbands still leave the heavy parenting to their wives. Some have watched their mothers or sisters sacrifice their lives to care for children and have decided they don't want to do that.

Joyce, an artist who died of cancer while this book was being written, said she was glad her first husband didn't want children. Getting pregnant had brought her sisters nothing but misery, and she had other plans for her life. "It was 1968 and I had my brand new bachelor's degree. I had a picture of life being all new and being mine. I wasn't interested in giving life to anybody else."

That marriage ended after three years when Joyce fell in love with a co-worker who was six years older and already had two children with his first wife. They immediately knew they were soul mates and were soon married. She accepted his decision not to have any more children, but told me that she didn't think much about it at the time because she was still growing up herself.

Even when Joyce's IUD failed and she got pregnant, they stuck by their decision to remain childless. She had an abortion. Shortly after that, they agreed that Tom would have a vasectomy. When she was in her early 50s, they occasionally talked about what life would have been like if they had had children. Joyce often said that she would have been a terrible mother, but conceded that no one knew that for sure.

The arrival of Tom's first grandchild helped ease any regret Joyce and her husband might have felt about their decision. "We are so pleased with that little girl," she said. "Now we finally have a baby, and she's the best possible kind because we don't have to diaper her. We visit her and give her back."

If we had been born 50 years earlier, Mary, Joyce and I would have been mothers and grandmothers. Before the advent of safe, dependable birth control and legal abortion, only infertile couples or those who abstained from sex could avoid pregnancy. The rest might bear a dozen or more children before their fertility waned. Nowadays, couples can choose to remain "childfree," a term many people prefer

65

to "childless," because they don't feel they are "less" anything. Me, I wanted kids, and I'm quick to correct anyone who calls me "childfree."

A woman's decision to give up motherhood for the man she loves could be seen as a beautiful, loving, romantic sacrifice. From another point of view, we could hate the man for depriving her of children.

I wandered into childlessness with the Disney movie mindset that if you want something badly enough, your dreams will come true. God, the Good Witch, or whoever would make it happen. Somehow, some way, without doing anything about it myself, I would have children.

But that's not how it works.

I write about everything that happens to me, so it was natural to start writing and blogging about childlessness. In my interviews and in comments on my Childless by Marriage blog (www.childlessbymarriage.com), I keep hearing the same story over and over.

A woman I'll call Minnie wrote to say she was relieved to find she wasn't alone and that there was a term for what had happened to her: childless by marriage.

Growing up, Minnie was the kid who "mothered everything in sight." She grew up wanting a houseful of children, but it didn't happen. At 23, she married an older man, and everyone, including Minnie herself, expected her to become pregnant right away. But this older boyfriend didn't want any kids. Since she wasn't using birth control, he practiced *coitus interruptus*. They kept talking about it, and she kept hoping they'd reach a compromise. Then his mom got sick and she wound up taking care of her, but still had no babies.

The husband vetoed adoption—too expensive and too chancy. He said he couldn't see her being able to handle the extra work, and he was just too old.

Finally Minnie thought that she had found the perfect solution: She would become a foster mother. But there were things that both of them had to do—TB tests, forms to fill out, referrals to be collected— and when I last heard from her, her husband hadn't done his part.

Childless by Marriage

Minnie is not happy. She can't let go of that dream of the big house and the minivan full of kids.

Laura T., a young writer who never wanted children, says she and her husband never discussed the subject before the wedding. It was a great relief to find out he felt the same way.

But it isn't always that convenient. Katreen, a 36-year-old writer and actress living in Luebeck, Germany, has seen what can happen if a woman waits too long. The man in her life has said he isn't interested in being a father, but she still hopes to change his mind. "I would never marry someone who does not want to have children." She doesn't want to follow the example of a friend who remained in a childless relationship for seven years. Now in her early 40s, she gave up her dream of motherhood for her partner, who already had a child. "What happens if the relationship ends?" Katreen asks. "She's faced with being single again at an age where it's near impossible to conceive—not to mention, find a man."

Jo, a British yoga teacher, knows exactly how that feels. She says she always wanted a family, but it didn't turn out that way. She loved a married man for many years. Friends encouraged her to let herself get pregnant with him, but she didn't think that would be fair. "By the time we broke up, I was 10 years older and had missed my chance. I eventually met someone else whom I liked, but he didn't want children. He had my last few years of being fertile and then he left me."

Shirley Price, who counsels engaged couples for the Northwest Catholic Counseling Center in Portland, Oregon, says engaged couples are usually full of optimism about the future. They look at the world through rose-colored glasses and are willing to accept anything as long as they can be together. She urges them to remember what they had envisioned for their married lives and warns that if there are no children, a lot of other things people take for granted won't happen. They will not be able to share child-related experiences such as school and sports with their friends. They won't have grandchildren, and they won't have children to care for them when they are old. Their decision will affect the whole family. Unless their siblings produce children, their parents will not become grandparents.

Sue Fagalde Lick

"Motherhood is such a primary image for women," says Bobbi Parish, a Portland-area marriage counselor who specializes in infertility. "Men are more attached to their jobs, but little girls start training to be mothers from the time they're old enough for their first baby dolls." Society can be hard on women who don't follow the usual path to motherhood. They will feel left out as most of their friends turn their attention to their children. "I see women struggling with it more than men." Women have a hard time understanding why men don't feel the loss as deeply, and men are baffled as to why their wives burst into tears when they see a baby at the supermarket, Parish adds.

Not all girls are raised to be moms. In fact, many of the women I interviewed had no interest in dolls or babies when they were growing up. A lot depends also on role models. When one's mother seems trapped and unhappy, the daughter may decide early that this is not the life for her. But as a doll-obsessed girl whose mom loved motherhood, I was fully imprinted with the expectation that I would have children and love it, too.

Tiffany felt the same way. When I first met her online, she was 38, working on her master of fine arts degree. She was engaged to marry a man who already had a daughter and didn't want any more children. She adored her future stepdaughter, but if she married this man, could she bear to give up the chance to have children of her own?

"Some days I freak out and want to leave my fiancé and run out to a bar and fuck some stranger and have his child. Seriously! Not that I've ever fucked a stranger in a bar before. That's how crazy this whole biological clock thing is making me."

Tiffany continued, "I am considering not marrying this person because I really want children, but realistically, I do not have enough time left as a fertile woman—if I even *am* fertile--I have no idea—to run out, find another guy, get to know him in any significant way, and then have a child. I've known people who've done that and it was disastrous. This is all complicated by the fact that I adore my fiancé and other than this issue, we do extremely well together.

"Also, I am sort of trapped by my stepdaughter, despite how much I love her—or rather *because of* how much I love her. If I left my fiancé, I would be leaving a family in the dim hopes of finding a different family. Basically, I'm looking at a lose-lose situation."

She did marry the man. At first, Tiffany put much of the hurt she felt over being biologically childless into her work. Eventually, she had a daughter, ending her years of childlessness.

Matilde, an immigrant from the Azores Islands, said her first husband, a Portuguese American, came to the Azores searching for long-lost relatives. "He found some cousins, and he also found me." We wrote letters to each other for one year. Then he came back to the Azores, and asked me to marry him. We got married in São Miguel in a civil ceremony, and I came here (to Boston) six months later. I had never been married before. I was 24 years old."

"Because of the Portuguese culture being so family-oriented, and knowing how the Azorean people feel about family, I guess I just assumed that he wanted children. I guess I never talked to him directly about the subject because I was intimidated by him and afraid to antagonize him too soon. I really wanted to marry him. I was deeply in love with him, and I desperately wanted to leave the Azores. No future for me there."

She was shocked to discover he not only didn't want children; he refused to have intercourse.

"I went into a deep depression when I found out that this man did not care how much I cried every time I talked about having a family. He walked away from me. Sometimes he would leave the house, just so he would not have to listen to me."

She said she was so depressed she couldn't eat or sleep and even contemplated suicide. Here she was in a new country where she barely spoke the language and had no money of her own and no family nearby. After two years, she filed for divorce.

Alas, when she married again, they had trouble conceiving. She checked out all right, but her husband refused to have his sperm tested. By then, she was 40 and gave up hope of ever becoming a mother.

Infertile couples who want children are forced to seek alternative ways to become parents. Treatments such as in-vitro fertilization are painful and expensive. No one can blame couples if they

69

decide the price is too high. Sometimes the man is the infertile one; he may want a child as badly as the woman does. But when no impediment exists, why wouldn't a man want to father children, especially if the woman he loves wants them?

Some men are just not ready to make such a big commitment, says Leslie Lafayette, founder of the Childfree Network. In her book *Why Don't You Have Kids?* she quotes Gene, a 37-year-old man who doesn't want children. "Were I to become a father, it would become the most important task of my life. While the choice is mine, I will not sacrifice a life filled with fun, love, adventure, socializing, learning, philosophizing, athletics, travel, fine arts and other adult pursuits to have kids. The cost for me is far too great."

While I was teaching at a conference in Georgia, everyone said I had to talk to Alek, a handsome bookstore owner who happened to be childless. His answer was short and to the point. He does not want to be a father because he doesn't like kids. What if a woman he loved wanted to be a mother? "It's not going to happen. No woman who wants kids would want me."

On the cab ride back to the Atlanta airport, I met Massoud, an Iranian immigrant who had a vasectomy before he met his second wife, Puran. He has two children from his first marriage and doesn't want more. Children just use up all your money and get in lots of trouble, he said. Puran, who wanted children, had a hysterectomy four years ago, so he got his wish.

Leslie Cannold writes in *What, No Baby?* that men who are up for the full commitment of marriage and equal parenting are "rarer than a size 8 at the end of a shoe clearance."

In her book *Younger Women/Older Men*, Beliza Ann Furman describes some of the reasons older husbands, like mine, might not want to jump into the daddy pool. They worry about money, whether they'd be good fathers, or about simply being too old. What if people mistake the older father for the child's grandfather? How can they put a kid through college while living on Social Security?

The younger woman may or may not understand his reluctance, but she faces a difficult choice. Is she willing to sacrifice the children she dreams of having to keep this man? It's possible that in the throes of new love and youth, she will agree to give up children then change her mind later. It's a decision that may not stay made for a lot of us, especially as we grow older and realize we have let someone else make one of the most important decisions in our lives.

But Furman hastens to add that some men, even older men, are eager to have children and will go all out to make it possible. Other men face the same dilemma as many childless women, wanting children but tied to a spouse who won't or can't give them babies. They, too, grieve their loss.

Nirpal Dhaliwal wrote an aching piece in London's *Sunday Times*, "The Men Who Are Desperate for Kids." It's not something men feel comfortable openly discussing with other men because it makes them look "soft," he writes, but he finds himself only interested in women with whom he could raise a family. Time spent in India with men who treasured their children made him want the same "real and uniquely powerful experience."

"Michael," who blogs about his marriage to a woman 17 years old than he is at himplus17.blogspot.com, experienced a situation similar to mine. He knew that by marrying a much older woman he probably would not become a father. At the time, he decided it was worth it. Two decades later, he says he realizes that "I've missed out on something fundamental to human experience." Although he wouldn't change his mind if it meant losing his wife Sheri, he questions the decisions he made when he was 27.

Tanya, 45, marketing director for a nursing home, tells me she feels sorry for the men she dates who want children. Divorced and the mother of two sons, she believes she could still get pregnant but has no desire to do so. When her dates express a desire to have children, she says, "I gently set them free."

Sometimes things seem to work out as if they were planned that way. Several women I spoke with found that they were physically unable to have children, suffering miscarriages or other problems that would make pregnancy difficult. They were glad to find mates who wouldn't pressure them into trying to have children. Karen, for example, lost a son who was born prematurely during her first marriage and was told extreme measures would be required with any future pregnancies. So it was a relief when her second husband wasn't interested in having children. By then, too, her career had become such a big factor in her life that she willingly chose not to try again. Now she is happy with her decision and cheerfully tells people she is "childfree."

I had just given a reading about childlessness at a writer's conference when I met Barbara. As I returned to my seat, she leaned close and said, "I'm 70 years old. I have never married and never had children. Are you still interviewing?"

That led to a long talk that night and another long talk over the telephone. Barbara is a delightful person, the kind who when asked about physical health in a childless old age, says, "I have a close personal relationship with my vibrator."

I wasn't going there, but I did ask what kind she uses. For purely journalistic reasons, of course.

After Barbara had one almost-marriage and decided he wasn't the right guy, the opportunity never arose again. She has dated. She enjoys men. But she never married. That has made her feel like an oddity in a world of couples, especially couples with children.

In her time, you simply did not adopt or get pregnant without a spouse, she says. For years, she was okay with her situation until one day, working as a nurse in California, staring at the babies in the nursery, it suddenly hit her: "I am never going to be a mother." She went through a long funk, especially when another job had her carrying newborns between the nursery and their mothers. She'd have tears rolling down her face as she delivered the babies to their happy mothers.

But did Barbara have a choice? Do you marry a guy simply for his sperm? She doesn't think so, but she grieves the loss.

What sounds good when you're 32 may not sound as good at 42. Unexpected emotions can surface all of a sudden. It may be a fleeting regret or it can be a full-force body blow. Every time I watch a baptism at church, seeing the mother, father and godparents surrounding this new baby with love, tears well up. I really don't want a baby now. I'm too old, too busy, but it hits me anyway.

Childless by Marriage

One woman after another has written to me with a similar story. She did or didn't want children when she got married, but now she definitely does and her man does not. She loves him, but she aches for a baby in her arms. What should she do?

Rebecca R., a 42-year-old MBA, wrote that when people asked why she and her husband didn't have children, "I say that my desire to be with him is much stronger than my desire to have a child." But in private, she admitted, "I'm pissed." She left her home country to be with Dave, who, although he had two children from two previous marriages, said he was open to the idea of having children with her. Later he informed her that he definitely did not want another child. He was the only guy she wanted to have children with. It was a puzzle with no solution. She stayed with Dave.

Not everyone is destined to bear children. Nor is motherhood the answer to all of any woman's needs. But each woman must choose for herself.

If I had it to do over again, I'd take off the rose-colored glasses long enough to see what I was getting into. I might insist on having babies, or I might choose to let that dream go.

I could claim my Portuguese heritage and blame fate—*o fado*. If I had been meant to be a mother, God would have made it so. But even my Portuguese grandmother would have said I was fooling myself. I was the one wearing a wedding dress and saying, "I do."

6
Who Knew it was a Sin?

*B*less me Father, for I have sinned. I have had sex, lots of sex, without making babies. Except for a few lucky experiments with the rhythm method, I used birth control. Pills, diaphragms, rubbers. Yes, I knew my way around a tube of contraceptive jelly. To be honest, I did not know it was a sin until I started writing about being a childless woman. You ought to tell the religious ed teachers to slip it in somewhere between lying, stealing and murder, or at least include it in the marriage prep classes. Maybe it was there, but I was too much in love to pay attention. Besides, I was already having sex and taking the pill. Wasn't everybody? It was the '70s. Maybe even you—no, never mind. I just wanted to get married. I figured I would have kids eventually. Surprise! I didn't.

Usually in confession, you say how many times you did the thing, as in, I kicked my brother twice, said the F word four times, and once I got too much change at the J.C. Market and didn't give it back. But I can't tell you how many times I did the sex thing. Who keeps score? I could tell you how many men I did it with, but does it matter? My actual father might read this. So Father with a capital F, forgive me for my sin. I know you're a good guy, and you'll let me off if I promise not to do it again. I'll keep that promise because menopause means never having to say, "Excuse me, I have to go put in my diaphragm."

*C*atholics are supposed to have babies. You'd think I would have known that birth control was a sin and that abortion was grounds for excommunication. But I had no idea, and I suspect many other young Catholic women are equally uninformed.

Looking back, I can see a gap in my religious education. When I was in catechism class, every Saturday from ages 6 to 13, the nuns no doubt figured we were too young to even think about sex (and in my case they were right), so it never came up. My mother's entire advice on the subject was: Don't.

For a long time, I didn't. But eventually, gushing hormones and young love led to petting in the car and sex in a sleeping bag. Which led to a trip to the San Jose State University student health center where they were passing out birth control pills like Tic-Tacs.

It was 1972, and the pill was still illegal for unmarried women in many states. Lucky for me, California wasn't one of them, but I lied to my parents about where Jim and I were going that summer evening. I probably said we were going to a movie. We walked into the brightly lit waiting room to find dozens of other students smoking cigarettes and chewing on their fingernails as they waited to meet the friendly woman doctor who demanded cash for a brief examination and a packet of pills. Up to that point, I had never gone to a doctor without my mother nearby. Nor had I ever kept such a big secret from my parents.

Once I started taking the pill, it was even harder to keep my secret. I suffered every side effect known to woman, starting with the beast of all yeast infections, for which I delayed treatment for weeks for fear my mother would find out I was having sex. It had nothing to do with sex, but I didn't know that. Finally I called Kaiser Hospital from the newspaper office where I was working and set up an appointment. I learned that the tetracycline I was taking for my acne, coupled with the pills I took for birth control, almost guaranteed a yeast infection. A prescription for a fungicide that I had to squeeze into my vagina at bedtime quickly cleared it up, but now I had to hide the medicine and do that under-the-sheets procedure in the dark.

The hormone dosages for birth control pills in those days were huge. Doctors were still working out how much estrogen and/or progestin were needed to prevent ovulation. In the 1970s, most women took pills containing 50 mcg (micrograms) of estrogen. Some took as much as 80 mcg. Today, most birth control pills contain 35 mcg or less of estrogen and low doses of progestin. The side effects I experienced, common in those days, are rare today. Back then, we bloated, we bled, we felt queasy half the time, but by God we did not

Sue Fagalde Lick

get pregnant, and that was the object.

The message I inferred from my mother's one-word instruction, coupled with the occasional magazine articles she left on my bed about girls in trouble, stressed that the big thing was to not get pregnant, to not embarrass the family, to not RUIN YOUR LIFE. I didn't. I took my pills faithfully. The current TV commercials about women worried about forgetting to take their birth control pills baffle me. Who forgets? You get up, you take your pill, then you hide the package under the prayer books in the nightstand. Or, if you're not religious, you bury them under your socks.

That first year, when I was engaged to Jim, I took three different types of birth control pills, trying to stop the side effects. I gained 10 pounds in a week, always wanted to vomit, and bled for 20 out of 28 days. I tested positive for diabetes, apparently mimicking the gestational diabetes some women get when they're pregnant. Each time things went wrong, I would try another pill.

Restricted to a sugar-free diet, my periods finally regulated, thinking I had found the right pill, I developed inch-high bumps on my legs. I cried out in pain if my pants brushed against them, and I saw stars if I tried to kneel or bumped my shins against the corner of the dresser. So much for the gymnastics class I was taking. My grade went from A to C because I couldn't do any of the stunts. I was lucky that long "maxi" skirts were popular then so nobody would see my legs.

Doctors at Kaiser Hospital suggested I might have something called Valley Fever. The antibiotics they prescribed didn't help. Stress? Dermatitis? No, these bumps were too big, one to two inches in diameter, hot and hurting.

Eventually I wound up sprawled on an examining table at the university medical center while every doctor, assistant, nurse and lab tech in the place checked out my bumpy legs. Finally the head doctor suggested, "Maybe it's the birth control pills. We could try a different pill."

No thanks. I was getting married in one month. I switched to a diaphragm, supplemented sometimes by condoms. That was the method my parents used, judging by the evidence my brother found in a drawer one day. Once I stopped taking the pill, I lost 10 pounds in a

76

week, and the bumps went away.

Feeling better, I wanted sex more than ever. One night when my parents weren't home, Jim and I made love in my bedroom. Mom found the used condom in my wastebasket the next day. She hardly talked to me the last few weeks before the wedding. I'm not sure which upset her more, that we were having sex at all or that we had used a condom, which she assured me was not dependable.

I'm sorry, Mom.

Having sex outside of marriage and using birth control were both sins. Jim was Catholic but wanted nothing to do with the church. I was Catholic, but my parents had dropped out after my brother and I were confirmed at age 13. I attended a couple of Masses on my own, but post-Vatican II, everything was different. Now we were supposed to sing folk songs, recite prayers I didn't know, hold hands during the Our Father, and take Communion in our palms instead of on our tongues. After all those years of Latin Masses in which all we had to do was keep still for an hour, I felt lost.

Meanwhile, my philosophy professors filled my head with alternative beliefs that made my religion seem about as real as the mythology we studied in European lit. I had been the kid who carried rosary beads around, prayed on my knees every morning and night, and honestly believed I would see Jesus in a vision just like those kids at Fatima saw the Virgin Mary, but by my early 20s, I cared more about Paul McCartney than Jesus and lost all control when Jim reached inside my clothes.

I didn't think much about sin in general, but if I had, I would not have thought about birth control. Back in second grade, when we were learning what to say in Confession, we never said, "Bless me father, I have sinned. I had sex and took Ortho-whatever to prevent me from getting pregnant." No, it was, "I hit my brother, I told a lie, I said a dirty word." And off we'd go to say two Our Fathers and three Hail Marys.

They didn't have teen religion programs in my day. I recently asked Sandy Cramer, who runs the religious education program at Sacred Heart Church in Newport, Oregon, what they say now about sex and birth control in the teen classes. "It's chastity-based," she replied. Meaning, DON'T HAVE SEX. Which renders the question of birth control moot.

Okay, so pretend we don't have sex until we get married. What are we told then? Around the time Jim and I were dating, the church began requiring engaged couples to participate in six weeks of lectures and discussions led by priests and married couples. I know we attended them. I know that we signed papers promising that we would raise our children as Catholics. But I don't remember a word about birth control. My friend Terry, who is a little younger than I am and has three children, had a different experience. "Oh yes," she said, "we spent several sessions on that."

I must have missed it. Just like I had the flu when we studied percentages back in grade school.

I know now that the Catholic Church does not allow any kind of artificial birth control. Welcoming children is a big part of the sacrament of marriage. Only Natural Family Planning, the so-called rhythm method, based on abstaining when the woman is fertile, is allowed. Sandy, the religious ed director, says she and her husband named their second child, the one they hadn't planned to have, after the priest who convinced them to try Natural Family Planning.

What I wonder—in addition to how couples can actually manage to abstain when the woman's desire is at its peak—is how any kind of abstinence isn't just as bad as taking a pill or slipping in a diaphragm full of contraceptive jelly. It all says the same thing: "No thanks, God. I don't want a child right now."

Anyway, I sinned. I sinned for the two years Jim and I courted and the six years we were married. Even after I started going to church again, getting used to the "new Mass," feeling devout in every other way, I did not know that birth control was a sin. I suspect I'm not alone. A huge gap exists in the church's education of its members. Once you have had all the sacraments, it's assumed that you know everything you need to know. Obviously, we don't.

Jim never tried to come between me and my diaphragm. No matter how hot the passion, he was happy to pause while I ran half-dressed to the bathroom, filled that stretchy beige mini-Frisbee with goop and maneuvered it into place. I did not know then how strongly he opposed having children. After he made it clear, I stayed with him, stressing that I, good Catholic that I was, did not want a divorce. Plus

I was sure he'd change his mind. Later, after I discovered his girlfriend and moved back to Mom and Dad's house, I learned that his refusal to father children was perfect grounds for an annulment through the church. Three hundred dollars and a pile of forms later, I was a free woman, as unstained as if I had never been married, never had sex. But for my problems with chastity and obedience, I could be a nun.

The official word from the Catholic Church, detailed in Pope Paul VI's 1968 *humanae vitae* and echoed by one pope after another, right up to the current pontiff: "To enter a marriage with an intention not to have children is to enter it without proper consent to the full meaning of marriage. Since there is no proper consent, the marriage is invalid and can be annulled at any time." In the eyes of the Catholic Church, I was never married at all because my husband never intended to have children.

Although I had heard people speak of annulment as a painful process, it was cathartic for me. My family testified with me that my husband had denied me the opportunity to have children. But was it all his fault? Wasn't I shoving motherhood away every time I used birth control?

Between marriages, let's just say I sinned some more. I did not want to be a 30-year-old unwed mother. I know, nobody cares in the 21st century, but God forbid I should have to face my parents if the unthinkable happened. Remember, to them, unwed pregnancy meant ruining your life. Now, almost half of the babies born in the U.S. are born to unmarried women, but this was a long time ago. For me, having a baby without a husband was unacceptable.

In those days, like many women I talked to, I might have had an abortion. In my mind, it wasn't, "I'm going to kill this baby," but "get this wad of cells out of me before it *becomes* a baby." I was not pregnant, have never been pregnant, but there were months when I was mighty glad to see my period arrive. It did not help that a certain boyfriend kept whispering things in my ear like, "Come on. Let me fill you up with my sperm. We would make beautiful babies."

No way. Not married, not getting pregnant. I ran for my

79

diaphragm.

Now I wonder whether I have come to believe that abortion is wrong because I have embraced the teachings of the church or because I have met so many women who aborted their only chance at motherhood. Perhaps it's both. I was lucky I didn't have to make that decision.

A long came Fred, adorable, responsible, loving, Protestant, and absolutely sperm-free, thanks to his vasectomy. Permanent birth control.

I did my typical doublethink and told myself we could still have a child. Relatives began bugging me again about having babies. I wasn't getting any younger, you know. Poor divorced Susie, remarried to such a nice man. Now it was time to get back on track and catch up. I fobbed them off with excuses, using my three new stepchildren as shields: Look, I have kids, instant family.

Grandpa Fagalde, who prided himself on the dynasty that grew from his loins, badgered me about having children. "What's wrong?" he would ask. "Why don't you want to have kids? What are you waiting for?" He just didn't understand, until finally one day, I blurted, "Fred's shooting blanks."

"Oh," he said, and that was the end of it.

M y experience is Catholic, but millions of women practice other faiths or none. In fact, in my survey of childless women, 97 percent said that religion played no role in their decisions about marriage and children.

Most religions are not as strict as the Catholic Church when it comes to birth control. The Episcopal Church, for example, which shares many practices with the Roman Catholic faith, differs in some key areas, including reproductive choices. "Children are considered a gift from God," says Rev. Susan C. Church, pastor of St. Stephen's in Newport, Oregon, but her faith accepts the use of birth control as a logical and sometimes necessary facet of life. Even abortion is not banned, although the church's ruling bishops have stated that it is a "moral tragedy." Church members are not all in agreement on these issues, she adds, noting that they continue to struggle with the tough questions.

Rev. Church is a childless woman who has never been married. She was once engaged, but it didn't feel right, and she did not opt for single parenthood. She admits to some regrets about not having children but also believes her childless state has brought her other gifts and made it easier to devote herself to her work.

Other Christian faiths may not forbid the use of birth control or abortion, but they do urge couples to have children. Barrenness is cited in the Bible as a tragedy or even a punishment from God. "Be fruitful and multiply," Genesis says, and many Christians take that advice literally.

R. Albert Mohler Jr., president of the Southern Baptist Theological Seminary in Louisville, Kentucky, had strong words about deliberate childlessness in a 2005 Baptist Press column. Couples who choose not to have children are selfish and sinful, he wrote. "Marriage, sex and children are part of one package. To deny any part of this wholeness is to reject God's intention in creation—and His mandate revealed in the Bible." He added, "Though childlessness may be made possible by the contraceptive revolution, it remains a form of rebellion against God's design and order."

Some Christians tell their members to go forth and multiply, but within reason. In fact, the 210th general assembly of the Presbyterian Church (USA) voted in 1998 to support family planning programs for all Americans and to limit family size to stabilize the world's population and bring human numbers into balance with other creatures "so that all children, present and future, may enjoy a habitat conducive to the realization of their potential under God."

As in the Catholic faith, most non-Christian religions decry abortion and virtually all disapprove of sex outside of marriage. Their views on birth control for married couples vary. In the Islamic faith, for example, interpretations of the scriptures range from a complete prohibition of birth control to allowing it for various reasons. Kathleen O'Grady, who did a study of world religious views on contraception, writes, "Those in favor of contraception argue that artificial birth control is morally the same as "azl" [*coitus interruptus*] and therefore to be accepted. Most Muslim traditions permit the use of birth control where health reasons are an issue or where the wellbeing of the family is concerned; this affords great flexibility and latitude in interpretation."

Conservative and reform Jews allow contraception for various social, environmental and economic reasons and leave the decision to individual choice, but Orthodox Jews condemn the use of birth control, except for health reasons.

Some rabbis have compared childlessness to death, but that's not the majority view.

In 2007, Rabbi Uri Cohen of the Jerusalem Center for Advanced Jewish Study for Women published a paper in which he countered an age-old ruling that childlessness equaled death. First of all, he says, all those years before Sarah and Abraham became miraculously pregnant, they weren't dead. They were sharing their spiritual gifts by teaching others and giving birth to them as faithful Jews. Second, the childless give life through their good deeds, When you teach or care for someone, says Rabbi Cohen, you plant a seed that brings life. Furthermore, the childless have more free time to do such things, so it's not all bad.

It is worth noting that in third-world countries where birth control is not readily available, couples have no more choice than our American ancestors did. No matter what their religion decrees, because of the lack of money and medical options, they either abstain from sex or have children.

I have found it interesting that in asking childless women whether religion was a factor in their decision, nearly all said that it was not. A few confessed to a little guilt but not enough to change their minds. Lisa, a craftswoman from Idaho, said, "I am spiritual and I believe in God. There are days when I feel like my choice to not have kids is a betrayal of the greatest gift that God has ever given women. I still struggle with that at times."

Ann, a teacher from the San Francisco Bay Area, fell in love with a widowed man who already had a daughter, Missy. He didn't want any more children, and they ultimately separated because she wanted to have a baby. But by then she was in her mid-40s and it was too late. Now, still grieving over the loss of this man and the girl she had grown close to, she wonders, did God want her to take care of Missy instead of raising her own child?

Childless by Marriage

For me, the question remains: If I had known that birth control was a sin, would I have used it anyway? Would I have been able to resist the double pull of sexual excitement and boyfriends who made it clear that if I didn't give in, they would move on to someone else? In this culture which glorifies sex and all too often makes fun of religion, would I have had the strength to say "no," to be the prude who pushes the boy away? I did try Natural Family Planning, briefly, but rather than abstain when I thought I might be fertile, I used my diaphragm. Dear God, I don't think I was ever strong enough to say, "No, not this week."

What about today's young woman? Is she operating in the same blind fog through which I grew up, torn between the all-knowing, all-seeing God and a boy with his hand on her breast? Perhaps this is why girls and boys had chaperones in the old days.

Here's another question. Even if I had waited until I was married, would I have been willing to accept the possibility that I might have had four, five, six, eight, ten or even more children, like some of the Portuguese families from the old days? My Aunt Genevieve was the youngest of 18 children. I wanted babies, but 18? I don't even think pets should outnumber their owners. Should children outnumber their parents?

If I had a big family, what would happen to all my dreams of writing and music? I'd like to think I'd carry on, like Julie Andrews in "The Sound of Music," but that doesn't sound realistic. My mother had only two children, and when she got a break between ironing and making dinner, she took a nap.

Is welcoming as many babies as God plants in my belly just too much to ask?

Why do I suddenly think of Fluffy, my friend Sherri's old black mom cat? She had a litter every few months, and after a while, she wasn't so fluffy. In fact, she looked pretty ragged. I'm sure she would have taken The Pill if she could have.

Will I be drummed out of the Catholic Church for even wondering about these things?

Come to think of it, was using birth control a sin if I didn't know it was a sin? According to the latest Catholic catechism references, the use of artificial birth control is a mortal sin, one of the big ones.

83

Sue Fagalde Lick

However, in order for it to be a mortal sin, three requirements must be met: It must be a grave matter, it requires full knowledge, and it requires complete consent of mind and will. So I'm not going straight to hell. I hope.

Although using birth control was a practical choice, not a religious one, I unknowingly violated the rules of my religion. If I had known, what would I have done? God help me, I don't know.

7
Flattened by a Film

You know that Steve Martin movie "Father of the Bride, Part II," where his wife and daughter are both having babies at the same time? When they showed the movie on TV, I sat on the floor watching it alone and cried.

It's supposed to be a comedy. It has appealing actors, delightful dialogue and a happy ending. So what's my problem?

The usual. I don't have a baby. I won't have a baby. I'm never going to have a baby. I don't have a grandchild, I won't have a grandchild, I'm never going have a grandchild. My father will never look at me with the kind of pride that Steve Martin gave his pregnant daughter or the adoration he showed his pregnant wife. I will never have an excuse to run around with stretchy clothes, an unrestrained appetite and that "glow" pregnant women are supposed to have. I will never have a little girl or boy to throw her or his skinny arms around my neck and hug me. I won't have a child to teach how to read, how to knit or how to bake cookies.

I won't have anybody to take me to lunch when I'm a widow or pay my bills when my brain turns to mush. I won't have anyone to throw me a party on my 90th birthday and fill a banquet room with my descendants. I won't have a doting granddaughter to write my biography when I'm dead but semi-famous. I won't—

Oh, stop. I thought I had settled all this. God had another plan. I unconsciously chose career and husbands over motherhood until it was too late to change my mind. I would have made a lousy mother anyway. I would rather write and play music. I have three stepchildren whom I get to share with their mother sometimes. I—don't want to talk about this anymore or I'll cry.

What kills me most of all is that I could have had children.

And I didn't.

Sue Fagalde Lick

I think about my brother watching his daughter being born, watching her grow up to be just like him, with a little bit of her mom and a little Aunt Sue mixed in. What a miracle. Creating life, watching it grow. Beside that, everything else looks puny and pale.

What have I done? Why did I marry men who didn't want children? Why didn't I marry Steve Martin?

So I watch this comedy about having babies and I cry, cry, cry.

I close the door so my husband won't hear me. I told him I was over it.

I *will never be a mother. I will never have children.* For years, I could not say those words. Even now, I'm uncomfortable with them. Logically I know it's true. That ship sailed so long ago it's scrap lumber now. But in my gut, I just can't say it. Never could.

How much more difficult it must be for the woman who has tried and tried to conceive and couldn't, whose pregnancies ended in miscarriage or stillbirth, or who has learned that her husband cannot produce viable sperm. No matter how many doctors and statisticians tell her conception is impossible, that hope is still there, flickering like a faint star in her gut. Maybe, just maybe . . .

I think the hardest thing is the indefiniteness of it. If one has a hysterectomy and knows that the uterus is gone, at least she knows it's impossible. If a woman decides, firmly and forever, that she is not going to have children, it has to be easier. But there is still a loss, and any woman who denies it is fooling herself. When you skip a part of life that most women have experienced throughout history, you have to notice that your life is different and always will be.

It's probably most difficult when you seem to be surrounded by women having babies. Even if they're having a hard time with it, you feel as if you're being left behind. Back in 1985, for example, my cousin Grace gave birth to her second child. Then a co-worker named Carol had twins. Then my niece Susan was born. After my mother called, I hung up the phone and wept.

A newspaper co-worker named Jean came back from maternity leave with baby pictures. That night I dreamed that Jean's baby was transferred from her womb into mine. I watched it grow inside me and be born. I cradled it lovingly, and everyone said I looked so right with a baby in my arms. But then Jean demanded her baby back. I woke up in tears.

In *The Childless Revolution*, Madelyn Cain writes of a Minnesota woman who prepared a grave in her garden and planned a funeral for the child she was unable to bear. She hoped that the ceremony would allow her to finally stop mourning and move on with her life. However, she kept putting off the funeral, unable to face that final letting go of her dream.

It's a hard thing. As little girls, we begin to think about what we would name our children, what they might look like, how we would raise them better than our own parents raised us. We practice mothering with our dolls, our pets and our younger siblings. As much as society today tells us we can do anything we want, the one thing most of us expect to do is become mothers.

And then we don't.

Even if we consciously accept that we will not be soccer moms, our subconscious minds hang on to the possibility for years after the decision has been made. How many nights have I dreamed that I was pregnant, awakening with my hand on my belly, sure that it will be swollen with child, surprised when it isn't? How many infants have I held in my arms in my sleep, bereft when I wake up in the morning with empty arms?

The hardest time was in my late 30s and early 40s when the possibility of having a child was still alive but fading quickly. I could see my chances of motherhood disappearing more with every passing day while a voice inside screamed, "Do something!"

As menopause approached, it got easier to handle being childless. But the baby dreams continued, as strong and as real as any moment of my waking life. I was 50 when I had this dream:

Fred is helping me take care of a newborn baby. I'm not sure who the mother is, but I'm nursing the infant, holding him against my skin. He is warm and sticky. I worry about who will care for him while I work. Later in the dream, I know this is my stepdaughter Gretchen's baby, but I'm still lactating, my breasts swollen with milk. I rush to her house every day to feed this child. I am always aware that he is waiting for my milk. On one particular night, I take the baby home to my own house, hurrying to the back room, lying on the

87

floor with him. My breasts are about to burst. There's someone else there, but I don't know who she is and I don't care. I care only about the baby and me.

I woke up brokenhearted. I had no milk and no baby.

At age 54, in the midst of menopause, I had another dream. This time the baby was about six months old and definitely mine.

I take her to the mall, where a band is playing old-time rags. The baby starts smiling and bouncing in my arms, and I realize this is my chance to teach her about music. So I talk to her about what they are playing, and I sing along with the band. We have a great time.

As we move on, a girl stops to talk to the baby. My little one giggles and reacts, as if they are conversing. This is the first time I've seen her do this. I am thrilled. Suddenly I'm so enchanted by this baby that I want to be close to her at all times. What a miraculous thing, this little person just being formed. I can't wait to tell everyone at home what has happened.

Then I wake up just enough to remember that I don't have a baby. Grief slaps me hard. I struggle to swim back into that dream and almost succeed for a while, but it slips away.

In an article called "Baby Blues," published in 2003 in the AARP magazine, Betty Rollins talks about how she was fine with childlessness until her 60s. Then it hit her. She finally had to come to terms with the fact that she would always be sad over it. I think that's how it is. Like the death of a loved one, it's a shard of sadness that stays with you forever.

Recently in the gynecology waiting room, I seemed to be the only one who wasn't pregnant or accompanied by children. When one new mom was called in, her husband took over care of their baby. Oh, how tenderly he touched that soft skin, how gently he lifted his daughter out of her carrier and cradled her in his arms. Why did I not marry a man like that, I thought. A few minutes later, I was in the examining room answering questions: How many children? None. How many pregnancies? None. Post-menopausal? Yes.

For those of us who expected to have children, who wanted to, giving up the dream of motherhood is a loss as deep as the loss of a leg or the loss of a beloved parent or spouse. The stages of

Childless by Marriage

grief are inevitable. I lived in denial for years. Then I felt anger, blaming my husbands for cheating me out of my chance to be a mother. Depression followed, realizing what I had missed, knowing it was my own damned fault. And sure, I bargained, trying to tell myself that my career made up for my lack of children, but in my heart I didn't believe it. Now I am moving toward acceptance, but I will never completely accept it.

Not every woman without children consciously grieves. Some are happy with their choice. Others are relieved it worked out that way. Sometimes, if I'm going to be completely candid, I'm glad to be free of the responsibilities of motherhood. Sometimes my dogs and husband are more than enough.

But I have felt the pain of loss, along with desperation as the last grains of fertility slipped through the hourglass. *Do I dump the husband before it's too late? Do I have an affair? Do I insist on artificial insemination? I've got to do something. Why do I have all these baby-making parts inside of me if I'm not going to use them? Every cat in heat finds a mate and has kittens. She doesn't think about it; she just does it. Why have I put up with lousy periods for 40 years if I'm not going to have a baby? Why have I used all this birth control when I don't even know if I could have gotten pregnant?*

Grief. Baby grief. Compared to the women who cannot have children, I dare not whine. And yet, I have, loud and long. Not long ago, while menopause was taking its time, the doctor told me that I might still be able to get pregnant. I felt this faint hope deep inside me, this *hey, there's still time.* The odds were impossibly long, the risks too great, the husband even less prepared to be a new father than he was 20 years ago. I would have been old enough to collect Social Security before the child reached junior high, and yet . . .

Then menopause arrived, shutting down the baby factory forever.

I'm not the only weepy one.

Chris, a bus driver, says she believes her decision not to have a child with an alcoholic husband was the right one, but the first word that comes to mind when asked how she feels about it is "heartbroken." It drives her crazy when her friends who are parents never stop talking about their kids, especially when they complain about them. "They are clueless about how lucky they are to have them."

Robyn says she chose art over motherhood. She also had health problems and found it so hard to support herself that she couldn't see how she could take care of a child. Still, she sometimes feels the loss. "Seeing my friends interact with their children can really tug at my heartstrings and make me wish things were different."

"I know it sounds funny," Robyn continues, "but I even have a list of names picked out if my life were different and I had a little one to give a name to. I also sometimes think about the many things I could do with my child, like paint, sing silly songs, dance, read them bedtime stories, celebrate holidays, and bring them to fun and interesting places. I could open doors of learning for them to learn anything they might be interested in, give them a sense of self-worth and security that I don't feel I had when I was growing up, and basically introduce them to the world in a loving, peaceful manner. I really do imagine it sometimes, the things I would do. But it doesn't change the way things are for me or the fact that it would be totally impractical and irresponsible for me to even think about having a child."

Talia, a journalist who had an abortion at her boyfriend's insistence, says, "I wouldn't advise my daughter, stepdaughter or any young woman to give up her child, unless there's a medical reason. And I certainly wouldn't advise them to remain childless. It's the loneliest feeling in the world and it's frightening as well—the thought that you won't perpetuate your genes, that no one will call you 'mommy.'"

Karey, who works in the travel industry, had an abortion at 17. She later married a man who had already had children and didn't want any more. Now 35, she says she wishes every minute of every day that she had children, and she often cries over it, "more often than anyone ever knows. It'll hit me in the middle of a workday, and I'll just sit at my desk crying. Thank goodness I work virtually. I cry in bed, I cry in the car, I cry in the tub. It's so painful, I don't know how to not cry over it."

She can never accept that she will never be a mother, Karey says.

"If I say that, I'm afraid I'll have given in, and I can't give up this dream."

In an essay called "A Small Conclave of Chairs" in *Nobody's Mother,* Rita Moir says, "This is the weird part about being childless and living far from your own blood kin: You end up without that organic connection to youth and regeneration. When there is death and mourning, there's no little kid in your living room giving you that 'life goes on' feeling. There's no family group snuggling around the hearth."

Considering that for most of mankind's existence, a woman's main role has been to bear and raise children, it is no surprise that childless women grieve. But different women experience childlessness differently. Some crave babies so badly they feel as if they will never stop hurting while others see their lack of children as a relief. They were spared an experience they weren't sure they wanted. Most of us end up somewhere in between, feeling both the loss and the relief.

Eventually, we do reach some sort of acceptance, a feeling that things turned out the way they were supposed to. As one woman told me, "If it was in God's plan for me to have kids, I would have. I've had a great career and a great life."

On a Jewish website called aish.com, A. Goodman writes about the years she spent feeling left out, first because she wasn't married and then, after she found a husband, because she didn't have children. She would hide in the bathroom or leave parties early because everyone seemed to be talking about their children and she just couldn't stand the pain.

Even at home, it was difficult. "I live next door to a family of 12 children. I hear their playful laughter, their voices soaring in unison around the table every Shabbat. I gaze longingly through my window as each takes his or her turn sitting proudly atop their *Abba's* lap or running for a reassuring hug from *Ima*."

But one day a thought came to Goodman: "Don't miss today!" By dwelling on what she lacked, she would miss the good things in her life. Overall, she says, "Life is about tests. God set up the circumstances for this most difficult one. I know it's a crucial one for

91

my soul, because it comes up over and over again."

In *What, No Baby?* Leslie Cannold notes that many women who wind up not having children were anxious to do all the things they wanted to do in life, such as going to college, building a career or traveling, before they had children. They feared they would regret the things they missed if they had children right away. On the other hand, they may regret the years they could have been having children. There's always going to be something they miss. Whether it turns into a great sorrow depends on whether they can accept the situation and move on.

Leslie Lafayette, founder of the Childfree Network and author of *Why Don't You have Kids?* writes, "We do not let go of important people in our lives without a sense of loss and mourning. If you have decided to step off the infertility treadmill or for some other life circumstance have reluctantly recognized that having a child is not in the cards for you, you have lost someone important. You have lost your child."

The grief is like a bullet lodged inside your heart. For a long time, you don't feel it, but then it shifts, hits a nerve, and hurts unbearably until it finds a new resting place. At least that's how it is for me. And it doesn't end with the loss of your own child. You also lose the chance to be a grandmother. Recently at a poetry reading, a woman brought her granddaughter. I had heard the woman say that she was "smitten" with this child, and now I could see why. About four years old, she looked like a tiny version of Grandma, with the same curly hair and dimples. They spent all evening together, snuggling, looking through the camera, talking and laughing. My friend was in the throes of grandma love, something I will never experience.

I envied her for this love affair and for the easy way in which she handled the child, clearly well-practiced from her years of motherhood. Yes, the child disrupted the program; yes, her grandmother had to take her out, and yes, the venerable poet at the podium stopped reading to comment on their exit, but Grandma didn't seem to mind.

The poems I read at that night's open mic drew praise and

Childless by Marriage

applause, but that dislodged grief bullet still hurt.

Just as real as the grief is the loss of a baby as an accomplishment. The woman who shows up with a new baby is suddenly the center of attention as everyone flocks around to praise the baby and by association the woman who produced it. In this society, having a baby is like winning the Oscar, the Tony and the Emmy at the same time. People shower you with gifts and acclaim. My having a baby would definitely have trumped my brother's passing the bar—until he had children, too.

It's as if there is a giant checklist for each of us, and no one is supposed to move on to the next step without completing all of the steps before, i.e., graduating from school, catching a man, having children, becoming a grandmother, and achieving something before you die. The last is optional; the rest are not, not for a *real* woman. (Childfree readers, hold your objections. We'll look at your side of the story shortly.) I read the obits, count the children, and sympathize with the women whose obituaries conclude, "She loved her nieces and nephews, and she adored her cat Mimi."

My mother, who quit working outside the home when I was born, always claimed that her biggest achievement in life was raising my brother and me and helping to raise my four cousins. Whatever else she might have done, that was enough.

Says A. in *Wanting a Baby*, "Our language needs a word for the feminine equivalent of machismo. Feminisa, or something. Just as the ultimate symbol of machismo is the erect penis, the essence of feminisa is the ability to create a living, breathing human being in the space between one's hipbones. I wanted to be able to do that, wanted to add getting pregnant naturally to my list of accomplishments in life."

In *Barren in the Promised Land*, Elaine Tyler May writes that in colonial times, women tallied their accomplishments by the number of children they had. Back in ancient Rome, childless women could be divorced or disinherited for their lack of offspring. Today, women accomplish wonderful things in many other areas, but if they haven't had children, there's a glaring blank spot on their resumes.

Prodded to admit their true feelings, most childless women and men confess that they have thought about the children they might have had. They have pictured what they would look like, imagined the things they would do together, and set aside family heirlooms to pass on. Now, when there is no one with whom they can share those things, a few pangs are inevitable. Only by facing the reality and the grief that comes with it can the childless woman go on to enjoy her life and the freedom that her sisters who are mothers won't be able to experience for 20 years or so. She can move, as Lafayette puts it, "from childless to childfree."

I'm not quite there yet. So I watch the silly movie and cry with the door closed.

Part 2

The Evil Stepmother

8
Instant Family

A waiter in a restaurant I frequented during my *Saratoga News* days asked me one day if I was a mother. I gave my standard answer: "I don't have any children of my own, but I have three stepchildren."

He rolled his eyes. "Oh, then you got kids."

Well, yes and no. A stepmother is a lot like a substitute teacher. The kids know she's not the real teacher, so they don't have to listen to her or do what she says. She has all the responsibility without the love and respect. If she sticks around long enough, they might get to like each other, but when the real teacher pokes her head in the door, they'll all abandon their desks, screaming, "Mrs. Smith, you're back!"

It also feels like being the babysitter or the nanny. When the folks come home, the dad gets out his wallet, hands you some money and says, "Thank you very much. We'll take over now."

One Christmas not so long ago, Fred, my father and I were at my stepdaughter's house, along with Fred's ex and her sister. When Michael arrived, his mother and I both jumped up to greet him. Then I suddenly realized, *oh yeah, she's his mother. Back off, Sue.* Fred's ex got the first hug.

As long as the real mother is alive, you can borrow the children for a little while, but you always have to return them. Like library books.

In fact, my role has often been less parent than facilitator. Over the years, I have bought birthday cards and Christmas presents to which I signed my husband's name. I made sure he called his children every now and then. When the kids visited, I provided food and clean sheets. I brought father and offspring together, then stood back.

Sue Fagalde Lick

When Fred and I met, Ted was 17, Gretchen was 15, and Michael was 7. On the night of our first date, Fred told me that he had to end our date before midnight because Gretchen was coming over. So he drove me home in his ratty red Ford Fairmont nice and early. His daughter may not even have known that Daddy was dating.

The first time I actually met the kids, Fred took me to his old house, a typical suburban ranch home in southeast San Jose. I remember a garden that needed work, lots of red brick around the fireplace, and a small kitchen that his ex-wife, Annette, was busy cleaning. It was a Saturday, and we were planning to take Gretchen to lunch.

Ted was in the garage. I got a glimpse of long blonde hair, cut-off shorts and scabs from a recent motorcycle crash. "Hey," he waved, busy with his bike. Fred worked and socialized with female recreation department co-workers about my age, so Ted probably figured I was just another rec leader, no big deal.

Gretchen was a different story. She refused to come out of her room. Forget lunch. In fact, she tells me freely now, "I hated you." At our outdoor wedding, sulking from the bleachers, she was still angry at me. I had no idea she thought I broke up her parents' marriage. Which I didn't. I started dating Fred after he and Annette split, but she carried that grudge for over 20 years before I had a chance to set her straight.

So, she hated me. I suppose it's natural for a daughter to resent any other woman being with her father. We did not have lunch together that day. I was mostly relieved. This was all new territory. *The Complete Idiot's Guide to Stepparenting* came out 13 years too late for me.

Michael was a different story. Drying dishes with his mom, he was a miniature Fred, complete with glasses, huge brown eyes and the same brown hair. He grinned and said hello. Hmm, I thought, he seems friendly. And he was. A sprite in thick glasses, he accepted me immediately.

While Fred and I were dating and later living together, Michael trailed along with us on alternate weekends, leaning over the back of the car seat telling knock-knock jokes and asking, "You know what?"

98

Childless by Marriage

I remember: Christmas stockings bulging with candy and toys. New bicycles. A little guy in flannel PJs turning the couch cushions into an obstacle course. Helping him cut his meat. Nosebleeds. Swimming competitions. Soccer games. Volunteering at Special Olympics track meets. Hunting for flecks of gold in the Sierras. Monopoly games. Impromptu piano lessons. Planting carrots together in the back yard. It was fun, and it did resemble parenting. But it was temporary.

Shortly before Fred and I were married, Annette, his ex, moved to Texas, taking Michael with her. The details of the divorce were still being worked out until just before our wedding. When the forms were finally signed and approved by the courts, Annette had custody of Michael and we were granted custody of Gretchen. Ted was legally of age, so neither parent got custody, but for about six months, we became the caretakers of his worldly goods and his cat while he stayed with friends and searched for a permanent home. Eventually he wound up with his grandparents in Victorville, California.

We were lucky that Fred only had to pay child support for one of his three kids, and it was not a burdensome amount. Other divorced dads tell horror stories about being financially broken in the divorce settlement.

So we had Gretchen. It's not easy taking on someone else's 16-year-old.

Having honeymooned down the California coast to San Diego and back, we arrived home on a hot afternoon, worn out and ready to begin real life as husband and wife.

First stop, naturally, was the bathroom. I saw my cosmetics spread all over the counter. What on earth? Had we been burglarized? For lipstick?

In the bedroom, I found some of my clothes tossed on the bed. Hey. "Fred, did someone break in?" I had been burglarized before and was always afraid of it happening again. Hurrying through the house, I found dirty dishes and beer bottles in the kitchen.

He came in, tossing his suitcase on the bed. "What?"

"Did someone break in?"

"No . . ."

Then it hit me. Oh. Wait a minute. Gretchen, who had been staying with her boyfriend's family, had a key.

"I think Gretchen was here," I said. "I can't believe she went through my stuff. And it looks like she had a party."

"I, um, I don't know."

That's when Gretchen and Ted walked in. Hiroshima was a puff of smoke compared to the blowup that ensued. "What were you doing in my personal things?" I asked.

If she were a dog, I would have seen the fur on the back of her neck go up. "I needed something to wear. What's the big deal?"

"Are you kidding me? Nobody invited you to go through my things. You weren't even supposed to be here. And who said you could have other people over?"

"Fine! I'm out of here. And I'm never coming back." As Ted went out to the patio to smoke a cigarette, Gretchen slammed out the front door and down the street, barefoot.

Fred followed, hollering, "Gretchen! Get back here!" He ran to catch up and grabbed her arm.

She spun out of reach. "No!"

This was one block over from my parents' house in the same quiet Leave-It-to-Beaver neighborhood where I used to walk to grammar school swinging my red plaid lunchbox.

Ultimately I closed myself up in my office and had a good cry while Fred brought his daughter home and tried his best to calm her down. I didn't come out until the kids were gone.

I could have handled that better. Not ever having had a sister, children, or even a roommate, I did not know how to share. Gretchen actually had a right to be there. But if that instant motherly instinct we hear about with newborns is a myth, you can imagine how unlikely it was that I would instantly feel motherly just because I had married Gretchen's father. I had taken on a job for which I had absolutely no training. I'd look at these tall blonde teenagers and wonder what this short dark Portagee was doing with them.

I tried. We enrolled Gretchen at my old high school, and I drove her there most mornings, feeling ever so much like my mother rolling into that parking lot where my best friend Sherri and I used to wait

100

outside the home economics building for our ride on rainy afternoons. When Fred and I went to parents' night, following her class schedule, each teacher said that our daughter was talented but her attendance was poor.

To the teachers, I looked like a mother, but I was merely playing a role. This unruly teenager was not my real daughter. I had no idea what kind of grades she had earned in elementary school, or even which school she had attended. It wasn't as if she was at home every night doing her homework. She spent most of her time at her boyfriend Brian's house. Many nights she didn't come home at all. Soon she announced that she was living there, that it was all right with his mother, and that she would take the bus to our house in the mornings so I could drive her to school. Fred went along with it. Nobody asked if it was all right with me.

G retchen had enrolled at my old school in September. By Christmas, shortly after we moved into our mobile home, she announced that she was pregnant. No wonder she had missed so many classes. She and Brian intended to get married. We took her to the Superior Courthouse downtown to get permission because she wouldn't be 18 before the wedding. We had to provide proof that she was pregnant, that Brian was over 21, and that he had a job. Permission granted, we alerted the retired reverend who had married us less than a year earlier than he had another job to do.

Meanwhile I was doing the mom thing. A journal entry from that time: "Such a long week, getting up at 6 a.m. to try to get Gretchen to school before the bell rang, failing half the time, with the traffic snarling things up so it's difficult to move. Driving, driving, driving. Talking to Gretchen about wedding plans, listening to complaints about her fiancé and her bridesmaids. Writing absence excuses at stoplights, fishing out lunch money, worrying that she won't make it to class or that she'll miss her doctor's appointment. Driving home alone, wondering whether I am doing all this out of love, guilt, insecurity or a desire to spite Fred's hands-off system of child care.

"She's 14 weeks pregnant, farther along than I thought, but still not showing, still jogging and doing aerobics. Sometimes I'm jealous; sometimes I'm glad it's Gretchen and not me. Sometimes I think I just want to be pregnant, not necessarily to have a baby to take care of. Sometimes, though, I think I'll go crazy with the thought that I'll never have one of my own."

In March, Fred and I hosted Gretchen's wedding in the mobile home park's castle-like meeting hall. Rev. Carl Stocking, who married us, performed the ceremony for Gretchen and Brian as well. We hired the same singer/pianist to provide the music. Fred's ex flew in from Texas, along with Michael in a pale blue shirt, brown pants and tiny cowboy boots, but I was the one helping Gretchen before the ceremony. She dressed in our bedroom, using the big mirrors on the sliding closet doors. "Can you tell?" she asked as I helped her cinch up her dress over her pregnant belly. I stood back and gazed at my stepdaughter. She looked so young, her long hair swept up into a snaggle of tight curls. "No," I said, staring at the slight bulge in her mid-section. Not that it mattered. Everyone knew.

I drove her through the park to the hall where the family was waiting. I made punch while Brian's dad, a cook, prepared the food.

I sang, I took pictures, and I helped Michael clean up when he spilled red punch down the front of his shirt. Meanwhile, my husband walked his daughter down the aisle.

Because we held the ceremony in a hall with folding chairs and no separate sides for friends of the bride or groom, I didn't have to endure that whole business of the mother of the bride being escorted to her seat. I know that at some point Annette and Gretchen's two grandmothers were seated, but I don't think I sat at all during the ceremony. I was too busy taking pictures, playing my comfortable journalist role.

My brother took pictures from the other side of the room. Since he had worked with Fred before we met and the groom was the nephew of another guy from the recreation department, everyone felt somewhat interrelated. My parents chatted with Annette's parents and Gretchen's new in-laws. It was all so very civilized—except for the young guys drinking out in the parking lot. Eventually the hard-core partiers crowded into our living room for booze and the opening of the presents. It was our home; Gretchen's mother was a guest and quietly maintained that role while I scurried around making sure everyone had food, drinks and directions to the bathrooms.

When the gifts had been loaded into the car and the guests had gone home, Gretchen wasn't ours anymore. She was a young wife. We moved into the in-law and grandparent mode. We visited the hospital the night Stephanie was born and attended Gretchen's high school graduation at the Fremont Adult School the following spring. She was already pregnant with Brandon, born the next October. We proudly took family photos.

As if it would last. For now, Gretchen was a teen mom. Ted, technically an adult, was baking in the California desert with his grandparents, and Michael was living in Texas with his mother. Fred and I settled back into our lives as happy newlyweds without kids.

9
It All Changes When They Move In

Before he came to live with us, Michael visited during school vacations. I temporarily gave up my office in the spare bedroom, moving my computer into our bedroom. I didn't mind. While Fred was at work, I'd take Michael to the pool, swim a few laps, then work or read in the sun while he paddled around. At Christmas he slogged through the mud with us looking for the perfect Christmas tree. We were buddies.

He only had to deal with me for a little while. Plus, since I was much younger than Fred, I was more fun. Once an amateur gymnast, I would do somersaults and cartwheels with Michael. I showed him how to play simple tunes on the piano. If he got whiny or refused to eat vegetables, it wasn't really my problem because he'd be gone in a day or a week. We didn't have to worry about school or homework or whether he was getting in trouble with his friends. That was all Annette's problem back in Texas. It was like having a visiting puppy: not my job to train him.

Besides, he was so cute.

In the morning, he was up early, sprawled on the couch in his PJs, wrapped in my grandmother's afghan, blearily watching cartoons on TV. He'd get his own breakfast of cereal and milk. A smart kid, he was good at entertaining himself. He could parlay a deck of cards and a sack of pennies into games that kept him amused for hours. When we went out, he came along, patiently enduring the boring parts.

On a trip to the Happy Hollow Park, he led the way, urging me to run with him or step across a pond on stones instead of going around ("Come on, Sue!"). We petted and fed goats and sheep, squawked back at the birds and tried out the rides and climbing apparatus. Like two playmates, we pushed our luck by staying late, hoping "Dad" wouldn't get home before we did.

Childless by Marriage

It was always hard to see Michael go, especially for Fred. It would have been different if he didn't live so far away and could visit every other weekend, but you couldn't do that all the way from Texas. Just when we got used to having him around, we were driving him to the airport again, hugging him hard and fighting tears as the little guy with the big backpack marched down the jetway. My sweet Fred would weep as he drove home. Suddenly the house was so quiet.

It was hard on Michael, too. One time, we arrived at the gate and discovered everybody gone. No Michael. "But he was supposed to be escorted by a flight attendant," we protested to a Southwest Airlines agent. She alerted security to make an announcement over the overhead speakers.

"We are seeking a lost child. Michael Lick, please contact any ticket agent. Your family is looking for you." We heard it over and over as we paced the empty ticket area.

Dear God. What if something bad had happened? What if he had missed his connection in Dallas? He was just a little kid. We called his mother. Had she heard anything? No, but now she was worried, too.

It turns out his flight had arrived early at a different gate. We found him playing behind a counter on the other side of the terminal. "Oh hi," he said calmly as if this happened every day.

But the happy-go-lucky child became an anxious adolescent. Growing up with divorced parents wasn't easy, and we heard tales from the other kids about Gestapo parenting by Annette's boyfriend. Every time Michael arrived, he complained of headaches and upset stomachs. Once, on Highway 101 somewhere around Tully Road, he threw up all over the side of the car. The transition was stressful for all of us.

Things got more complicated when Michael moved in. I took him shopping for school clothes that first year. Remember, I had no mothering experience. I didn't know what his mom had done before. So I went with an unlimited budget. If he said he needed it, he got it. He couldn't believe how much I bought. I was like Santa Claus in September. He came home raving. "She bought me Dockers, she bought me tee shirts, I got new shoes . . ."

Sue Fagalde Lick

Michael went off to his first day of junior high in his pegged acid-wash jeans and untucked shirt, his backpack slung across his shoulders. He seemed confident and ready for new challenges. I was so proud of him.

I felt motherly, but I didn't know what I was doing. Michael did all right at school, but he spent his non-school hours in his room watching the TV his maternal grandparents had sent him. When he fell off his bike and came home bleeding, Fred was the one who took him into the bathroom and cleaned up his wounds while I remained at my desk.

When it was time for the school physical, I took Michael to the doctor, but I had no idea what illnesses or immunizations he had had before. As we sat in the waiting room at Kaiser Hospital, I could feel Michael's nervousness as he fidgeted beside me.

"Don't worry. They're just going to ask some questions and listen to your heart. You won't have to get any shots or anything."

A nurse appeared in the doorway. "Michael Lick."

I followed the nurse and Michael followed me down the hall to the examining room. The nurse picked up a clipboard. "Okay, Mrs. Lick, I just have a few questions."

I smiled at Michael, who was busy playing with the zipper on his jacket. See?

"Has Michael had the measles?"

I looked at Michael. He shrugged.

"Have you?"

"I don't know."

The nurse frowned and checked a box on her form. "How about chicken pox?"

Again, I looked at Michael. "Maybe," he said.

"How about his vaccinations? Is he up to date?"

By this time, I was thinking, oh nuts, why don't I know these things? Time to 'fess up. "I'm sorry. I'm his stepmother, and I don't really have that information. I could call—"

"Well, we'll just take care of it today."

The poor kid ended up getting three shots. I felt like such a traitor. I should have gotten his medical history from Annette, but I didn't know they would ask those things. I wouldn't blame Michael if he never trusted me again.

A mother who carried a baby in her womb, bathed him, diapered him, nursed him, and took care of every inch of his body can naturally gather him into her arms, even when he becomes a resistant teen. They fall together easily, like pieces of a puzzle. As a stepmother, you don't even know whether he had chicken pox or measles growing up or where that scar on his forehead came from.

Michael and I were reluctant to touch each other, even to sit close enough for arms or thighs to come together at a movie theater. We were physical strangers. He was somebody else's teenager, all bones and smells and resentment. I assume it would have been different if he had come out of my body. That physical closeness would have been there from birth, but that's not how it is with most stepchildren.

For a while, I tried to hug Michael every morning before he left for school, just as my mother had always done with my brother and me, but it was awkward as I clutched his stiff, bony shoulders for a moment before setting him free. By the time he grew taller than me, we didn't hug anymore, and it was a relief for both of us.

As a stepparent, there were other rights I didn't have. For example, I couldn't share my religion with him. I continued to go to St. Julie's alone, practicing a faith not shared by my husband or his kids. I was shocked one Christmas when Michael asked, "What's that hut?" meaning the nativity scene. In this mostly Christian country, how could he be ignorant of the story of Jesus? Yet it was not my place to teach him, at least not without his parents' permission.

I couldn't share my music with him either, except for forcing him to listen to my performances until he was old enough to stay home alone. In the early days, Michael had shown an interest in playing the piano. I offered my books, marked them up with finger numbers, coached him through simple Christmas carols, and suggested to his mother that he should have piano lessons. But it didn't happen, and his interest had waned by the time he moved in with us.

Ironically, as an adult, he joined a band, playing his own keyboards and amps, but I saw a talent that could have gone farther and was powerless to do anything about it.

At least we got him singing with us. Fred and I belonged to a small vocal ensemble that went Christmas caroling every December. One year we dressed Michael up in a white shirt and red bowtie and brought him along to sing at the airport. He stood next to me, singing with the sopranos because he still had his squeaky high voice, higher than mine. We frequently challenged each other to see who could hit the highest notes; he always won.

I never had the right to say where he or any of the kids would be on Christmas, Thanksgiving, Easter or Fourth of July. It was Annette's call. As I wrote in my journal in 1995, "She takes him over like a possessive she-bear, and all I am is the woman who lives in the same house as he does. I cook, I show people where the bathroom is and stand back while she embraces my would-be son, buys him new clothes, has long, intimate talks and takes him to visit his real grandparents."

Yet I was the one who got the calls from the scoutmaster's wife seeking cookies for the Court of Honor. I was the one who sat in the emergency room when he crashed his bike and dislocated his shoulder or when he sprained his ankle playing volleyball.

And I was the one who sat in the classroom every back-to-school night listening to his teachers talk about homework and grades and hoping he'd do his assignments.

It was my only shot at motherhood and not a very comfortable one. It was like he was a boarder, somebody who just lived there.

Discipline was a disaster. How does a stepmother of a kid she barely knows tell him what to do and make it stick? When I told his father what he had done wrong, it felt more like a big sister tattling than a parent seeking discipline.

The school would call me to report that Michael was cutting class or flunking a subject. I would tell him he was grounded. Within 24 hours, Fred would commute the sentence. I could not make my stepson do homework, help with chores, or get up in time for school. I could not keep him from sneaking out at night. I couldn't even make him put on a clean shirt for my grandfather's funeral. Instead, he stayed home and pouted.

I tried too hard, making rookie mistakes. For one birthday, we invited all of Michael's friends. I cooked for two days. They didn't eat my fancy quiches and spinach dip. They spent most of the party watching "Friday the 13th" videos on our TV and spraying canned soda at each other in the patio. I didn't know how to stop them. I had to call Fred, the real parent, to yell at them.

I had not planned my life around an adolescent boy with all the quirks, smells and needs that he brought into our home. It was all about writing and music for me. I scarcely had time for a husband, and now, in addition to dealing with his older siblings, I had a growing boy living with me.

And I do mean growing. Once the tiniest kid in the class, Michael became the tallest. His voice deepened from soprano to bass, and he turned into a real teenager. He still spent a lot of time closed up in his room, and I didn't know what to do about it. I had so much work, and Fred was often busy with his tax business. I was going to school, too. My professors acted as if we had nothing else to do except read entire Dickens novels overnight or spend days at the library, but I had a family to take care of. I rarely got to my homework until midnight, and it soon became apparent that I couldn't do it all. I had quit grad school when Jim and I got divorced, and now I reluctantly did it again. My days were marathons, trying to balance work and family. And always, always, it was clear this boy at the end of the hall was not completely mine.

I was torn between wanting to be the mom and wanting to be free. I loved going on a field trip to the technology museum with Michael's class. The other mothers complained about the problems they were having with their children. Mine was great, I said. He was, then.

By Sept. 1990, as he started eighth grade, Michael was taller than me. He was growing so fast I could almost see it happening. At meals, the former picky eater started cleaning his plate and asking for more. He wasn't a little boy anymore.

That summer, when I took Michael to the airport for his return to Texas, an America West worker addressed him as "sir."

But the person inside that body hadn't caught up with his bones. His acne-pocked face looked so innocent, so vulnerable, like a blank piece of paper waiting for the world to write on it, and I couldn't control what might be inscribed there.

Sue Fagalde Lick

In June, I took Michael for a so-called counseling appointment before he flew to Texas. At the high school, he sat mute as "Ms. Louden" hastily told him he would be in college prep and meet the University of California requirements. She filled out every class choice for four years—an absolutely killing schedule—as he said nothing except a quick "uh!" when we walked out.

Why didn't he speak up for himself? Why didn't I?

At the airport, Michael was just as quiet, solicitous of me, but not talkative. I learned later that his mom just dropped him off at the curb, but I went all the way to the gate and watched at the window until he was out of sight. He kept looking back, a little pleased, a little puzzled, this oversized boy in blue shorts and white tee shirt towering over grandmothers and businessmen. He didn't say much, but those dark eyes were taking everything in and his mind was working.

Watching a cute little boy turn into a man was one of the most amazing things I had ever seen.

Yeah, aw, that's sweet, but you know what? While Michael was gone, we picked out our new house and moved. Imagine that, especially for a kid who had been shuffled around so much. Welcome back, son. We live in a different house now.

Michael's new bedroom became his nest, piled with clothes, books and funky smells. His buddies would come laughing down the hall past my office, enter that room, and I'd hear the door close. Once they reach their teens, boys turn to their friends for everything. Moms, even real moms, are mostly there to provide food and money and sign papers for school.

Sometimes I got things right. One night, 49ers football player Ronnie Lott was supposed to be signing autographs at the grand opening of his new fitness center and I had arranged to cover it for the *South Valley Times*. I took Michael and his friends, expecting to score big points. Unfortunately, the editor had given me the wrong date and Lott wasn't there. But Michael and his friends were more interested in rock music than football anyway. Renee Fox, a disc jockey from "Hot 97.7," the radio station all the kids listened to, was the featured celebrity that night. The guys were too shy to talk to her, but I introduced myself and dragged Michael over to meet her. He was geeky and bashful but thrilled when Renee reached under her table

110

Childless by Marriage

and pulled out a 97.7 tee shirt for him. It was two sizes too big, but he couldn't wait to wear it to school and brag about where he got it.

By the time Michael turned 15, I had learned a lot about teen birthday parties. We survived this invasion of teenagers much more successfully than the first time. Actually, it wasn't too bad: four hours of loud music, balloons popping, chips getting ground into the carpet and young men hollering "Hey dude!" I opted for pizza and chips, which is all they wanted. I bought soft drinks in bottles instead of cans and had no illusions of joining the party. Fred and I spent part of the party in the patio and part dining in my office. The music was loud, but we were able to tolerate it. We were wiser. The kids were also older. The boys' voices had changed, and the girls had breasts. The kids sneaked off in couples to neck in the dark. I even saw Michael with his glasses off and his arms around a girl, but no clothes came off, and, to our pleasure, Michael helped clean up.

Before the party, the mother of one of Michael's friends had called. She thanked me for having the party because now she wouldn't have to have one at her house. She offered any supplies we might need and she wished me luck. I smiled. It wasn't so bad.

When Michael turned 16, I gave him my old car. A few months later, he loaned it to his girlfriend, who totaled it. That was the car I had bought for myself with the money I got when my grandmother died, when I was too poor to even keep the previous car running. In one night, it was gone.

Michael had been pacing around that morning, waiting for me to see it. I glanced out the window, thought I was imagining things, then looked again. "Oh my God."

I walked outside. Bright sunshine sparkled off a cracked window and crumpled bumper. The damage went all the way around the front.

When I came in, he was telling his father what had happened. He stopped mid-sentence.

"Sorry," he said, slipping his backpack over his shoulder.

"Me too."

And he went off to school on his bike.

Maybe a real mother would just be grateful that no one was hurt, but I wanted to throttle him, especially as I watched my chocolate brown Honda Civic get towed away the next day. The insurance

111

company had declared it too damaged to fix. That was *my* car.

Somehow the years passed. Michael graduated from high school, turned 18, registered to vote and signed up with the draft board. We're lucky no one was being drafted then. He had transformed from a tiny kid with big glasses and huge eyes into a tall, handsome adult with contact lenses. He had outlived zits, puberty and trigonometry and was looking at college catalogs. We had done it.

The year Michael turned 20, Fred and I moved to Oregon. We invited him to join us, but he declined. By then, he was sharing an apartment with friends. We knew he was struggling to balance college and work. When his mom announced that she was moving back to California and said he could live with her if he got in trouble, we were relieved. Once again, he would have a mother-in-residence to watch over him. I warned her about her son's late hours; she spilled the beans about his girlfriend sharing his apartment. By comparing notes, mother and stepmother, we both knew the whole story.

10
Hell Breaks Loose

Three years after Gretchen's wedding, Fred and I returned from a vacation to Bandon, OR, to find a series of tearful telephone messages. She and Brian had gone out drinking, come home drunk and gotten into a fight in the parking lot at their apartment complex. The police came, and somehow two officers were injured.

Arrested on minor charges, they managed to stay out of jail, but their problems continued. Brian had turned violent. Gretchen often called us, crying. She said she loved Brian so much, but she was afraid to be alone with him.

After a beating sent Gretchen to the hospital, she sought refuge with us. When she and the kids arrived about 5 p.m., I was typing a *South Valley Times* article, on deadline, hoping to get to the office to turn my film in by 6. Suddenly there they were, the kids with their hands in my stamps, erasers, staple removers, favorite pens, and important papers. Within 10 minutes, Brandon had broken the knob off my piano lid. Within a half hour, they had cookie crumbs, newspapers and water glasses all over the house and yard. Both kids were stubborn and cranky and wouldn't obey or listen to anyone.

It was no wonder the kids were acting up. They had watched Brian attack their mother. Brandon had clung to Gretchen. Stephanie had gotten a stick from the back yard and waved it at her father, telling him to "leave Mommy alone." The first words out of her mouth when they got to our house were, "Do you know what my Daddy did?" Then she described it, even demonstrating how he had tried to strangle Gretchen.

Fred didn't say much about any of this. Just home from work, he settled into his chair with a glass of wine and a book. He was sympathetic, but when I think about how most fathers would react, I'm surprised. My dad would have killed any man who hit me.

They only stayed overnight. Gretchen took the kids home the next morning while Brian was at work. Repentant, Brian moved out, but the kids continued to see him at his mother's house. After another incident, when Brian called Gretchen names, hit her and refused to let her take Stephanie home, she called her mother in Texas and arranged to send the children there for a couple months. They would be safer with their grandmother, she felt.

When we went to the airport to see the kids off, we met Gretchen's new boyfriend, a bartender named Dave. Brian showed up, too.

"Uh-oh," I whispered to Fred as we saw our handsome son-in-law approaching.

But Dave saw him, too and went off to smoke just outside the terminal entrance. I joined him. I soon found myself bonding with him. We were both outsiders. He was closer to my age than anyone else there, and he seemed like a decent guy, despite two failed marriages.

The kids had no idea what was up. Brandon ran joyfully to the new play equipment while Stephanie clung to her mother's pants. I don't know what Gretchen said to him, but Brian walked away without talking to us.

Gretchen stood at the gate with tears streaming down her face.

It's a good thing we liked Dave because soon he was living with Gretchen and the kids. It wasn't long before we attended Gretchen's second wedding. She married Dave in Reno, and I got to play mother of the bride again.

Arriving at the Vagabond Hotel an hour before the wedding was scheduled, Fred, Michael, Ted, and I changed our clothes and drove to the courthouse, across from the Heart of Reno chapel, with its heart-shaped neon signs. The bride and groom came from their hotel in a white limo. Dave looked spiffy in a new pin-striped suit. Gretchen looked like a movie star in her snug-fitting off-the-shoulder ivory suit, her golden hair falling in soft curls. She and Dave held hands and smiled at each other.

Getting the license took longer than the wedding. The two older women working that Sunday afternoon had trouble understanding that the Newark where the kids lived was in Alameda County, California, not New Jersey. As for the rest of the form, including previous marital experiences, blood tests, etc., check, check, stamp, stamp, and it was done.

License in hand, the bride and groom walked across the street to the chapel.

It was just like in the movies, so tacky it's hard to believe they were serious. We purchased flowers and boutonnières in the lobby, and we picked one of three gaudy little chapels, the red and pink one. In seconds, the boys and I were seated and Fred was walking Gretchen down the short aisle to Rev. Warren, a pudgy guy with a Southern TV preacher accent. As the video camera whirred, the reverend asked everyone's names, including the bride's and groom's. He whipped through a five-minute ceremony. They exchanged rings, they kissed, the recorded music swelled, and it was over, $200 please. Was it real? Did it count? Fred and I rolled our eyes at each other.

Apparently it was legal. We drank champagne in the kids' hotel room, to the accompaniment of jackhammers just outside. We exchanged sincere words of love and blessing and had a wonderful dinner downstairs as a family.

We settled into the in-law/grandparent role again. The kids grew up calling Dave "Dad." He had a daughter of his own, Sabrina, so Gretchen became a stepmother, too. Now we had something in common.

But don't get any pictures of us having this warm fuzzy relationship with Gretchen and her new family. We didn't visit or talk often. When we did go to their house, we spent most of our time watching TV or talking to the dog, a Rottweiler named D.O.G. We were all busy with our own lives.

Gretchen had her problems, but the early years of our marriage were tough times for Ted, too. I had no idea how much his parents' divorce tore him apart. As the oldest child, he probably resented the changes his family had undergone more than the other kids. His parents got divorced, his mother moved to Texas, his father remarried, their house was sold, and where was he? Looking for a home. Those were dark days, which he has requested that I not write about here. I'll just say that the years he lived in Victorville, plus his jobs working nights and weekends when he lived nearby, made it difficult to form a close relationship. I don't see him much now, but we get along.

Today, Fred's children are in their 30s and 40s. We talk on the phone once in a while, exchange text messages, and meet on Facebook. I mail Christmas and birthday gifts. On Christmas or my birthday, they might call or send a card, but probably not. I like to think that if I had raised them, they would be more attentive, but I am not their mother. I did not get to teach them how to be adults. Whatever influence I had was brief and intermittent.

When you're married to a man with children, how you relate depends a lot on how he relates to them. If the kids live with him, it's a whole different story than if they live with their mother. Their ages, visitation arrangements and whether the parents get along make a big difference, too. Does it make any difference that Ted and Gretchen were adopted? I'll never know for sure. They both think Michael got most of the attention, but I doubt that Fred would have been closer to them if they were his biological children.

I noticed early in our relationship that he didn't pay much attention to his kids. It was a time when Ted and Gretchen were both having a lot of trouble. Gretchen disappeared for days at a time with her boyfriends. Although all three kids were deemed gifted, Ted and Gretchen struggled in high school and did not graduate with their peers, although both earned their diplomas later.

One night in bed, I confronted Fred. "Don't you care?" I asked, straining to see his face in the dark.

To my amazement, he started to cry. "I do care," he said.

I touched his damp cheeks, wishing I hadn't started this but needing answers. "Sometimes you don't act like it. How come?"

"I don't know."

I put my arms around him, kissed his wet cheeks, and stopped asking questions.

I still wonder after all these years why he wasn't more involved in his children's lives. Was it the way he was raised with two working parents? His mother was not fond of children. Did that rub off on him? Was it that he had lived hundreds of miles from his parents and his brothers most of his adult life? But I remember stories of Fred's father leading their Boy Scout troop. I have seen home movies of Fred and his brothers goofing around in the pool or playing ball. We have black and white pictures of Fred with his grandparents and his cousins. It looked like a close family.

Did Fred feel shut off from his kids' lives after Annette ended the marriage? Or did it start before that? My brother and other former co-workers tell tales of drunken recreation department parties. Fred had an active social life that included parties, softball games, art and wine festivals, and other events that didn't seem to include his wife or kids. While Ted and Gretchen were small, he earned a master's degree, taking night classes after working all day.

He was also working a second job doing income tax returns, which I soon learned meant that you couldn't talk to him from the end of January through April 15. Did he stay busy to avoid his teens' troubles? To avoid the responsibilities of caring for little Michael, the child who was born well into their marriage when they believed they couldn't conceive? Or did his kids get in trouble because he was so busy with other things?

Once Fred and Annette were divorced and we were married, we could have done so much more with his children. They might have rejected us, but we could have tried harder. I had all this mother love to give and never felt free to give it because Fred stood in the way. Over the years, I have been the one connecting my husband with his children, making the phone calls, sending the gifts, suggesting we visit. If I didn't, I suspect there would be no contact at all.

Several years after we moved to Oregon, Gretchen met us for dinner at La Paloma in Santa Clara, the same restaurant where Jim and I had discussed our impending divorce many years earlier. Gretchen had recently left Dave, her second husband, claiming he was doing drugs. She and a dark-haired man came roaring into the parking lot on motorcycles. We were disconcerted because we had expected her to come alone. We wanted a chance to find out what had happened with Dave. But here was this new guy, Matt.

Gretchen had barely shed her leathers and settled into a pitcher of margaritas when she suddenly lit into Fred. "I've been thinking a lot, and I have to get this off my chest." Chug. "You were not a very good father. You were never there for me. It hurt me deeply, especially when you moved to Oregon as if we didn't matter at all."

Stunned, Fred began to cry. Matt politely went out for a smoke. I gulped my drink. Fred stuttered and sobbed as she went on and on about what a rotten dad he had been. All he could say was, "I'm sorry." He kept saying it over and over. "I'm sorry, I'm sorry."

I wanted to disappear.

Did that evening change things? Not for the better. It was too late. When the margaritas and chips ran out, we boxed our dinners and went back to our hotel while Gretchen and Matt sped away on their bikes.

Take one work-obsessed stepmom who doesn't know how to jump into the parenting pool and one father standing like a wall keeping her out of the water, and that's what happened.

11
You're Always the Temp

When the real mother is still around, the gap between stepmother and stepchildren is like a canyon full of rattlesnakes.

It's always part-time, halfway. For our first Christmas in our new house, I had planned a big Christmas Eve party, inviting some friends, my parents and all the kids. Only Ted and Gretchen showed up, and they didn't understand why I was serving linguica dogs, beans and potato salad. Because my family always did that, that's why. We were so different, these tall, blonde young adults and this short, dark Portuguese woman.

Gretchen looked beautiful in a white sweater, white slacks and a red jacket. Her long golden-blonde hair was beautifully waved. Ted seemed moody and anxious to leave. We ate our food, exchanged gifts—expensive sweaters for them, housewares for us—and sat awkwardly. The kids shared secret jokes and experiences with each other. They talked about the Christmas feast they were planning for Annette's relatives. We were not invited or given a chance to see Gretchen's children, who were with their dad on Christmas Eve and would spend Christmas Day with Annette's family. I felt jealous and left out. Busy planning their party, they didn't stay long. I was left with a ton of beans, potato salad, and Portuguese sausage.

Looking at stepmotherhood from another angle, I got something real moms rarely experience: breaks from parenting. The older kids never stayed with us for long, and Michael spent weeks away with his mother. I missed him, but I got to focus on work, had private time with Fred, and didn't have to compete for the telephone. I also didn't have to deal with invasions of Michael's friends when I was cleaning the toilet or working in my bathrobe.

Sue Fagalde Lick

We had some challenging days and nights, but having Michael only part-time made me appreciate little things like watching him go off trick-or-treating or goofing around with his buddies. It also gave me the option of calling for backup from his mother, something biological moms can't do. Blessed with a cordial relationship, Annette and I were able to parent as a team.

My friend Mary believes step-parenting is the best way to be a parent for someone who is as busy as she is teaching music lessons, directing choirs, and performing. She barely has time to eat, but she enjoys her stepchildren and step-grandchildren. She also enjoys resuming her activities when they leave.

I admit that I do, too. So many baby boomer women have learned that women's liberation freed us to do anything we wanted outside the home PLUS taking care of home and family. It's an impossible load. Remember Arlie Hochschild's classic book *The Second Shift*, which showed how women were wearing themselves out trying to maintain both careers and families with minimal help from their husbands? Step-parenting might be the perfect way to have it all.

At our wedding reception, Ted, who was a week shy of his 19th birthday, said to me, "Now I guess I should call you 'Mom.'" "Not unless you want to," I replied, a little stunned.

I guess that was a mistake. In the nearly 30 years since that day, Ted has never called me Mom. Nor have the other two gotten into the habit. To them, I am Sue. I guess it makes sense. They already have a mother.

Most stepmothers go by their first names. Even in the case of my aunt, who bristles when I refer to my cousins from my uncle's first marriage as her stepchildren, they call her Suzanne, not Mom.

My friend Lee Ann, who took care of her stepdaughters after their mother abandoned them, feels as close to them as any mother could, but they usually use her first name. She does hear from others that they sometimes refer to her as their mother, just as she refers to them as her daughters.

It's so much easier to take the "step" out of the language. We probably all drop it sometimes and just say mother, daughter, son, but then we come up against the need for accuracy, especially when there's a biological mother hovering in the background.

Cheryl from Michigan doubts that her husband's kids will ever call her Mom. "The boys remain close to their mom, and I can't imagine them not feeling as if they were betraying her if they'd call me that. They've always called me by my first name. I have wished there was some in-between term which is more familial than using a first name, but unfortunately there really isn't."

Laura D., a massage therapist from Texas, wouldn't expect her stepchildren, who are almost the same age as she is, to call her Mom. She laughs when asked what they do call her. "Sometimes Bitch. No, I'm just kidding. We were friends before I got married to their dad."

The problem of what to call each other is as hard for the kids as it is for us. When introducing us to their friends, stepchildren occasionally leave out the step. Michael did that when he'd parade his posse through the house and point to me. "That's my mom; she's a writer." I loved it, and I'm sure it was less awkward for him.

It makes a difference how old the stepchildren are. Joyce's steps were already adults moving into middle age when we talked. "Dad and Joyce are our names," she said.

Just as Fred and I became "Dad and Sue." Here's a secret. If I picked out a gift and their father had nothing to do with it, I wrote "Sue and Dad" instead. My own little code.

I would love for someone to call me Mom and mean it.

Stepchildren get you into the Mom Club, but it's a conditional membership. At any time, especially if the real mother is alive and nearby, you can be outed as NOT A REAL MOTHER.

When Michael moved in with us, he had no friends to play with and no outside activities. He spent all his time in his room reading or watching TV. When we asked if he'd like to try sports or scouts or something, he just shrugged and said no. Having both been Scouts in our youth, we signed him up for Boy Scouts anyway. It was a good thing. He made some friends and had something to do.

The poor kid got dumped right into the heart of it. The winter campout was his first event. This boy who had never really camped got dragged out shopping for a snow suit and other gear, then dropped

Sue Fagalde Lick

off at 6 a.m. to meet the other Scouts, all strangers.

It was snowing and cold. He got so nervous he threw up in the car, and somehow he melted his rented snowsuit on the campfire, but he stayed with the Boy Scouts. Over the years, as he grew too tall for his green shorts and too broad for his original khaki shirt, I sewed on badges until my fingers bled—those things are thick!—and I baked dozens of cookies.

The Scouts were big on ceremonies. One required the mothers to wear a red ribbon and go up front to have their sons fasten on new pins every year. Although Michael gave up Scouts in high school, I still have those pins and treasure them. Will I ever give them to his real mother? Not a chance. I baked the cookies.

For eight years, I was the mother who attended school conferences and answered calls from the teachers. I wrote the notes when Michael stayed home sick, and I got used to groups of adolescent boys trooping through my house.

I even tried to discipline him, especially when he started skipping school, sneaking out at night and getting low grades in his junior and senior years of high school. I was the one who argued with him about how Ds are passing but not good enough. His father, bless his heart, didn't get involved.

But, in the years when I was mother-in-residence, any time his biological mother came to town, she could show up at the door, receive the kind of hug I never got and spirit him away. I often heard Michael on the telephone talking to her, keeping his voice too quiet for me to hear what he was saying. That's step-parenting. In terms of fitting in with other women, it's better than not parenting at all. When people asked if I had children, I could answer, "Yes, I have three stepchildren." If I said it quickly and firmly, I could head off questions about having any of my own.

I could show photos of my gorgeous stepdaughter and her beautiful children. I could compare Michael's junior high and high school experiences with the other kids'. I could talk about Christmas dinners and birthday parties just like any other woman my age. But it was a role I was playing, not really me.

122

Childless by Marriage

When your husband's child moves in, for a day or a lifetime, suddenly there's competition between you and the kid. The child has an advantage in the biological connection and having known your husband longer than you have. Your needs take second place. You want to go to a concert, but the son has soccer practice. You want to have sex, but you can't be alone. You want to go to a fancy restaurant, but the child wants a hamburger.

Parenting requires sacrifice. I'd like to think it's easier if the kids are yours to start with. You can work your way into it through the planning and pregnancy and the months when the child hasn't learned to walk or talk yet. Maybe some biological imperative makes you willing to share everything you have. After all, the child is part of you.

But it's different when you inherit someone else's children overnight.

A *U.S. News and World Report* article by Art Levine notes that about 40 percent of remarriages involve stepchildren. Studies show that the conflicts between children and their stepparents cause those marriages to break up more often than those without.

It's a two-way battle. The kids may blame the new wife for breaking up their parents' marriage—even if she didn't—and they probably worry that you're going to take their dad away from them. So they kick, scratch and hit, figuratively if not literally.

Meanwhile, the father may feel guilty for leaving the kids, for not being there all the time for them. He may neglect his new wife while trying to make amends with his children.

Plus, there's this tendency on both sides to tattle, especially when you're considerably younger than your husband. *Do you know what he did? Did you see what she did?* It starts to feel as if you're all children vying for the attention of the same parent figure. That's nuts, right? I'm supposed to be the adult. But I'll bet most stepmothers would admit to feeling that way sometimes. They also find themselves thinking or even saying, "Hey, I'm your wife. Listen to me." And maybe he does; maybe he doesn't.

In an article called "Second Wives Do Have Fairytale Powers," Angela Phillips writes about Louise, who had a hard time spending weekends with her husband's children. When they had screaming fits,

123

Sue Fagalde Lick

she wondered why her husband didn't stop them. At meals, all the kids would fight to sit next to their dad while she felt like an "appendage."

Louise added, "I'm sure they found my presence as strange as I found theirs, but when a six-year-old suddenly says, 'I'm going to take my Daddy away and lock him up and put you on the rubbish dump,' it is hard not to feel rejected. Then, instead of comforting me, my husband would be cuddling her and saying how much he loved her. I felt terribly jealous."

A woman who calls herself Cool Steppie discusses her experiences on her web site. Conflict dominated her early years with her stepdaughter. If the child acted up, the husband took her side. Steppie felt as if she was doing all the work for none of the credit. "Somehow I had become the wicked stepmother. I found myself short-tempered, irritable, insanely jealous, angry, a ranting, raving lunatic at times, and ready to give my stepdaughter a one-way plane ticket for the middle of Antarctica . . . .

"She was a devil-child to me but a complete angel to him. Because I couldn't control her or be a 'good enough mother' to her, I was told that I was too immature to have children of my own. I think that all of this would be enough to turn ANYONE into a wicked stepmother!"

Things got better for Cool Steppie. They settled into a relationship of love and respect. "I realize now that all of her actions were pretty much normal and that she was fighting me not so much for me but for what I represented: never having her parents together again."

It's inevitable that the stepmother and stepchildren would be jealous of each other, having to share their father. In the case of a woman who will not have her own children because her husband already has these kids, the battle becomes more intense.

It's particularly difficult for stepdaughters who see the stepmother coming between them and their fathers when they're used to being Daddy's Girl.

Step-parenting, especially in the early years, is messy. It's war. With luck and time, you work out some kind of truce. Maybe you become friends, even feel like family. Maybe you just agree not to

124

hurt each other for the sake of the man you both love. Or maybe you agree to never be in the same place at the same time. Option number one feels like the best choice, but every family is different.

When I telephone Fred's kids, I often refer to myself as the wicked stepmother. Thank God, they laugh and tell me I'm not wicked, but I always wonder what they really think.

What about all those fairy tales? Cinderella's stepmother treated her like a slave. Snow White's stepmother ordered her to be killed. Hansel and Gretel's stepmother left the children in the woods in the hope they'd get eaten by the witch. There are many more lesser-known tales of wicked stepmothers. The father is rarely mentioned. I wonder where he is and why he's not sticking up for his kids. But more important, why is the stepmother so evil? Is it jealousy? Are the children a bother or an obstacle between her and her husband? Are they so angelic that they make her look bad?

Well, I hope no real-life stepmother is out to murder her stepchildren, but competition definitely arises in step-parenting situations. You want your husband's full attention, especially if you haven't been married very long, but so does this child. *Daddy, Daddy, Daddy.*

There's also resentment.

Sarah from Virginia worries about seeing her stepsons have kids when she doesn't get to have any. Her husband's a great dad, but she says, "I'm not going to watch my husband bounce somebody else's kids on his knee."

Looking back, I felt that, too. When Gretchen got pregnant less than a year after I married her father, I definitely saw a little unfairness in the situation. I was going to be a step-grandmother when I had barely gotten a grip around the edges of being a stepmother. It seemed ironic that she was swelling up with child while I was in the midst of a raging barren menstrual flow.

I don't feel like a wicked stepmother. Wicked stepmothers are old and mean and ugly, and they boss their husband's children around. I'm not like that. I hope.

Sue Fagalde Lick

Families are complicated, no matter how they're arranged. We had just had a tearful confrontation with Michael over wrecking my old car when Fred's birthday came along. Fred's parents flew in from Las Vegas, my parents joined them, and all the kids showed up. It was a noisy, laughing, loving crew. They were dressed up, personable, and smiling, the kind of kids everybody wants.

Gretchen's children, staying with their dad, telephoned, giving me a warm glow when they called me Grandma. I served an elegant dinner and impressed our parents. I was surrounded by step-children who were friendly, loving, and helpful. They even did the dishes. Fred was delighted to have everyone together for his birthday. At that moment, I couldn't think of anything that was missing in my life. As we went to bed that night, I kissed Fred. "Thank you so much for giving me this family."

The warm feeling has come and gone over the years. Being a stepmother is not exactly like having your own kids, but I don't *not* have children either.

The best Christmas of my life occurred at our house on Safari Drive in San Jose. Mom and Dad, Fred's kids, our son-in-law Dave, Gretchen's two kids and Dave's daughter Sabrina were all there. I had cooked and decorated. We had crowded under the Christmas tree to exchange presents. We had eaten our turkey dinner, and now we were relaxing like the families on TV.

Gifts and wrapping paper were scattered all over the house. The air smelled of turkey and pumpkin pie. The boys and men gathered around Fred's computer, and the girls shared the piano bench with me, improvising accompaniments to "Little Drummer Boy" and other corny Christmas songs. It felt so good.

But it only happened once. Most holidays, everyone was scattered, the grandchildren to their respective non-custodial parents, Fred's kids with their mom and her parents, us with my parents. That's the way it goes when families are broken up by divorce into Legos that sometimes fit one way and sometimes another.

Childless by Marriage

I come from parents with strict old-country standards. They had not progressed far from a time when people didn't get divorced, when women didn't drink, when you stayed in school, got a good job, got married and had kids—in that order. Ted and Gretchen didn't follow that pattern, and Mom and Dad had reached an age where they expected people to bend to their wishes, not the other way around.

My parents never accepted Ted, Gretchen and Michael as their own. On the rare occasions when Michael would call one of them Grandma or Grandpa, they didn't respond, but what else was he supposed to call them? Mr. and Mrs. Fagalde? Ed and Elaine? Poor kid. Divorce gets everything all scrambled up. At one point, Gretchen's son Brandon had so many grandmothers and great-grandmothers, he looked at me and said, "Hey, uh, *Aunt* Sue?"

I could have pushed harder to bring my parents and Fred's kids together, but it takes more than one person to make it work. During my mother's life, I think we spent two Christmases with my parents and my "kids" in the same place. The first one, at Mom and Dad's house, was particularly interesting because my brother's wife and Gretchen had both just had babies, so my mother and I were new grandmothers together. We have pictures of my niece Susan and Gretchen's son Brandon taking naps on their blankets in the den, Susan in a red sweater and red-ruffled panties, Brandon in a tiny tuxedo.

But the folks didn't invite them back; they never reached out to them. Michael lived with us, so he was an unavoidable part of the package. But as for Ted and Gretchen, my parents didn't send gifts, didn't know when their birthdays were, didn't include them in their thoughts or their plans. Nor did the kids reach out to them.

Perhaps I didn't stick up for my stepchildren as much as I should have, but I felt pretty bad when my mother died and my father refused to include Fred's children's names in her obituary. "She didn't know them that well," he said. Ouch.

A re stepchildren satisfactory substitutes for having your own? I asked other women.

No way, said Laura, the Texas massage therapist.

"I was not 'mom' to them—just Dad's wife," said Lisa, also

127

from Texas. "No, they were not satisfactory as substitutes. I never tried to make them my kids—that would be unrealistic."

Likewise for Sarah, who left her home in Scotland to be with the man she loved, who had two sons. The boys seem to think she split up their dad's first marriage, she said, so they were not close. "I've never been a stepmom; I'm always Dad's wife." If the boys' mother is present, she added, "I don't even exist."

No, said Chrissie, a New Zealand writer. "They aren't substitute children, and I don't want them to be. We're just friends, with a shared interest in a man who happens to be their father and my partner. Everybody's happy!"

Sometimes they feel like hers, said Karey, who had an 8-year-old stepson when we talked. "He lives with us fifty percent of the time. I play the mother role when he is with us in the sense of packing his lunch, checking his homework, tucking him in at night. It's very fulfilling, but it's not enough. I've been in his life since he was 2, so he doesn't recall life without me and the transition was very easy, as we never went through the 'you're not my mother' phase. But his bio-mom is very much involved and she very much likes to remind me of my place and let everyone know she is the mother and I'm not. She likes to rub it in that she had a child with my husband and I didn't."

Absolutely yes, said Lee Ann. Her stepdaughters' mother dropped the girls on the doorstep one day, and Lee Ann became their *de facto* mother. "She just dumped them off at Jon's with no plans, no nothing, right after his second year of law school." The girls were covered with sores from lying in urine after wetting the bed. In the divorce proceedings that followed, he won custody because the children had been so mistreated.

Lee Ann and Jon weren't even married before Lee Ann was parenting his children. "We coordinated our school, work and kid schedules so the kids would never be left alone anymore. We couldn't afford babysitters. I took it upon myself. I was a 'we' already, having to take care of these girls."

The girls were 2 and 8 when they moved in. "I gave them their first birthday parties," Lee Ann said. She also attended school conferences, provided their clothing and saw them through their first periods and their first dates.

Childless by Marriage

When she and their father split up, Lee Ann remained the mother figure to his daughters. "They really became my kids," she said. She did all the mother stuff as they grew up, and now, as she battles MS, they watch over her. "I'm so lucky in that regard really that their mother was absent. They were so desperately in need of an adult in their lives that we were able to have a deep bond." She said raising them is the biggest accomplishment of her life, so yes they were a real substitute for having her own children.

Lee Ann's cousin Marie, who lives in Montana, said the same of her two stepdaughters. "They just love me, and I love them." At the time, the oldest was trying to get pregnant. "I'll be so delighted to be a grandmother."

Yes, echoed Chris, who mothered her two stepsons and is now enjoying grandparenting. The years of motherhood flew by. She was closest to Billy, the youngest. "This one was probably closest to my heart because he had no relationship with his own mother and had nothing to do with Phil, his fisherman dad. This little boy was really abandoned by the parents, so he stayed with us while his dad fished. He came to us at 2 or 3 years old, and we really bonded." When she saw her sister taking on the challenges she had already faced, she'd say, "I've already done all that. I did do my job being a mom."

And finally, a big yes from Bonnie, who has stepchildren from two marriages and now step-grandchildren from the second marriage. They all get along well. She talks to them and receives Mother's Day cards and feels she's closer to the grandchildren than their real grandmother is. "My stepson and grandchildren have been the best substitute I could ever want. But I wonder if they will still be as close to me if my husband is not around someday."

That sliver of doubt is always there. A couple years after Michael moved out and we relocated to Oregon, I was filling out a Who's Who form. When I got to the space where it asked for the names of my children, I hesitated. Should I mention Michael, Gretchen and Ted? I did. They are listed as stepchildren.

When they're in your lives, especially when they live with you like Michael did, you start to feel as if maybe you really are a mother. But it's like playing a long-time role on a soap opera. When the show gets canceled, you're an actor, not the character you played.

129

Sue Fagalde Lick

Just before we sold our house in San Jose, Michael moved into his first apartment and never looked back. We saw it only once. Gretchen helped us paint our house and pack the moving van, but Ted never returned our calls.

Once we got settled, they mostly telephoned when they wanted something, usually help with their taxes. When I tried to engage them in conversation, they repeated like a broken record, "Can I talk to my dad?"

Sure, I'm just the lady who answers the phone.

12
Grandma Sue?

One of the strangest things about being a childless woman married to a man who has children is that we sometimes become grandmothers and even great-grandmothers without ever having been mothers. Things can get complicated, especially if we have had no practice with little ones.

Some women dive in and develop wonderful relationships with their step-grandchildren, completely filling the emptiness caused by not having children. I was not one of those women.

Not long ago, Gretchen blasted me for not being involved enough in her children's lives. She's right. I wasn't. If you average it out, I probably haven't seen them more than once a year. They were not available, Fred was not interested, or we were "busy."

If only I could have been more like my Grandma Rachel.

Rachel Meynell Fagalde was married three times, but she remained childless. By the time she married Clarence Fagalde, she was probably menopausal. I'll never know why she didn't have children with her previous husbands. I didn't ask; I wish I did. But when we talked, it was always about me. That, I think, was her secret to terrific grandparenting—that and the fact that she didn't have to compete with her husband's ex.

My biological grandmother, Clara Fagalde, died when I was two years old. I don't remember her at all, nor do my brother or my cousins. She was just a name on a plaque in the mausoleum at Oak Hill Cemetery. So Rachel had an open field, and she played the grandmother role full-out. She asked questions about what we were doing, showered us with gifts and treated us like little adults whom she adored. She spent most of her tiny social security income on us grandkids and her beloved nephew and nieces.

Her stepsons and their wives found her annoying. She cooked terrible tasteless meals, read letters and articles out loud to folks who

Sue Fagalde Lick

didn't want to hear them, drove like a maniac, smoked cigarettes in the kitchen, and put on airs. A native of New Brunswick, Canada, she claimed ties to British royalty and thought anything English was the bee's knees. When she discovered Fred was half English and had an ancestor who came to America on the Mayflower, well, wasn't he wonderful?

An amateur writer and artist, Rachel covered every wall with pictures and every flat surface with books, magazines and papers. She praised my poems and childish stories and encouraged both my writing and my music. I remember her teaching me Christmas carols at the piano in the back room at the ranch house before they moved to the beach. My library is filled with classic literature inscribed "to my dear little Susie," love "Gramma" Rachel. She always put the "Gramma" in quotes.

Rachel gave me books about famous writers and passed on her copies of *Writer's Digest.* I'm glad she lived long enough to see me publish many articles and my first two books. My business card was thumb-tacked to her bulletin board in the kitchen when she died.

Yes, she was big, loud and useless in the kitchen. Now that I think about it, she didn't know the physical part of parenting any more than I did, but she made up for it by caring about us. When she visited our house, she wanted to see my room. She wanted me to show her what was new, what I had written, what craft projects I had made. I felt that she was really interested. She sent me long letters in her illegible scrawl. They described her life, her days, and her thoughts. Sometimes she included one of her own poems. She might talk about the birds in the yard or the fish Grandpa had caught or the church ladies' supper. But she also asked about me and my life and wanted to know what was going on. So I wrote back, and I told her.

When I think about it, here's another reason Grandma Rachel got to be a real grandma. My parents visited her and Grandpa often when they lived on the ranch in San Jose and almost as often after they moved to Seacliff, just south of Santa Cruz. We didn't dare go near the coast without visiting them, even if our main destination was the beach. It was that way for my cousins, too.

After we became adults, we continued stopping at the house right up until 1991, when Grandma Rachel died of cancer and

Grandpa Clarence moved to a nursing home. We all spent a lot of time together, and she really was our grandmother. I couldn't imagine calling her Rachel without the word Grandma in front of it. At her memorial service, wearing green and gold earrings she had given me, I talked about how she had been my mentor and helped me start my career. Afterward, my mother, in tears, said she wished she could take credit for those things. Well, Mom was too busy doing the nuts and bolts of motherhood. Grandma Rachel never had to worry about taking a child to the orthodontist or feeding her three times a day, so she had time to write letters and encourage a kid's dreams.

Rachel seemed just as much my grandmother as Anne Avina, my mother's mother. Grandma Anne knew all the motherly skills, the cooking, sewing, and cleaning. She taught us about Jesus and helped us with our prayers. She knew how to take care of babies, and she gave us plenty of gifts, too. But she wasn't our buddy, and perhaps because she lived nearby, we didn't make the effort to visit as often. When she came to our house, she sat in the corner chair like royalty. The closest she got to our bedrooms was visiting the bathroom. Yet we loved her, too, in a different way.

F red and I had been married only seven months when Gretchen showed up at Christmas with the news that she was pregnant. Our relationship had gone from her refusing to come out of her room when I visited to reluctant one-word conversations to a grudging agreement that we were stuck with each other.

Now she was going to have a baby.

Stephanie arrived in August, followed 14 months later by a little brother, Brandon. Although Gretchen and her brothers called me Sue, I was "Grandma" to her kids. I didn't look or feel like a grandmother. In my mind, grandmothers were plump, elderly ladies with too much face powder, shiny blue dresses and support hose. In my preppy wardrobe, running around doing concerts and covering stories for the newspaper, I did not fit the image. I'd only been married a little over a year. Most women get a couple decades of practice before someone hands them a grandchild.

Besides, how could I be a grandmother when I had never been a mother? "Grandma Sue" sounds strange to me even now, when

133

Sue Fagalde Lick

Stephanie and Brandon are adults. I had sat through my share of uncomfortable baby showers where I dodged questions about my own plans to procreate. My gifts tended to be toys because I didn't know what babies needed. And I had spent lots of time in ob-gyn waiting rooms with young women whose pregnant bellies stuck out. But I had never been in a maternity ward before the night we went to visit Gretchen and our new granddaughter. My only birthing experiences came from TV shows.

We sat awkwardly on plastic chairs beside Gretchen's hospital bed, watching her hold her baby. I didn't reach out for Stephanie like most mothers would. Neither did Fred. I couldn't offer any advice or share any experiences. We just listened to Gretchen, made appropriately admiring comments and went home.

My mother and I were grandmothers to infants at the same time. My brother's daughter Susan entered the world three and a half months before Gretchen's son Brandon was born. We have pictures of all the wee ones romping in our back yard that spring. When someone called "Grandma," my mother and I both turned around.

I felt like a fraud. My mom was a fully qualified grandmother. She had earned the title. She gave birth to her son and daughter in her twenties, raised us all the way from diapers through chicken pox and braces, through dating, wisdom teeth and learning to drive, through college and our first and second weddings. Round and soft, she was built perfectly for cuddling babies, and babies instinctively knew it.

When I held them, they always cried.

At bedtime, Mom read to us and made up wonderful stories to lull us to sleep. When we coughed during the night, she got up and spooned cherry-flavored syrup into our mouths. On Friday nights, she helped us with our catechism lessons, and other nights she drilled us on our spelling words. She put up with our perpetual bickering and was constantly knitting, crocheting or sewing something for us. The cookie jar was always full.

When my niece Susan was born, my mother was there to help. We have photos of her and my dad with baby Susan. My folks look exhausted and deliriously happy. And yes, they were holding the baby.

When Gretchen's kids were born, I was going to school, working for newspapers and singing with the Valley Chorale. I could write a feature in my sleep and knew hundreds of songs by heart, but when it came to children, I didn't have a clue.

Yet there I was, Grandma Sue.

The little bit I experienced felt good. Not the crying baby part, but other things. One time, the kids arrived while I was painting the kitchen. I ordered Stephanie and Brandon to keep out, but they didn't listen, traipsing over the paint-speckled plastic on the floor. My arms ached from painting the ceiling. I worried about every drip and line, and here came two unleashed toddlers who never obeyed a word I said. As Stephanie crackled and slipped toward me, I was about to scream at her to get out of there, but then she stood, hands on her three-year-old hips and stared at me, a serious look on her pudgy face. "Grandma," she asked, "How come Grandpa makes you work so hard?" Laughing, I put down my brush, gave her a kiss, and took a break. You need children around for those moments of innocent sanity.

A few months later, I came home from a chorale workshop exhausted and looking forward to dinner out and an evening of quiet reading, but Fred had committed us to babysitting while Gretchen and Brian went to a concert in Santa Cruz.

Before they arrived, I went around babyproofing the house, mostly hiding things I didn't want damaged.

The two little redheads entered like they were shot out of a cannon, screaming, "Hi!" and racing around the house. Gretchen brought crayons and coloring books and strapped the kids into huge plastic coloring bibs, but they didn't sit still for long. Coloring? Nah. We tried to eat a quick, disjointed dinner, then settled in for a four-hour film fest, but the kids screamed, ran and wrestled with their Uncle Michael for hours. They were still in motion as "Bambi" played on the TV screen. I'd never seen the movie, but they had all the lines memorized. When Bambi's mother got shot, Stephanie ran back and forth across the living room screaming, "Mother, where are you?"

Finally during 'E.T.' they started to slow down, spreading out blankets, then fighting for the same space. Stephanie fell asleep

Sue Fagalde Lick

scrunched up in the big chair, and chubby, blue-eyed Brandon wound up on the couch between me and Michael, eyes wide open watching the movie, asking with every other breath "Who's that?" "What's that?" "What they doing?" At one point, he reached into his nose, picked out a string of snot and handed it to me. I thanked him, not realizing at first what it was. Despite the snot, it was sweet having him next to me.

By the time Brian knocked softly on the door, both children were asleep and we had their toys gathered into a pile. Brian and Fred each picked up a sleeping child and took them out to the car. Stephanie promptly woke up and started fussing about Brandon hitting her. Off they went into the night and we fell into bed, exhausted. I fell asleep thinking maybe this grandma business really could fill the void left by not having children.

Then Gretchen's marriage went bad, and she sent the kids to her mother in Texas. Just as we were getting close to the little ones, we watched them board a plane with Michael, who at 14 1/2 was a veteran of many flights between Austin and San Jose. Brandon, 3 1/2, didn't realize what was going on. He was excited about being at the airport. When he spied the new children's playground, he screamed "Wow, look it" and ran into the middle of it. At the gate, he watched the planes, fascinated as they zoomed down the runway and took off. "Look, it flyded! It flyded." He was a little disappointed to find he didn't get to ride one of the big silver American Airlines planes, but had to take the dumpy one parked outside the gate. But he wasn't too worried.

Stephanie, who looked like Brandon's twin, was almost five. She stuck close to her mother, except for a quick trip through the playground. She was proud of her new dress and her curly ponytail, but as we approached the gate, she was quiet, eyes big in her freckled face. What's going on here, she seemed to be thinking.

Soon they were gone, one on each side of Uncle Michael. He was in charge now.

Gretchen stood near the gate, tears rolling down her face. Brian stood next to her, movie star handsome in a tank top and white jeans. He silently watched his children go, then turned and walked away.

Childless by Marriage

As I pictured the kids riding that airplane alone, I felt as if Fred and I should take them in, but we didn't have the space, couldn't give up our jobs and couldn't afford preschool or day care. It really wasn't up to me anyway. Fred didn't seem to want them at our house. He liked his quiet adult life, coming home from work to a glass of wine and a good book. I loved this man with all my heart, but there were a few things we would never agree on. He was finished raising kids; I never got started.

As the years passed, the grandkids and I were not destined to be close, partly because their grandfather, my husband, never extended himself to be around them and partly because their lives were overloaded with grandparents. When they were young, they had Fred and his ex-wife Annette, Brian's mother, father and stepmother, and two sets of great-grandparents. When we visited them, we usually ended up sitting like lumps on the couch while the kids played around us. Perhaps we should have jumped up and tried to get involved, like Grandma Rachel used to do, but we didn't.

The Christmas after Fred and I moved to Oregon, we spent the holiday at Gretchen's house with all the kids and grandkids, plus Michael's girlfriend and his mother. Michael grabbed me in a long, sincere hug that warmed me hours later, but Annette, who had moved back to San Jose that year, was the mother-in-residence now. She knew a lot of things about the grandchildren that we didn't know, including that Brandon's school grades had soared since he had stopped taking Ritalin (he was taking Ritalin?) and that Stephanie had a baby doll for which she was collecting clothing.

Brandon, immersed in his gifts, called for my attention. "Sue!"

"That's Grandma," his sister corrected him, but he couldn't seem to get the word out and settled for a silent shrug.

All night, I heard, "Grandma" or "Mom" and told myself to keep still; they didn't mean me. As Annette reminisced with Fred over old times and talked about people I thought of as *our* friends, as she taught Michael to swing dance and I saw the missing half of Fred's dance steps, I felt like an outsider. I was back to the substitute babysitter role I had played when we first got married. I have nothing but affection and respect for Annette. In a different situation, we

137

could easily be friends, but it was all too clear she was the mother and grandmother. I was just Sue.

The years passed. When Fred and I moved to Oregon, Stephanie was 9 and Brandon was 8. Visiting once a year, with no contact in-between, does not lead to lasting relationships. On birthdays and Christmas, we sent checks and gift certificates, not really knowing what the kids wanted or needed. When we shared Christmases, Fred's ex was there, too, and she always came up with exactly the right present, the one they were longing for.

Visiting a few years ago on the night before Thanksgiving, we ate dinner at Gretchen's house, then went out for dessert at the restaurant where her brother Ted worked. Brandon rode in the car with us and told us about his plans to study computers and get a great job. We were amazed to find him so grown up and sensible. He was also about six-foot-five. When did that happen? At the restaurant, Stephanie told us about her job at Starbuck's, and we realized that those cute little kids had turned into young adults. We missed it.

I talked with Stephanie on the phone a few months later. She was working in the pastry shop at a local Safeway store by then and had a lot to say about her work and the "old" people she worked with. I loved listening to her babble on. This was cool. If this was grandmothering, I liked it.

But then she found her father, Brian, dead of a drug overdose at his mother's house. He was lying on the floor of the bathroom. Stephanie started screaming for help. She sobbed as an ambulance came and took him away.

I wanted us to be there for her then, but I couldn't get anyone to return my calls. From 700 miles away, with no support from my husband, what could I do? I knew the real grandmothers would be there. We never heard anything about a funeral, if there was one. I sent a sympathy card.

Shortly after that, Stephanie stopped talking to her mother and stopped talking to us, too. I telephoned Fred's ex for an address to send a Christmas present, but she had promised to keep Stephanie's location a secret. Eventually she moved back in with Gretchen, but we had no connection with her by then.

Childless by Marriage

We lost touch with Dave's daughter Sabrina when Gretchen and Dave split up. Then Brandon joined the Marines. He got married in San Diego and didn't even invite his mother. Both he and his wife were training for service in the Middle East. I worried about him, but I also suspected that if I ran into him on the street, he wouldn't know who I was. Now he's a father to a little girl named Serenity. Technically, Fred and I became great-grandparents. In reality, we were just names on a Christmas card.

We watched these kids grow from afar. They were like sparkling lights on a lake that we could see but never touch.   Yes, I had the three stepchildren, but none of them called me Mom, Mama, Mother or any of those things. I had no clue how to be a grandmother. I still don't. I send gifts and cards. I'm friendly when we're together, ask questions about their lives, and cook delicious meals, but I never fit into the grandma place. I was just Grandpa Fred's wife.

Part 3
The Mom Club

13
The Annual Mother's Day Rant

Mother's Day pisses me off. Every year I write about how painful it is for women who are not mothers. You'd think I'd be able to let it go. I could just accept my wilting chrysanthemum from the misguided usher at church or the waiter at Denny's, smile and nod when strangers say "Happy Mother's Day," shrug off the lack of Mother's Day cards from my stepchildren, and move on. Do I really need to explain to every single person I meet that I AM NOT A MOTHER AND MY MOTHER IS DEAD?

Sorry for the capital letters, but that's how I usually think it, how I write it, how I say it. Not this year. Perhaps my menopausal hot flashes are actually flashes of inspiration, but now I'm thinking, I don't care, lower case. I see the ads all over TV, the newspapers, even at the side of my Yahoo page on the Internet. Flowers for Mom, breakfast in bed, diamond pendants (Come on. Who buys their mother diamonds?), and it occurs to me that I get to pass on this holiday. I don't have to send cards or gifts or take anyone out to brunch. I don't have to do anything I don't want to do. I can choose not to stew over whether my stepchildren will call or send me a card. It's not my holiday, that's all. Like Father's Day. Or National Secretaries Day. Or Brussel Sprouts Appreciation Day.

It appears I have come full circle. For the first 22 years of my life, Mother's Day was about other people—my mother and the grandmothers. My role was to buy and deliver cards and gifts, just as I did to Dad and the grandpas on Father's Day. When I got married, I added a mother-in-law to the gift list. People started hinting that I too would soon be a mother. But I was young, and Jim kept saying, "Not yet." That's what I told everybody who pressed me about joining the great Mother's Day gift grab: "Not yet."

Not yet became "not with you." Jim and I got divorced. Cross off one mother-in-law.

Still no problem. "You're young. You have time," people said. I went on honoring the mothers and grandmothers, who were all older women with corsages on their bosoms. I hadn't even grown a proper shelf-like bosom yet. Mother's Day was still okay. I didn't mind if other people got presents and I didn't. When I was 30, Grandma Anne, my mother's mother, died. But I still had Mom and Grandma Rachel left. Mother's Day went on as usual.

At 33, I married Fred, who presented me with three stepchildren, a vasectomy, and a new mother-in-law. Now Mother's Day became a little trickier. As a stepmother, did I qualify for Mother's Day honors? My mother and the other women in my life thought I did, but to the kids, I was just "Sue," the woman who was sleeping with their father.

In view of the vasectomy, the outward sign of my husband's disinclination to have any more kids, my chances of bearing children became about as good as those of a nag with a limp winning the Kentucky Derby, but I spent a few years in denial. Surely if I wanted it badly enough, my wish would come true.

As age 40 approached, Mother's Day took on a whole new complexion. You don't care who wins the race if you don't own a horse and haven't bet any money, but now I wanted to bet and couldn't get to the track. I'd have to find some sperm in a hurry or forget about it. As my childbearing clock ticked toward tilt, I was not a good sport.

Because I have spent most of the past 20 years singing and playing guitar and piano with church choirs, a lot of my reflections center on that. As you read on, remember, I'm Catholic. We're supposed to have babies.

May 13, 1991, age 39

Every year on Mother's Day, when our pastor asks all the moms to stand so the ushers can give each one a flower, I always wonder what to do.

I'm not a mother, technically. I have never been pregnant. I have no children of my own, although I always wanted them. Telling people that I have three stepchildren stifles their questions about why

144

Childless by Marriage

I never had a baby. But when it comes to Mother's Day, I'm not sure how I fit in.

This year, I stood up in the choir section at church, nudged by my fellow singers who hear me talking about my kids all the time. As I accepted a yellow carnation, I noticed my friend Sara sitting at the end of the row with tears in her eyes. Unable to conceive, she and her husband have been struggling unsuccessfully to adopt a baby. Oh hell, I should have been sitting, too. Maybe I should have given her my flower, but I was treasuring it too much to let it out of my hands. Then we were singing the final song and she had fled out the side door.

Father Richard paid tribute to moms in his homily and added special prayers for them in his blessing. Then I went home, and nobody said "Happy Mother's Day" to me.

I knew Michael had sent a card to his mom in Texas, and I was waiting for his card to me, but it never came. "Oh well," I told myself, "Don't dwell on it." I was planning to take a gift to my own mother that afternoon. There was no question she deserved special treatment.

Grandma Rachel, my dad's stepmother, died last month. Fred and I are out of grandmothers, but we have our mothers left.

I urged my husband to call his mom, and I reminded Michael to telephone his mother. You're thinking I'm so good. Not really. I placed my wilting carnation in a vase in the middle of the dining room table, hoping my husband and stepson would see it and feel guilty. I mentioned what other people were doing for Mother's Day, hoping they'd take the hint.

Being male, they didn't.

May 11, 1992, age 40

I survived another Mother's Day by keeping too busy to think. I'm 40 now, and my eggs probably look like the cracked ones at the bottom of the pile at the supermarket, the ones that are leaking all over their cartons.

Church was hard. Father José went on and on about the glories of motherhood. His blessing just for mothers almost killed me. Once again, he had the moms stand and receive carnations. I waffled.

145

Sue Fagalde Lick

Diane, who has two teenage daughters, said, "You're a mother. Stand up." Reluctantly, I rose to my feet. I laid my yellow flower along the bottom of the music stand while I played the closing song.

That afternoon, I threw a party for my parents and my brother and his wife. It was relaxing, loving and fun. Until . . .

"What did Fred's kids give you for Mother's Day?" my sister-in-law asked.

"Nothing." I busied myself refilling the potato chip bowl.

"Not even a card?"

"Nope. I'm not a mother."

That's when Mom chimed in. "Don't ever say that."

"Sorry. How about some more dip?"

I wouldn't really care about Mother's Day except that the media, the church, and almost everybody else is pushing presents, cards and special honors for "Mom." I feel left out.

It occurred to me at church that I do lots of mothering, not only for my stepchildren, but for my writers club and other groups I lead, plus pets and plants. I use my creative energy to write, cook, do needlework, etc. I have done everything a mother does except give birth.

Yeah, right. As if knitting an afghan is the same thing as pushing a baby out of your body.

May 1993, age 41

I hate Mother's Day. For a month before it happens, we are blasted with signs, TV commercials and articles about motherhood. Tributes to "Mom" fill the newspaper columns while the advertising sections are packed with gift ideas. On Mother's Day itself, shoppers jam the stores looking for last-minute cards and presents, youthful flower-sellers line the streets with Mother's Day specials, and even the cartoons in the Sunday paper all seem to have something to do with Mother's Day.

As I progress through the day, everyone, from the cashier at the supermarket who wants to know what my kids got me to the waiter at lunch who hands me a carnation in honor of Mother's Day, seems obsessed with this pseudo-holiday. They all mean well, but they don't understand.

146

Childless by Marriage

Just because I look like a mother doesn't mean I am one. I have never been a mother and can never be a mother, not by choice or broken body parts, but by circumstance. The world assumes that if I'm doing my part, I'll have children like everyone else. Check the statistics, folks. One in five women of my generation is not a mother.

It's hard enough the rest of the year. I cry every time a birth is shown on television, I envy my friends as they cuddle their little ones, and I get tongue-tied when people demand to know when I'm going to get pregnant. You're not getting any younger, they remind me. What clued them in, the bifocals, the gray hairs or the nifty shelf my bosom is becoming? When I tell them that I can't have children, they get quiet and embarrassed. "Oh, I'm sorry, I didn't know."

Of course not. It's not something you go shouting from the rooftops, but on Mother's Day you might as well have it tattooed across your forehead. "Barren. No gifts for this one."

May 9, 1994, age 42

Another Freaking Mother's Day.

I skipped church, partly because of my schedule, but mostly to avoid the annual ritual in which mothers are asked to stand and receive a carnation, with lots of rhetoric about the glories of motherhood. That's fine for those who are mothers, but it's like root canal for the rest of us.

Skipping Mass didn't stop my annual depression attack, although there was one bright spot. Fred bought me a great card which says, "You're not my mother. You're my wife! Since there's no 'Wives Day,' happy Mother's Day." I'm keeping the husband. As for the kids, I received no acknowledgement of the day from Michael, Ted or Gretchen. As expected.

I went to visit my mother. She loved the flowers I brought and almost made me cry when she hugged me and told me I was a good mother, too. Somebody's in denial. By insisting that I'm a mother, she can pretend to be a grandmother.

Is it tomorrow yet?

The tide begins to turn.

147

Sue Fagalde Lick

May 15, 1995, age 43

"Happy Mother's Day!" boomed Dan, he who is famous for climbing on top of a desk and yelling in the junior high science class he teaches. Subtle he's not.

"Don't say that. I hate Mother's Day!" I shrilled with all the tact of one of his 13-year-old puberty-crazed students. We were standing on the church altar at the time, getting ready to sing for the 9:30 Mass. God should have stricken me dumb. But he didn't. He left me to stew over it for the rest of my life, adding it to the pile of stupid things I wish I'd never said.

How could Dan know I wasn't Michael's mother? According to the school office, I am his mother-person, the one they call if he breaks his arm or skips class.

Later in the Mass, at the Sign of Peace, Dan said, "Happy Mother's Day" again, more softly. He said it to all the women. "Thanks," I replied, chastened. But I never brought myself to wish anybody else "Happy Mother's Day." Looking back, it seems pretty selfish. All I could think of was my own pain. So if I'm not a mother, no mother should be honored? I really am 13, aren't I?

I had planned to leave town, but stuck around to wish my mother a happy day. Then she snuck off at the last minute with Dad to Morro Bay for a romantic weekend. "Don't buy me anything," she said on the phone. "You spent too much on the microwave you got me for Christmas." Yeah, right. I know my mother. I left a pot of daisies and a card on her front porch.

Fred's mother, Helen, lives far away, and my grandmothers are dead, so I didn't have any other mothers to visit. I decided might as well go sing with the church choir.

I dreaded the end of Mass, when Father Richard would call on all the mothers to stand and receive a special blessing and a carnation. But this year Father Richard's own mother had died, and he changed his speech. He addressed his tribute to *all* women who nurture others by their work, their love, and their lives. Hooray! I jumped to my feet. God bless Father Richard. Happy Mother's Day to me.

Motherhood comes in many forms. I nurture my stepchildren, my dog and cat, my husband, my staff, my friends. I nurtured Grandpa Fagalde in his last months. I even nurture the houseplants.

148

Childless by Marriage

Growing a baby inside me, giving a human being life, is the ultimate expression of a woman's nurturing power, but God knows I do nurture. I give birth to a whole newspaper every week. Try that, Hallmark.

I had so dreaded the annual church tribute to mothers that my emotions boiled to the top. My lips twisted out of control. I couldn't look at anyone. Thank God the last song was a jazzy number that took all my concentration to play.

But I still had to shed those tears. I cried in the car, and I cried in the bathroom at home. I cried it all out before I faced Fred. I know he feels guilty. I didn't want to hear "Oh, babe" again.

When I stopped sniffling, I discovered that Michael had left a Mother's Day card on the kitchen table. Wow. But he didn't sign it.

Next Mother's Day, I won't be here. I'm planning to organize an unmothers camping trip. We'll go far away from all media, well-meaning churchgoers and big-mouthed junior high science teachers. First one to mention Mother's Day gets to sleep with the bears.

I have no notes from Mother's Day 1996. I know I didn't go camping. We were too busy packing. By May 1997, we were living in Oregon, far from both mothers. I had joined another choir at another church. The ritual was similar, but most of the women in this choir happened to be childless, two by marriage, one by hysterectomy, one by choice. We claimed sisterhood in our unused wombs. In fact, most of my new friends seemed to be childless. Or else their children were grown and gone. At 45, I knew I wouldn't be having any babies, and I was too tired to care.

Besides, more important things were about to happen that made my Mother's Day rants sound like the whining of a spoiled brat. What follows is just part of it.

May 2002, age 50

Fred's mother died of lung cancer last December. We had barely finished cleaning out her house when my mother was diagnosed with cancer in March. Her doctors were not sure where it started, but tests showed it had already spread throughout her body. They tried chemotherapy, but all it did was make things worse.

149

Sue Fagalde Lick

By May, she was so thin she held her pants up with giant safety pins. She didn't have the energy to buy new clothes, so we all bought them for her as Mother's Day gifts. Fighting tears, I wandered through Wal-Mart and Fred Meyer picking out soft shirts and drawstring pants that might fit. I knew it was the last gift I would buy for my mother.

I boycotted Mother's Day Mass that year. In my journal, I wrote, "I have figured out how most women handle Mother's Day once their mothers are gone. Their kids come and honor *them*. Soon I'll be out of luck on both ends."

We spent most of the day sorting Fred's mother's stuff, boxes and boxes of papers, pictures, dishes, and sewing things that we had piled up in the den. It looked as if we would never finish. I vowed to clean out my own junk so nobody else would have to do it when I died.

"It's good to hear your voice," my mother said when I called her. My voice was usually so like hers that people routinely mistook me for her when I answered the phone at home. But this time, her voice sounded low, drug-slurred, and despondent. She was fasting in preparation for a colonoscopy on Monday. What a rotten way to celebrate the day. The new clothes fit, she said, but I shouldn't have wasted my money. Just wear them, I thought.

The conversation petered out. We said, "*Adios*" as usual.

I dissolved into tears.

Fred and I went back to sorting his mother Helen's ancient bank statements.

That evening, my stepdaughter Gretchen, now a stepmother herself, called to wish me Happy Mother's Day. We had bonded after Helen's death. She said she had wanted to send something but never got around to it. Oh well. No word from her brothers. None expected. I didn't really care. I just wanted Mother's Day to be over.

We lost my mother in July. She never wore any of her new clothes. I brought them home, finding comfort in the warm, stretchy fabric. I might not be a mother, but in private, I started dressing like one.

150

Childless by Marriage

May 11, 2003, age 51

Jessie, my piano teacher, was guest-directing the choir at Sacred Heart. Just before we went into the sanctuary, she put her arms around me. "I thought you might be missing your mother today."

Well, dang it. I had a grip on my emotions until then. I was grouchy but in control. Out came the Mother's Day tears, but not because I didn't have children. Who cared anymore? I was out of moms.

Throughout the Mass, the urge to weep swept in and out. Toward the end, Father Jack had all the mothers stand up. I sat, reached back to pat Lori, she of the hysterectomy, and my face fell apart again. *Study the guitar frets, study the sheet music, fight it off.*

Three years later, past the initial grief, denial, and depression stages, I was still working on anger.

May 12, 2006, age 54

After all these years, I still weep when I read about someone welcoming a child or grandchild. Columnist Bob Welch has done it again with his piece about the birth of his grandson in his book *My Oregon*. He speaks of the wonder of this new generation, the drama of the birth, the miracle of new life. I'm already reading through tears when he ends with the zinger, the first words his daughter-in-law spoke to her son: "I'm your mom."

Oh. Crap. Why did I have to read this two days before Mother's Day? Why didn't somebody warn me? A least, a certain talk show host let us know in advance that today is the big Mother's Day Show. I'll just do something else at 4:00. But I'm sitting out in the sun reading this pleasant book, which has already gotten to me a couple times with columns about the author's parents and children, and here comes this baby getting born. Like I haven't already wept through every TV birth shown in the last 20 years. It could be a sitcom, with the laugh-trackers guffawing in the background, and I'm sobbing on the sofa.

Just. Kill. Me.

I think the worst thing about being childless by marriage or not quite getting around to procreating is that you know it's your own fault. You can't blame God or fate or doctors. You could have done it, but you didn't, and now it's too late. It's Mother's Day again. Everywhere you look is another ad for what to buy "Mom" or where to take her on that special day: brunch at the Embarcadero, a garden tour, a bracelet with the names of all her children or grandchildren etched into rubies, emeralds and diamonds.

I already know where I'm going and what I'm getting for Mother's Day. Nowhere special and nothing. Okay, I take that back. I might be handed a carnation at church or some restaurant under the mistaken impression that a woman my age must be a mother, heck a grandmother by now. And I'll say thank you and keep it until it dries out and falls apart. I used to argue the technicality, but I surrendered a long time ago. I mother my dogs, my husband, my students, my geraniums. Whatever.

Mother's Day hurts even more now that my own mother, mother-in-law and grandmothers are all dead. I used to be able to deflect all that childless energy into honoring the mothers in my life. Not anymore. Now it's just me and my dogs, who are also childless. They got fixed before they knew what was happening. There are no mothers or babies around here.

I plan to duck and cover for the duration of the Mother's Day bombardment. Let me know when it's over.

And then, I found acceptance.

May 13, 2007, age 55

Menopause has finally occurred. My only feeling is gratitude. It's not like I was going to use that uterus anyway. Time has eased the anguish of lost mothers and grandmothers. This year, I lit candles at church for both moms. "Happy Mother's Day," I whispered, then prayed I wouldn't screw up the songs, the same prayer I pray every Sunday.

I still wish I had children. I'd be a grandmother by now. I miss our mothers and grandmothers, but today is just another day. I went through all the stages of grief, and now I'm done.

Father Brian, a priest of minimal sentimentality, didn't bother with flowers. While everyone was already standing for the final

Childless by Marriage

prayer, he asked the mothers to bow their heads, said a few words, and moved on. Father, Son, Holy Spirit, don't forget coffee and donuts in the hall, and the gift shop is open. Amen.

Mother's Day is okay—for other people. As for me, I'm waiting for Fourth of July.

153

14
Chatty Cathy's Mom

The little girl wandered around the auditorium at the monthly Fiddlers' Jamboree clutching her doll. Now and then the girl talked to the doll and stroked its plastic hair. When the fiddle music got lively, she danced with the doll, looking back to make sure her mother was watching.

Across the room, a woman with thick glasses and scraggly brown hair displayed a real baby as if it were a trophy. Suddenly this mousy woman had a claim to greatness: She had borne this baby. It was a newborn, its navel not yet healed, its head a soft bobble buried in blankets. She held it carefully and proudly as admirers gathered around.

Meanwhile, I cradled my guitar and watched a tall woman in tight black jeans, a striped tank top and a cowboy hat serve cake to her fat daughter, whose buck teeth matched her mom's. The mother had the MC proclaim that it was Shannon's eighth birthday. After feeding her a giant portion of chocolate-frosted birthday cake, she hauled the kid onto the stage with her violin to squeak out a horrendous rendition of "Twinkle, Twinkle, Little Star" and an even worse "Red River Valley."

The mother stood by, smiling, sure that her fiddle-playing friends were impressed by her little prodigy. The woman overseeing the show held her hand over her mouth the whole time. I couldn't tell whether she was laughing or horrified.

Just when I couldn't stand much more of this mother-child adoration, I noticed the first little girl had dropped her doll on the ground and gone in search of other amusement.

The toddler is a mother in training—as I once was. I learned my lessons well, but I was trained to be something I didn't become. As I sat in that sweltering auditorium, nervously awaiting my turn on stage, I felt like a girl who had gone to a party and forgotten to bring her doll. What did I have to show off? Just a nicked-up guitar and a couple of country songs.

I once had a hundred dolls. I lined them up on my dresser and counted them. My math was probably off, but they were my children. Every year at Christmas, there seemed to be a new doll I just had to have. If Santa didn't bring her, I'd die. One year Santa brought a three-foot-tall walking doll I named Patty. My friend Sherri got one, too. We walked them down the street toward each other so they could be best friends, just like us. My dolls always had dark hair and eyes like me. Sherri's dolls were blondes.

Each new doll I received spent the first night sleeping against the pillow next to me while the others slept with the stuffed animals at the foot of the bed. It's a wonder there was any room left for me. I named the newcomer, kissed her and wrapped my body around hers to protect her from the night terrors.

The next morning, I dressed her, combed her hair and brought her to breakfast with me, setting her up against the milk bottle, pretending to feed her bits of toast and eggs. I took her to school with me, never wanting to leave her alone. I knew she was just a cloth or plastic doll, but she was a real person to me.

Back in the 1950s, the big innovation was baby dolls that drank and wet. You inserted the tip of a rubber bottle in the hole between their lips and squeezed the milk or water down their throats. Rather quickly, the liquid came out a hole on the other end.

Sherri and I fed our "babies" outside in the patio. That was our house. It never seemed odd to us to be two mothers sharing the same house. Our husbands were nonexistent or off at imaginary jobs. Like our mothers, we spent our days taking care of the house and our babies. We talked to our dolls all the time, telling them how sweet they were and how much we loved them. We taught them what we had learned about Jesus in catechism class, along with the ABCs, the times tables, and the capitals of all the states in the U.S.

Betsy Wetsy and Tiny Tears led to Chatty Cathy, who could talk when you pulled the string in her back. "I'm hungry." "I'm thirsty." "I love you," she said. Then we got Barbie and her curvaceous friends. My black-haired Barbie had a best friend named Sandy, and

155

they hung out with Sherri's blonde Barbie and Ken. We invented boyfriends and careers for our dolls. Mine were always in show business. Sherri's Barbie was a stay-at-home mom.

We watched our children grow up in that redwood patio with the cracked concrete floor. We cooked our pretend meals in the brick fireplace that my father and grandfather had built together, and washed the dishes in the sink Dad had made from scraps of wood and old pipes.

I was a good mother to my dolls, but all too soon I faced the empty nest.

When I was 13, growing breasts and having my first periods, my mother decided I didn't need dolls anymore. "You're getting too old," she said. "It's time to give them to Goodwill or to the Malleys." The Malleys, who lived behind us, had seven girls and one boy. They probably couldn't afford Barbie and her canopy bed, her orange Austin Healey and all those clothes. But this wasn't like giving away my outgrown pedal-pushers.

"No," I protested. "They're mine." My children. How could I give them up?

Mom was not one for sentiment or saving things. Barbie and her entourage went to the Malleys, and most of the other dolls were tossed into a bag for Goodwill. I kept only a few, the ones Mom couldn't find. My favorite, Chatty Cathy, sits on top of my bookshelf right now, looking down with a goofy smile. I change her outfits to match the seasons, choosing from a red and white trunk full of clothing, some store-bought, most made by my mother while I was off visiting my grandparents. Chatty Cathy gargle-talks like an old lady who's had a stroke. One of her shoulders is cracked so her arm falls off if I'm not careful. She doesn't have any teeth. But I love her anyway.

Mom ditched my dolls as a sign it was time for me to grow up, date, get married, have flesh-and-blood babies and take care of a real house.

Well, I have taken care of lots of houses. I got married—twice—and I got to play mommy with my stepchildren, but I never had my own real babies, so I still talk to Chatty Cathy.

Childless by Marriage

Most of the women I interviewed denied any interest in dolls. If they did have them, they had Barbies, not babies. Over and over the answer to my question about whether they treated their dolls like their children was "No." Emphatically no. Their response to the next question, the one about having pets they babied, was almost always yes. Most of the women are younger than I am. Did they not grow up with dolls? Are dolls passé? Were dolls more important in the '50s and '60s? Is everybody playing computer games now?

I went shopping to find out. First I did online research, then I visited Wal-Mart and Fred Meyer with my tiny voice recorder.

At Fred Meyer, I watched as a mother dragged her daughter over to the doll department and asked her to choose which color stroller she wanted. The girl, maybe 7 years old, sighed. "Purple, I guess."

It seemed as if raising a doll was just too hard. I mean you have to pick out the clothes, keep them fed and diapered, and buy the stroller, playpen, crib, and sleeping bag. You need a station wagon to carry all their stuff around. And if you touch them wrong, they talk back.

Today's baby dolls are awfully cute and lifelike. I wanted to scoop one off the shelf and hug it.

Along with the baby dolls, I found older dolls, including the Bratz line that has been demeaned for teaching shallow values, and lots of Dora dolls. Barbie's still around, slightly more realistic-looking than she was in the '60s before feminists protested that nobody could have those big breasts with such a tiny waist.

It's encouraging that today's dolls come in multiple ethnicities. You can buy La Baby or Fiesta Dora with instructions in Spanish. The Bratz dolls are a vague racial blend, possibly Eurasian, part Latino, a little black. In other words, who knows and who cares?

On the other hand, it worries me that so many dolls come with names, prefab dialogue and written histories. Let the little girls name their own dolls and make up their own stories. That's part of the fun, having those conversations that start, "Let's say we're going to the store and . . ."

Sue Fagalde Lick

P eople don't think you're crazy if you hug a cocker spaniel, stuffed or real, but they do wonder about grown women strapping dolls into car seats.

A line of dolls designed for adults is gaining popularity. Called "Reborns," they are disturbingly lifelike. With prices ranging from hundreds to thousands of dollars, these faux babies are stuffed and weighted to feel like real infants. Their mohair tresses are rooted into their heads strand by strand. Some have heartbeats and a mechanism that makes the chest rise and fall as if they're breathing. In fact, they look so real, an MSNBC Today Show report said police have smashed car windows to rescue these "infants" that have been left in booster seats in parked cars.

Reborns reportedly offer some comfort to adults whose children have died or moved away, as well as to those who are childless. They also seem to have a calming effect on nursing home residents. Their owners cuddle them, dress them, and take them for walks in strollers. They talk to them as if they were real. Of course these dolls have some big advantages over real babies: no messy diapers, no endless crying. They never outgrow their clothes or become too big to hold against your breast. Plus, you can leave them behind when you don't feel like playing with them.

Is this too odd? Is it a sign that childless women never grow up? Or are the owners of these "reborns" simply exhibiting the same feelings most of us share? After all, I treat my puppies like babies to the point I call myself "Mommy." I hug my stuffed bear, José, and every now and then I still put a new outfit on Chatty Cathy. I would have hugged the baby dolls at Walmart if I didn't think anybody would see me.

Monica Walsh, a Reborn owner quoted on "The Today Show," said, "I don't really worry too much about what people think about me. I just try to make myself happy, and it makes me happy to collect dolls. I feel like a little girl that just never stopped loving dolls."

Play is preparation for adulthood, product reviewer Doug Phillips wrote on his blog in September 2007. "One of the most iconic symbols of childhood play is the doll. Dolls have always served an important role in culture, primarily in preparing daughters to be mothers." He says the baby dolls help girls identify with motherhood while the dress-up doll "allows her to imagine her own future building a culture of hospitality for her family."

Phillips contends that today's dolls are tools of propaganda that reflect today's roles for women, factoring in political correctness and feminism.

It's interesting to look at how childless women related to their dolls. In an essay called "Patchwork" in the anthology *Nobody's Mother*, Mary Jane Copps says she was the youngest child. When her siblings went to school, she found boxes of baby clothes and dressed the dolls that she found. For Christmas she received a life-sized baby doll, which she christened Noreen and dressed in all the clothes. Later her mother gave her a baby carriage for the doll and she spent many days walking the baby up and down the block. Copps had no doubt she would become a wife and mother. Unfortunately, by the time she was in a position to start a family, she had moved into early menopause.

Chris, a school bus driver, had some dolls but preferred playing outside with her brothers. "We never played mommies. We wanted to be like my older sisters who went to proms and all that stuff and not the mommy stuff. I wonder if that has to do with seeing my mom have 10 children." Of those 10, she says she's the only one who is not a parent.

On the other hand, Marie mothered her baby brother. "He was my doll. He was the one that was my real baby."

Karey, who manages corporate travel, says, "I *always* knew I'd grow up and have children. Did I treat dolls like children? Of course. I always knew I'd be a mother, so playing house was natural."

Jan also admits to loving her doll. "I only had one doll, and I loved her above all else. I'd cuddle her close at night to warm her soft plastic skin and talk to her. I kept Elizabeth until I was in my early teens and she was worn, bald and naked."

And what do we make of this from a woman named Talia? "Yes, they were my babies. I'd even make my Barbie doll pregnant!" Does that make her a wannabe grandma?

Barbra had no such illusions. When asked if she treated her dolls like children, she responded, "I'm not crazy, just childless."

Sue Fagalde Lick

I only had one brother, and we were both in diapers at the same time. I never had a chance to practice on a real baby. In families with lots of siblings, girls who are drafted to care for their brothers and sisters sometimes work so hard at it that when they reach adulthood, they feel they have already mothered enough. Now they want to be free.

Dolls are different. You can leave them behind and go play hopscotch; they just wait with their stupid smiles. But after a certain age, you can't play with dolls anymore, at least not where anyone can see you.

Was I being trained to be a mother? Absolutely. In addition to my hundred doll children, I had a miniature baking set with which I made real cakes, and I started drying dishes and stirring the gravy as soon as I grew tall enough to reach the sink and the stove. I became an expert at ironing and clothes-folding. From the looks of it, Mom's work started early and didn't end until she was dozing in front of the TV in the evening. I was her apprentice.

My older dolls were always in show business. They were Doris Day, Ann Margret or anybody who sang and danced. It was always, "Gotta get dressed and go to the club." They didn't have any children, but maybe that was coming later. They were gone before I figured out the rest of the story.

15
Exiled from the Mom Club

A 100-year-old woman is asked how she feels about not having children. Move on to another topic, she tells the interviewer. It's stupid to waste time talking about it.

After thinking about the subject more than most people, I sometimes feel that way, too. Move on. It happened, we did other things with our lives, and that's that.

But that isn't that. Our lives are filled with constant reminders that we are different, that we are not now and never will be bona fide members of the world's biggest women's club, the Mom Club.

"Be prepared to be the proverbial square peg in the round hole in any number of situations if you insist on living childfree," warns Childless by Choice founder Leslie Lafayette in her book *Why Don't You Have Children?*

Those situations include walking into a gynecologist's office where the walls are plastered with baby pictures and all the other patients seem to be pregnant; finding all the other women at work talking about Little League, day care, ear infections and other motherly concerns; and discovering that lifelong friends who have become parents suddenly have no time for you. If they can fit you into their schedule, they're still going to focus all their attention on the kids while you find yourself watching television or studying the pictures on the wall—pictures of children, of course.

On a flight from San Jose to Portland, Oregon, the woman in the next seat looked about my age. I liked her casually upswept sandy hair, her smooth skin, and her turquoise eyes. We seemed to share the same middle-aged weariness and the same anxiety to get back to Oregon. Sitting with our headphones on, we exchanged a few pleasantries. She noted that her son was cleaning the house for her. "How nice," I said. Then she asked whether I had any children.

Wham. When I said no, the door closed so quickly I could feel the breeze. For the rest of the flight, she read her book, and I stared out the window, listening to Mozart and watching the Siskyous pass by through cottony strands of cloud. I can't help it if I don't have kids, I thought, reminding myself that my life was full of other wonderful things.

Meanwhile the smell of the soggy cookies the toddler behind me held in his sticky hands was making me sick. Such a beautiful child, but that smell! I guess only a mother could stomach it.

On another flight, I rode home from San Francisco with a dark-skinned woman in front of me and her two children, a teenage boy and a girl about 12, beside me. The whole flight, the mother leaned over the seat, talking to her children. "Do you want something to drink? When we get there . . ." It was as if no one else existed in the world except the woman and her kids. I was invisible, a non-person. I was not a member of the Mom Club.

Lafayette quotes a friend, Karna, who did not have a baby until she was 43. "Did it make a difference in the way I was treated by my friends who are parents? I was admitted to the club. I started receiving invitations to things again—like their kids' birthday parties! I had something to talk about with them. It wasn't until I became a mother that I realized how exiled I had been, and how different I had felt.

"There's no question that they saw me as really different from them, not like them at all, because I had no children."

In a *San Jose Mercury News* article, Kathleen Donnelly quotes a woman named Catherine from Berkeley, who says, "The hardest part is you're excluded from a huge club. What happens is all your friends become friends of the parents at the nursery school once the kids come along, and you lose each other. That was the reason I wanted to have kids, and I knew it wasn't a good enough reason."

I know exactly how they feel. The last time I saw Marti, who used to be a close friend, she was so deep in kids that we never had the lunch she promised when I came to visit. I found myself alone in the living room talking to a parakeet.

This is the woman who worked side by side with me at a community newspaper, sharing stories, gossip, and occasional games of crumpled-paper volleyball. People said we looked like sisters, both of us with dark hair and olive skin. I was the one she called when Josh, her first son, was born. Now she had Jason and had fully gone over to the mommy side. She was active in the PTA and laughed at the idea of getting another job. My life was all about work. We didn't have much to talk about anymore.

On an outing to Happy Hollow Park and Baby Zoo in San Jose, Marti always seemed to be out of sight, playing with Josh while I got stuck pushing the screaming bald-headed baby in his stroller. I had no idea what to do and felt as if the whole world knew it.

Oh, and then she sat on a curb to nurse the baby while I chased her popsicle-stained kid, who wanted to know what the monkey's genitals were. "That's his pee-pee," I lied.

When Josh turned five, Marti asked me to provide entertainment for his birthday party. Imagine a woman who knows nothing about kids and has no idea what music children listen to frantically trying to memorize a Raffi record. I sat cross-legged on the lawn with my guitar, surrounded by kids who gathered so close they could touch my legs, arms and face with their sticky hands. They wanted the same song over and over again.

It was my first and last children's birthday party gig. Marti and I didn't see much of each other after that.

More recently, I have been deeply involved in my church choir. It's great; it's a family. However, at least once a week, I find the moms wandering off together at the end of rehearsal or after Mass discussing music lessons, youth group activities, or sleepovers. I have discovered that their families have whole relationships that do not and never will include me. Maybe if my stepchildren were the same ages as their kids . . . but they're not. Even my stepchildren's children are older than their children. That's another problem with marrying someone so much older than you are. Standing there in the chapel, alone in the crowd, I realize the only one I have left to talk to is Jesus so I pack up my guitar and go home because you can talk to Jesus anywhere.

The moms seem to know all these children's songs with related gestures, and they know about games, toys and TV shows that I have never heard of. I don't know the secret handshake, so I can't get in.

Sue Fagalde Lick

It's like high school. You make friends with the people who take the same classes you do. You and Marisa sit next to each other in Spanish so you know each other and eat lunch together. Sally is taking French, and you don't know her at all.

A friend told me she had gotten in line at 4:15 a.m. at Circuit City to buy this thing for her daughter for Christmas. She had a cold and sounded miserable on the phone, but she had to get it. I had never heard of this thing and had to ask what it was. It's a $250 computer game that apparently everyone with kids knows about. I can't believe even a totally child-besotted mother would do that, but I've heard of other mothers doing similar things. When the last Harry Potter book came out, mothers everywhere hit the bookstores at midnight for a hardback that became available at a cheaper price just a few days later. My mother would have laughed at the idea, but maybe times have changed, and I missed it.

Not being welcome in the Mom Club is just this little burr under my skin. If you're childless, you know what I mean.

As Kamin Mohammadi wrote in *The Guardian*, "The joys of parenthood are hard to share, and as for the gap in experience that suddenly opens up, the new parents might as well have taken a trip to Mars."

Parents flock together like Canada Geese. It's actually the kids' fault. Remember when you were a child and a new family moved in on your street? The first thing you wanted to know was whether they had any kids your age. If they did, pretty soon you were doing everything together, right? Kids naturally seek out other kids, and their parents can't help getting to know each other. They see each other at school, soccer, the orthodontist's office, piano lessons, and at church. Wherever kids go, their parents have to go too, so parents find their friends among other parents.

Mothers have common concerns and life experiences that a childless woman does not share. Game Boy? Is that over? I don't know. Bratz dolls? When did they change the ages for First Communion and Confirmation? How come I'm the only one who never knows when the schools are closed? I'm not in the mother loop.

When mothers get together, they talk about their kids. The

164

Childless by Marriage

childless woman may want to discuss her own experiences, her work or her hobbies, but the conversation inevitably veers back to the children. Maybe that's why I often wind up with the men talking about cars and football. At least I know something about those things.

Alison, 28, a childless business consultant, said things have changed since her friends had children. "Girls' nights, which we have a few times a month, have gone from chatting about work and guys to lots of talk about babies, etc. I'm feeling like the odd man out and at times a little jealous of their lives. Day to day I am pretty much fine, but I am feeling now like every time I turn around, the concept of family and having children is being thrown in my face. I see it on television, in the movies and in everyday situations. Funny how when something is on your mind you start to pick up everything that is associated with it."

It's as if we're living in a parallel universe, and ours doesn't include children. When I come to church choir on Wednesday nights, I drive my Honda past a whole line of mommy vans all parked in a row. The kids and their mothers are in the church for religious education classes while those of us who aren't tied up with the kids practice music. If we run into the moms in the halls, they're distracted, gathering their chicks and talking to each other. "Can you give my son a ride to soccer practice?" "What are you bringing for treats?"

The differences became obvious recently when I was called for jury duty. Waiting in the hallway, we seemed to be quite a diverse group: a lady firefighter, a Walmart worker, a hotel owner, a real estate agent, an engineer, several Georgia Pacific lumber mill workers, a stay-at-home mom, a marine science center administrator, a nurse, a teacher, and a Native-American jewelry-maker with rose-tinted glasses. I met a young guy doing his first jury duty and an old man who needed headphones to hear what the judge was saying. It seemed like a nice cross-section of rural Oregon, BUT when the hugely pregnant defense attorney questioned us about our lives and experiences, nearly everyone had children. It was the first thing out of their mouths. "Well, I have three kids and . . ."

So what did I say? I said that I was a writer and a musician. And they stared at me.

165

Sue Fagalde Lick

Not having any children made me an odd duck in that room full of Canada Geese. This sampling of Lincoln County residents was all ages and occupations, but they were nearly all parents. That's how it is in small-town America, where I live now, and in suburbia, where I grew up. If you haven't had kids, you have missed the main road and gone off on a side road. Bye-bye, Canada Geese.

Sometimes it looks as if the world is splitting into parents and non-parents. Read Elinor Burkett's *The Baby Boon: How Family-Friendly America Cheats the Childless* to get a good taste of it. In fact, read any "childfree" blog or online forum and see what the folks there say about the "breeders" who are gunking up our world with babies.

Many childless women are truly ticked about what they see as the extra benefits mothers get in the workplace. They take time off to care for sick kids or to attend their extracurricular events. They leave at exactly 5:00 rather than stay late. They make personal calls on business time checking on little Kaitlyn or Taylor. Meanwhile, the women without children feel that they are expected to pick up the slack. *Hey, you don't have kids. You can stay late. You can work the weekend. You can fly to Pittsburgh for the meeting.*

I never felt that antagonism in the newspaper business. The women there either didn't have children or criminally neglected them. The news doesn't wait for Mom to pick up her kids after school. She's lucky if she gets lunch. But in the real world, you can hear the drums of war getting louder all the time.

Karen, whose stepson lives with her and her husband half the time, says, "I live in a major family-oriented neighborhood. I've had to walk my stepson to the bus stop many times. Let's just say, I am not a part of the mommy-group and they make that very clear. There seems to be this instant bond these women share and it's a members-only club. It's very hard to be treated like an outcast."

Meanwhile, the mothers are massing in protest that women without children are immature, selfish and don't really know what life is all about. It happens at all levels. In 2005, for example, Angela Merkel, then a candidate for chancellor in Germany, was roasted for not having kids. How could she possibly represent the experiences of

166

most women when she didn't know anything about it? A woman without children couldn't claim to support women's rights, critics said. More recently, the same types of comments were made about U.S. Supreme Court justice Elena Kagan, who is also childless.

Antagonism or not, parents and non-parents definitely live different lives. An article in *American Demographics* describes a significant financial difference. "As consumers, this diaper-free brigade wields considerable financial clout." Their studies show childless couples spend more per person in almost every consumer category than their married-with-children counterparts. Without the expenses involved in child-rearing, they simply have more discretionary income.

The *American Demographics* story notes some important factors besides simply not having children that might give these couples more money. In general, two-income childless couples have more education than those with kids. They also work higher-level jobs. One might argue that childless women move up the ladder because they don't take time off for maternity leave and childcare.

They also don't need a mommy van or a childproof house, and they can travel without the added expense or the constraints of finding child-friendly activities and scheduling their trips around the school year. It looks good.

It also looks selfish to some people. Have Fred and I enjoyed the financial benefits of exclusion from the Mom Club? You bet. Nobody ever hassled us about it because Fred already had his three kids, but it's there. We've traveled a lot, we turned our extra bedrooms into offices, and we have rarely had to include offspring in our budget or our schedules. If we want to leave town, we just take our dog to the kennel and go.

16
Why Don't You Have Kids?

Did you ever lie about not having children? I have.

Once in a game called Two Truths and a Lie at a writers' gathering, the lie I told was that I had two sons. The truths were that I was a professional singer and that I had published three books. I won the game; nobody had any doubt that I had 8- and 10-year old sons. I gave the boys names and everything.

And yes, I let people think I was a mother when I was writing for *Bay Area Parent*.

One of my assignments was a piece on the cost of childbirth and Baby's first year. Knowing nothing, I called hospitals for quotes and drove around to the various baby supply stores taking notes on what they had and how much it cost. As if I knew what I was doing. It would have worked out better if I had sat down with some actual parents who were willing to go through their receipts for the past year or at least make a list of the essentials. I mean, what did I know? Did I include breast pumps, vaccinations, itty bitty shoes? I know more about what a dog needs than what an infant requires, but I did my best. It was published and paid for. All I can say for sure is that babies cost more than dogs. A little kibble, some Milk-Bones, an occasional rabies shot, and you're good to go.

Side note: Does it ever occur to those stores that advertise "baby sales" that it sounds as if they're selling actual babies? I'll take two boys and a girl, please.

I let people I interviewed think I was a mother because I didn't want to have to explain my situation. I usually got away with it, but there were times when I got caught. I did a story on birthing suites for *Bay Area Baby*. As we walked down the hall of the hospital toward the elaborate new room with its big bed and chintz curtains, the nurse in charge asked me where my children were born. I had to confess that I didn't have any. Likewise, when people asked about teething, potty training, or the terrible twos, I didn't have an answer. Michael was almost 12 when he moved in with us; my mothering knowledge only goes back to sixth grade.

Short of actually making up fake offspring, we childless women sometimes use other people's kids to grab a place in the conversation. I have used my stepchildren, my niece and nephew and even my own childhood for source material.

Eloise, a high school teacher, says she talked so much about her best friend's children just to feel included and match the other mothers' stories that she realized she was overdoing it. She decided it was more important to listen to the others' stories than to match them story for story with her own.

Not having children was a handicap in her previous job as a social worker, Eloise adds. Some of the mothers she was trying to help openly challenged her credibility when they found out she didn't have children. Being so close to her friends' kids that she was like their second mother wasn't enough. She decided the best she could do was facilitate the discussion, but she couldn't tell mothers how to do their jobs. Eventually, she changed careers.

Don't you love it when you go to have a gynecology exam or a mammogram and they hand you a form that asks "How many pregnancies have you had?" As if it were inconceivable (pun intended) to have never been pregnant. It doesn't take me long to fill out that form. I check "none" and leave the rest of the page blank.

"'Do you have children?' is the first question that women in their twenties are always asked," says Patricia Mahlstedt, M.D. a clinical instructor in the Department of Obstetrics and Gynecology at Baylor College of Medicine. "So women are expected to be mothers first and foremost. Part of the pain and suffering of infertility comes from the weight of that expectation and the fact that women without children are not seen the same way by others."

Even if the woman is childless by choice, the question keeps coming up.

Some of us take it better than others. For example, Tiffany Lee Brown, who married a man who was content with the one child from

169

Sue Fagalde Lick

his first marriage, told me she gets a little steamed.

"I want to wring someone's damned neck and/or burst into tears. Baby culture is everywhere, everywhere, everywhere, all the freakin' time. I hate that it is assumed that this is part of every female's path. It would be impossible for society at large to be sensitive enough to avoid setting me off emotionally, but I guess I still wish it could happen."

In an article for *Oregon Humanities*, Brown wrote about how bringing up the subject of childlessness is a real conversation stopper. Despite all the good things in her life, including a loving relationship with her stepdaughter, she says the need to procreate hits her sometimes with the intensity of the need for food, water and sex, but her friends don't understand. "Why don't you just get a puppy?" they ask.

In her article, Tiffany says her doctor told her to avoid babies, young children and pregnant women because it was so upsetting.

Erica Rothman wrote in the Childless by Choice Newsletter about her 10-year struggle to decide whether or not to have children. Ultimately she decided against it, but she definitely felt she was working against the tide.

"We are at a very interesting point in women's history: Women have an option about whether or not to have children, but the notion is still so new that society hasn't fully condoned it. If we break the norm and do not want children, there can be a psychological price to pay. I have made a decision that not only goes against the culture, but has also disappointed people (my parents) and has confused people, who expect that I am a mother. There have been times when I felt that other people wondered if there was something wrong with me, that I must justify my 'difference.' It is difficult to confidently stand with a decision that society does not want you to make. Women who become mothers are not asked to defend why they decided to have children (unless they are unmarried, or have eight children, and/or are on welfare), so why should I?"

Barbara, who never married or had children, says people make assumptions. "Number one, they'll assume that I have been married and they'll assume that I am a grandmother, especially here in Ashland because there are so many retired people and they all have families and they all have grandchildren. Sometimes it feels like yes, I missed the boat when I have to say no, I'm not married, no, I don't have any children. And some people will be rude. It doesn't devastate me, but it makes me feel uncomfortable."

Barbara doesn't go into detail when people ask why she doesn't have children. She just tells them her life didn't work out that way.

But other women who are sick of the question are a little more outspoken.

One of my favorite answers is: "Because I've seen yours."

First runner-up: "No, I don't have kids. Do you want to give me yours?"

Second runner-up from an elementary-school teacher: "I say I have 200 kids a trimester and one stepdaughter."

And here's a very tactful answer suggested by Christopher Clausen in an *American Scholar* article titled "Childfree in Toyland": "If I could be sure of getting one just like yours, I'd do it in a minute." It's guaranteed to change the subject on a pleasant note, he says.

Of course, Clausen's wife doesn't always exercise such tact. "On one occasion my father, always an outspoken man, took my wife aside and blurted experimentally, 'Chris should have given you a child.' To which she responded: 'I would have given it right back.' My parents never raised the question again, but after Nancy and I had been married twenty years, my mother-in-law was still asking her when she planned to start having a family."

Most of us aren't clever or tactful. We never know what to say. One time when I was taking pictures of the new dog at a Montessori School, a little girl came up close and tugged on my slacks. "Are you a mommy?"

I squatted down to her level. "No," I said.

"Are you a teacher?"

"Nope."

She put her pudgy hands on her hips and stared at me. "Then what are you?"

"A reporter."

Disgusted, she turned and walked away.

"I hate the question," Karen says. I hate even more being told at each annual that I need to have kids soon as I'm running out of time. As if I didn't already know this." As for non-medical people who ask, she used to say she had a stepson. Later, she said she did not have any children. More recently, she says, "Ask my husband."

Jill, a music teacher and "dog mother," doesn't let it bother her. "No. Now I get 'em back; I talk about my dogs. I get irritated when people feel sorry for me. I really detest that, because I think I've had a good life. I don't believe you have to have a husband or kids to be happy."

From earliest recorded history, the childless woman has been seen as a tragic figure to be pitied. Only recently has the arrival of easy access to birth control given women a choice, and many people are still trying to figure out how to react when a woman says, "I'm not going to have children."

"It's natural," they say, or "You'll be sorry later," or "You don't know what you're missing."

Rebecca R. tries to cut the discussion short by simply saying that she has no kids, but if she has to explain, she tells people that her desire to be with her husband is much stronger than her desire to have a child. End of discussion.

Although childless women from North America, the UK and other parts of Europe sometimes feel disapproval from their parenting peers, it's nothing compared to what happens when they visit other parts of the world. Rachel, a freelance journalist who spends a lot of time in Russia, says, "People there are very shocked by my choice and criticize it openly. I also had an argument with an Israeli friend for the same reason."

Jo, a yoga teacher, felt nothing but disapproval when she worked in Costa Rica. As soon as people found out she was unmarried and childless, they shunned her. She overheard people saying she was "selfish." They absolutely could not understand how a woman could get to be in her late 40s without being a wife and mother.

Bela, a PhD. who works at a university in India, says she has suffered greatly because her husband refuses to consult a doctor about their fertility problems. His mother recommended herbal medicines and trusted an astrologer who promised they would have three children. The children didn't come. Bela finally convinced her husband to try medical intervention one time. It didn't work. His family decided she had "destroyed his life." She has been harassed by her husband and his mother for not providing children and for interfering with nature. But she feels she had no choice. "Once you are married there is no way to change your fate."

Compared to Jasu Bricha, Bela is lucky. *Express India* reported Dec. 12, 2008 that 32-year-old Jasu committed suicide by setting herself on fire. Her parents told officials she could no longer bear the harassment she had received, especially from her in-laws, for being unable to conceive during 16 years of marriage. Jasu's parents, like Bela's, apparently didn't consider the possibility that the problem lay with their son.

In an article titled "Where have all the Children Gone?" Vijay Nagaswami, a Chennai-based psychotherapist, described the growing number of what Indians are calling VCCs, voluntarily childless couples. In India, the norm is babies soon after the wedding. Couples who don't follow that path suffer considerable questioning from family and friends. How can they deny themselves this wonder? Are they selfish? It's all right if they seem to be infertile and grieving over their loss. But those who make it known that they are perfectly happy without children are likely to be seen as greedy, selfish, childish, and just plain foolish.

Nagaswami stresses that the decision must be and usually is mutual, not imposed by one partner, such as a husband who doesn't want to have children. If the couple agrees, they can back each against the pressures of family and society to change their minds.

In comparison, my situation has been easy. Most people are satisfied that I have stepchildren and a busy career. But that doesn't stop strangers from asking me whether I have children. Recently while I was visiting a nursing home, one of the residents, who has dementia, asked me how many kids I have. When I said none, she shook her head and turned away. Even there, my childless status set me apart.

Sue Fagalde Lick

Just as there's a Mom Club to which I'll never be admitted, there's also a Grandma Club. Now that I'm at that age, I'm surrounded by doting grandmothers. In fact, my friend Georgia is jetting off to Eugene this weekend to hear little Madison sing in some choir. If her grandkids play football, perform, have a birthday, or just get the blues, she's there with them. Sorry church choir, gotta go. Well, Madison is one of the cutest kids I've ever seen, but it's that whole Grandma Club thing again.

I met up with it big-time at dinner before a writers' gathering Fred and I attended.

"I never thought I'd fall in love with her, but I'm absolutely smitten," Carla said of her 2-year-old granddaughter. "I thought she'd be amusing, but I wasn't prepared for this. I can't get enough of her."

Uh oh, Grandma talk, I thought as I sipped my *pinot gris*, well aware that I was getting tipsy. We were at the Chowder Bowl at the big round table in the corner, having our monthly writers' dinner before our official meeting at the library. Two of our party were actual famous writers, the rest of us getting there. I had never heard Carla, a local publisher, poet and political activist, discuss anything but writing and local political brouhahas. Suddenly it was the Mom Club all over again, except now, in our 50s and 60s, it was the Grandma Club.

"What's her name?" asked Debra, guest speaker and mother of four daughters.

"Marian."

"Oh, that's sweet."

Then Debra and her husband Barry, the famous writers, started going on about their grandson and how brilliant he was, how at four he was already using four-syllable words.

Carla told how little Marian was already sitting at the computer making typing motions--with all ten fingers.

It got worse--and this was at a gathering of writers, where we might have been discussing literature, politics, publishing, or the state of the world. But have I mentioned my theory that mothers fall more

174

Childless by Marriage

deeply in love with their children than with anyone or anything because their children are literally part of them? I fully believe that and know that I would be among the worst child-obsessed mothers and grandmothers if I had children to obsess about.

It was actually a relief when Barry started trashing the government.

Every day is another reunion of the I-made-a-baby club. *See, here he is. I made a life. You made a . . . what? A book, a quilt, a pie, a PhD? Yes, but I made a person. My grave will say "beloved mother." Yours will just have dates for when you were born and when you died. You were never a member of the club.*

17
Free to Be Childfree

❝I have no intention of having children," announced Chyler, the 29-year-old woman my stepson had brought home with him for Christmas. At that moment, she was sitting at the breakfast table with a hot pad on her belly and a cup of tea in her hand, bemoaning her cramps and possible endometriosis. Her doctor had suggested a hysterectomy, but she said she didn't want it. The side effects were worse than the problem.

"You're probably right," I said. "Besides, if you had a hysterectomy, you wouldn't be able to have children."

That's when she made her announcement. She wasn't going to have any kids anyway. Then, to our amazement, Michael added that he didn't intend to have children either.

Wow. Chopped off that branch of the family tree.

We had just met this woman, who was as beautiful as any fairy princess and talented in so many ways that when I told my friend Carol about her, she responded, "We hate her."

No, no we didn't hate her for being beautiful and talented. We hated her a little for expecting to be being waited on for cramps, a malady for which my mother had always insisted one take a pill and move on.

But it was her "I refuse to have children attitude" that bothered me. I have seen this attitude more and more, especially among teens and 20-somethings. *We don't want children and we aren't having any.*

Chyler broke up with Michael, crushed his heart, and for that we probably do hate her, but that still leaves us with the son who doesn't want to be a daddy. Having grown up when everyone supposedly wanted children and it was a tragedy if they couldn't conceive, I find this hard to grasp. Especially when I was as thrilled with the little taste of motherhood I was getting this Christmas as our old dog used to be when my husband came home from work. The hug we exchanged when Michael arrived was one of the best presents I received. He had moved to Portland, so we were his closest family now. I was happy to get up at 6 a.m. to chop fruit, grate cheese and bake cinnamon rolls for a special breakfast. I knew as I peered out the window into the night still lit by stars and full moon that THIS was what had been missing in my life. If I could do any part of my life over, I'd have children.

Why didn't Chyler want children? Her tone—and her cramps—did not allow for questions, but I keep asking this. I want to understand where this "no kids" decision comes from.

While recruiting people to interview, asking everyone I knew and putting the word out on the Internet, I stressed that I was looking for women who were childless by marriage, who had sacrificed motherhood for their husband or partner. That didn't stop dozens of voluntarily childless women from responding. They seemed anxious for someone to listen to them and understand their choice. Harassed by pro-baby relatives, friends, co-workers, and society in general, they wanted someone to see that they weren't crazy or selfish, that they had perfectly good reasons for choosing not to have children. Many said they had known from early childhood that they didn't want to be mothers.

My own mother's generation never considered that choice, but this is the 21st century, with choices that didn't exist 50 years ago. So I offer here a chance for the childfree among us to explain themselves.

Here are some sample responses:

* Gina, 42, a court reporter: "I don't feel there is anything to be ashamed of. I am proud of myself for not needlessly, unconsciously breeding just because I got pregnant or [because] it is what is expected in society. I don't dislike children; I just don't want any, even though I am exactly the kind of person that should be raising children. I think that statement is true of most of the childless women I know, but it is a Catch-22. I don't believe we would be the strong, educated, thoughtful women we are if we had children, because we wouldn't have had the time that is necessary to explore ourselves and become the women we are."

Sue Fagalde Lick

* Joyce, 54, also a court reporter: "I don't think I would have married a man who wanted children. I believe people need to make very clear, conscious choices to have children, and I believe that 99.9 percent of people don't do that. There are too many neglected and unloved children in the world now. If someone is going to have a child, it is the parents' responsibility for one of them to stay home and nurture that child. Too many have children and dump them on nannies or in day care. What were they thinking? Nurturing a child is the most important job on the planet. If you're not willing to do what it takes, then don't have a child. I knew I wanted a career, and it would not be fair to a child for me to have a career. People treat their children as if they are property or a potted plant. I work in the court system and see the tragic results of parents who don't know how to raise their children or simply can't be bothered with it. It takes a huge toll on society."

* Robyn, 40, an artist: "My art always came first. My paintings were my 'babies.' My art was the number one priority in my life and if I couldn't give that kind of energy and time to anything else, I felt it would be irresponsible for me to have children, who need 200 percent of a parent's time, love and attention.

"I think that the world needs people, particularly women, to give birth to many things, not just children. Some of us have children. Others of us make art, cure illnesses, write books and leave other legacies behind. As women, I don't think we should feel obligated to have children just because we can. We have the capability to do so many other things, and we have so many choices. Having children is just one of those choices, and it's not particularly the right one for every woman."

Susan Maushart writes in *The Mask of Motherhood,* "While fatherhood remains one option among many, motherhood revokes the whole concept of free will. It is with motherhood that the myths of equal opportunity and shared autonomy bite the behavioral dust."

In her essay "Autumn Fruit," Patricia Frank writes, "My birth canal has not birthed, my arms have not cradled a child and these breasts have not suckled. I am without progeny. How do I feel about that? Pretty good."

Childless by Marriage

I heard from quite a few women who simply said that they don't like children and don't want any. Kids are parasites, one said. They suck the life out of you, said another. If I'd had children, my life would be ruined, said still another.

My father would say, "Yeah, so? That's just the way it is." But he was one of those boomer-era parents who never considered not having children. Lucky for me and my brother.

What about Chyler, Michael's ex-girlfriend? Is it simply that she was so wrapped up in her career and her many hobbies that there was no room in her life for children? Was there a clue in the helpless dying act she put on when struck by menstrual cramps? Are today's young adults too childlike to raise children?

What about Michael? He just doesn't want to. Period.

I mentioned this later while dining with friends. Our hosts had two children, but their neighbors, both 60-something, said they had never wanted children. The woman, Orpha, a round and loving motherly type with blonde hair and gold jewelry glittering over her black dress, said her mother was so terrible she never wanted to be a mother. Her husband, a longtime Hollywood cartoonist with a leprechaun face, said his mother had abandoned his family when he was a boy. This couple had had a full and wonderful life and served as extra parents for their young neighbors and their dogs. That was enough for them.

It's not a new thing, this childlessness, but I'm betting those who made the choice decades ago were never as definite or as open about it as young Chyler calmly sitting at the table on Christmas morning declaring to people she had just met that she had no intention of ever having children.

For decades now, we have witnessed antagonism between parents and the self-proclaimed "childfree." Not child*less*. That would imply they're missing something.

People can have children or not. It's certainly their choice, but the anger of the childfree frightens me. Were they not children once themselves? Do they not understand that you have to have children in order to have grownups? How can folks who fight for the right to

179

drink their lattés with their poodles and pugs at their side object to children? Is it because children talk? Because they can't be choke-chained? Well, that's true, but when they get old enough, kids can drive you to the doctor when you break your hip while your beloved pooch will just look up and say, *Where are my treats*?

Am I right?

Jonathan Kay, a Canadian writer for the *National Post*, wrote in his blog that a story about the disconnect between parents who bring their kids to restaurants and non-parents who think kids in restaurants are an abomination had brought him lots of feisty e-mails and blog comments, the worst of which follows:

"Mr. Kay, I hope we never have the misfortune to have your family ruin a nice restaurant near us, because I could hardly resist the compulsion to empty ice water into the faces of both you and your broodsow of a partner. Attention, Mr. Look-My-Sperm-Works, your job as a parent does not end at ejaculation. Would you please show the rest of us the Get Out of Courtesy card that they gave you when your wife [birthed] your first replicant? Polite parents do not assault diners with their loud brood of assmonkeys."

Wow. Good thing these guys will never meet in person.

I agree that some children don't have sufficient manners to eat in upscale restaurants, but others are well-behaved. Besides, how are you going to learn good manners if you never eat at a restaurant until you're old enough to date? When I was a child, we ate out often. My brother and I knew that we had to be quiet and eat or face our father's anger. No, he wasn't an abuser, but he could frighten you into submission with a look.

Kay's column sparked quite a response. At childfree websites such as www.selfishheathens.com, members urged each other to flame Kay at will. And flame they did. Selfish Heathens discourages parents, aka Breeder Trolls, from joining. No, discouraging is putting it too mildly. They use language I don't dare use here. This is a perfect example of the anger some childfree people feel toward those who have children. Their Satanic symbols and angry verbiage scare the heck out of me. That's probably their intention, would-be breeder troll that I am.

Childless by Marriage

Not everyone is as frightening as the Selfish Heathens, but many are militant about non-parenting. Remember Zero Population Growth? The movement's bible, Paul R. Ehrlich's *The Population Bomb*, published in 1968, was required high school reading for my generation. The book told us that the world would soon be so overpopulated that it would self-destruct. People started having fewer babies. This coincided with the arrival of legal birth control and women's liberation, so Ehrlich wasn't the only influence on their decision, but birthrates definitely started going down.

Forty years later, citizens of some countries, including Canada, Japan and Germany, aren't having enough babies to reproduce themselves. Entire cultures could disappear in a few generations. But the childfree have grabbed onto a new environmental issue, global warming. They tell us all these people breathing out carbon dioxide are wrecking the planet.

Kay quotes the British Optimum Population Trust, which put out a briefing statement on the subject. It concluded: "Population limitation should be seen as the most cost-effective carbon-offsetting strategy available to individuals and nations."

Kay's response? "I would much rather live in an overheated world teeming with assmonkeys than a Kyotified utopia in which human life was measured against carbon credits. And thankfully, my broodsow feels the same way."

More reassuring comments about Kay's blog include a note from a mother of seven children who are being taught to treat the earth gently. They are helping the problem rather than making it worse. She concludes, "We do not need to worry much about those who remain "childfree" on purpose, for they will soon all disappear."

So there.

The *Greeley (Colorado) Tribune* published a commentary in which the writer, a parent, tells how much she appreciates her childless friends and honors the choice they made. She hopes her daughters grow up to understand that they don't have to have babies if they choose not to.

Jerry Steinberg, founder of NO KIDDING, an international social club for childless and childfree couples and singles, praised the writer's mutual respect for everyone, wherever they stand on the baby-making question.

However, some of the comments were less than kind. A reader protested the use of "childless" vs. "childfree," chastised the writer for accepting gifts from her childfree friends with no reciprocation and finally blasted her with, "Which is precisely why most childfree people avoid friendships with—to be blunt—breeders."

Gack. Using the word "breeders" as a pejorative against people who have children makes me think of Margaret Atwood's science fiction novel, *The Handmaid's Tale*, in which less fortunate women are hired to breed babies for the wealthier women who can't be bothered. It also makes me think about breeders in the animal world. These breeders are humans who choose the strongest, smartest and most attractive bitches and studs, bring them together to mate, then sell their offspring for money. The rest of the animals, the mutts and strays, are to be spayed, neutered, or put down.

Are we starting to apply the same concept to humans, but in reverse? Only the poor, uneducated and inferior people are dumb enough to breed? Is that what the childfree are saying?

I guess some animosity is inevitable. I have heard all the stories about how the people with children skip out of work early, leave unfinished tasks to their childless colleagues, get better benefits, fawn over their kids, and fail to include those without children in their conversations and their social events. I know. Been there, lived that.

I feel left out at least as often as I feel relieved not to be connected to a whiny child. But if no one had children, sooner or later, we wouldn't have people. I say God bless those with the courage, love and energy to raise children. It's a hard job. But also God bless those who for whatever reason live their lives at the end of the family tree.

Let's just not fight about it.

I'm standing at my book table in Lincoln City, Oregon on the rainiest, coldest, most miserable day of the year. It's the "Plein Air" festival, expected to be a happy mix of painters painting, sculptors sculpting, musicians playing, and crafters and artists selling their wares, but for the half of us who didn't bail out, it's not fun. I can't imagine why so many people have brought their tiny dogs in little raincoats and their toddlers in shiny jackets. They're certainly not buying anything. My single buying customer must be a mom; she sees me shivering and gives me the gloves she just bought. I'm so grateful I could weep.

Two women in their early 30s meander over to check out my books. They ask what I'm working on now, and I tell them it's a book about childless women. They look at each other and grin. "We're childless," the dark-haired one with the white knit hat and the multi-colored wool jacket says.

"Really," I say. "Are you childless by choice?"

"Yes," they chorus.

"About once a year," says the dark-haired one, who's from Latvia, "my husband and I ask each other, 'Should we have a baby?' and we say no. My art is my baby." She makes ceramic vases.

"Well, yes," I agree. "It is hard to be an artist and raise a family."

"I just have too much else to do. I don't have time for kids," says her curly-haired artist friend in the yellow slicker.

"But someday," I suggest, "you might be lonely."

Immediately comes the standard answer I have heard at least a hundred times, no exaggeration: You can't count on your children to be around when you get old. They move away. They're too busy. "Look at my family," says the Lat. "My mother's all the way in Latvia. I hardly ever see her." Then she twists the knife. "What about your momma and daddy?"

"Well," I say, "My mom died, and my dad lives in California, which is far away."

"You see!"

And they go back to their art. Yes, I see. Many women have told me that they couldn't have their careers and raise children properly, too. Many famous writers and artists, including Louisa May Alcott and Georgia O'Keeffe, never had children. As someone who barely finds time to buy groceries or shave her legs—without kids—I can identify with the difficulty of trying to do everything in one lifetime. But if *I* had kids, it would be different. Of course, everyone says that, too.

Sue Fagalde Lick

I understand why people might want to be childfree. I don't have to have kids to see that they can wear you out. We're not that far from the mama bird who spends all day flying back and forth regurgitating food into the open, cheeping mouths of her nestlings. I'm sure, if she could speak English, she'd say, "Damn, they're always hungry. What I'd give to eat a meal of my own in peace."

And yet, what healthy female bird doesn't lay eggs? It's not a question of choice. It just happens. The way nature works is that as one generation grows up, gets old and dies, another generation is born to replace it, whether you're a robin, a daffodil or a coyote. Except we humans sometimes choose not to participate. In my own family, people have had so few children we're disappearing. Pretty soon we'll all fit in one row at the funeral parlor.

I get it. Kids force you to stay home when you want to go out. They talk with their mouths full. They cost a fortune—the latest estimates are over $200,000 from birth to age 18. They always need more, more, more. Children are like puppies that pee on the carpet and chew up your favorite shoes. They need training. But that's the deal. First you get to be a kid, ignorant, helpless and served by grownups. Then you're a parent, teaching your children everything you know and helping them to grow up strong and healthy. Finally you're a grandparent or even a great-grandparent, and all you have to do is remember them on Christmas and their birthdays and step in for occasional babysitting. If you trained them right, your children will take care of you in your old age. When you die, the next generation takes your place. That's how it goes. If you don't have children, there is no next generation.

It's instinct. It's biology. We're hard-wired to mate and procreate. Most people seem to be able to do it easily, but thousands, perhaps millions of infertile couples struggle to become parents. They put everything they have into the often futile effort to get one sperm and one egg to come together as an embryo that becomes a fetus that becomes a baby.

In a *Chicago Tribune* column, Dennis Byrne suggests that human instinct causes us to want children and that the childfree advocates are fighting their own instincts.

184

Childless by Marriage

Susan Jeffers offers a different view in her book *I'm Okay, You're a Brat*. First, the urge to parent is not instinct; it's cultural conditioning, a lifetime of being told that's what you're supposed to do. Second, she believes that magic that's supposed to happen the first time we hold our babies in our arms is a myth. "Most are not that thrilled. Some are horrified at this sudden responsibility that has been thrust upon them and [they're] surprised at how they feel because society has told them incessantly that motherhood is magical and glorious."

If we're really going to live according to nature, the Childless by Choice literature maintains, we should stop flying in airplanes. We should live outdoors, hunt for our food and not wear clothes. Furthermore, in the natural world, when a species risks extinction, it makes sense to produce more offspring. When there are too many of a species, the animals stop breeding, bear smaller litters or die of starvation or disease. Thus, with more than six billion people on earth, we don't ALL need to breed.

So, are we the stupidest animals on the planet or are we starting to practice intelligent population control?

Religious people might suggest we are taking into our own hands decisions that ought to be left to a higher power. Are those who choose to be childfree selfish, putting their own desires above those of their potential offspring? Is there an angel up in heaven who is supposed to be theirs and won't get his chance at life because they take the pill, tie the tubes, have the vasectomy, or abort?

Or are they doing a good thing? People who don't want children might change their minds when they have their own, but they might not. They might be terrible parents and are thus wise to pass.

On the other hand, children aren't babies forever. One minute they're in diapers, the next they need school clothes, the next they're asking for the car keys. And one day, one wonderful day, you turn around and realize you have created this grownup person who looks like you and who will carry on the family name and story. For me, it's always going to be child*less*, not child*free*.

Sue Fagalde Lick

For some couples, the decision not to have children is a painful one made for very good reasons.

Women have told me they held off because certain physical or mental illnesses ran in their families and they didn't want to pass them on. Others have said their husbands appeared likely to be alcoholic child-abusers. An Episcopal priest felt she could not give herself to both the church and her own children.

Barbara admits that during her child-bearing years she was an alcoholic. In addition to the drinking, she came from an abusive family. Her parents never encouraged her to marry or reproduce, and she says she really didn't know how to go about having a normal family with children. Now 32 years sober, she knows she would not have been a good mother.

Karen, a 38-year-old writer, says she was delighted when she discovered the term "childfree." Physically unable to bear children, the concept changed her whole perspective. She stopped feeling as if she was missing something and started spreading the word that it was okay not to have children.

But it gets fuzzy. Women who have had bad upbringings fear they would inflict the same on their own babies. Maybe they wouldn't. Having witnessed the worst, they might be wonderful parents.

Some childfree advocates believe we already have too many people. Looking at the gridlock on the 280 Freeway in San Jose at 5:30 any weekday, I'd buy that. But wait, we don't all have to have cars. I don't think it's the existence of children that's destroying the environment. It's what the grownups are doing to it.

It takes a village to raise a child, Hillary Rodham Clinton wrote. "Children exist in the world as well as in the family. From the moment they are born, they depend on a host of other grown-ups: grandparents, neighbors, teachers, ministers, employers, political leaders, and untold others who touch their lives directly and indirectly. Adults police their streets, monitor the quality of their food, air and water, produce the programs that appear on their televisions, run the businesses that employ their parents and write the

186

laws that protect them. Each of us plays a part in every child's life: It takes a village to raise a child."

Indeed. A little girl comes up to me at the mall and grabs my leg. I don't know who she is or to whom she belongs, but before I ask these questions, I bend down and find out what she needs. If she has a question, I will answer it. If she's lost, I'll find her mother. If she's hurt, I'll do what I can to make her feel better. To a child, every woman is a mom, a safe place she can go when she's lost in the mall.

In her essay "The Barren Sister" in *Nobody's Mother*, Adrienne Munro writes, "I dream, not of having children of my own, but of parenting when and where and whom I can—as a sort of universal parent, a Mother at Large, if you will. I don't need to produce a child in order to mother; I can mother in a hundred different ways. I can love the children in my life . . . I have not borne a child, but I am a universal parent; in a hundred little ways my love can change the world."

In a book called *Childlessness Transformed*, Brooke Medicine Eagle describes how among the Crow Indians when a person has no children, all the children are her children, not just humans but every life form. When a woman, parent or not, passes through menopause, she moves into the Grandmother Lodge. These "grandmothers" are responsible for all the children of the earth. "The Grandmother Society looks around to see that everyone is cared for and nurtured, not just their children or not even just the children of our family or our clan or our small group, but the children of all the Earth."

I'm such a hypocritical flip-flopper. The other day while I was getting my hair cut, I had a long discussion with Karlia, my stylist and the mother of four. I told her about the Selfish Heathens and other childfree groups and about how so many women I interviewed had had abortions. She and I shared our outrage at men who forced women into abortions, doing the get-rid-of-it-if-you-love-me routine. Forget that, we agreed.

You have to give Karlia credit. She adores her kids, all born by C-section. She works her schedule around their needs. But Karlia doesn't make me feel weird for not having kids. I know she'd jump on anyone who dared call her a "breeder," but she has plenty of other

187

Sue Fagalde Lick

things to talk about, from show business to politics. Her children may be the most important thing in her life, but she recognizes there's a world out there.

I was all pro-children while talking to Karlia. The next day at the gym, however, I felt a little of that Selfish Heathen anger. No, more than a little.

Here's what happened. I was happily pedaling the exercise bike, warming up for my workout, when in walked a man, a woman, and one, two, three children under the age of six. There were two girls and a boy, the girls both dressed in pink, the boy wearing glasses, all three bubbling with energy.

Hey, I thought, isn't this supposed to be an all-adult gym? Didn't I read somewhere that no one under 16 was allowed? But we have new owners, and they have kids. Who knows what the rules are now?

The mother, slim and blonde, wearing a white tee shirt and black workout pants, climbed aboard a treadmill and started walking while the dad, red-haired, freckled and pudgy, with a cross printed on his tee shirt, led the kids into the tiny lounge, stuck a video into the machine and told them to sit and stay put.

Well, kids are not dogs. They did not sit. They did not stay. The older girl was out in a flash, running next to her mother's treadmill, bouncing off the other machines, parking herself on the box where I needed to do my calf extensions. Get away from there; it's for grownups, I thought. Get out of my gym. Git!

But I didn't. I waited until she moved, then did my 24 up-downs and moved to the next machine. By the time I hit the rowing machine, all three children were playing with the barbells that had been lined up on a bench by order of weight.

The wife wore a pained expression. She knew the kids were annoying. But the husband was like a bigger child, too busy complaining that the machines weren't up to his standards to notice his wandering offspring. Judging by the shape of his shape, how would he know good machines from bad?

Does this remind anyone of the man who complained about broodsows and their offspring ruining his meal at a nice restaurant? Yes, I confess. Switch restaurant for gym, and it was the same thing. Get those dang kids out of here.

Childless by Marriage

The gym wasn't just a place to lift weights. It was my sanctuary, where I didn't have to think or worry about anybody else, just work my body to the beat of loud music. But now, my mind buzzed with bitchy thoughts.

When I went to move the bar for my standing pushups, the dad had left his weights on it. Did he not see the sign! I removed his weights. Grrr. Okay, so he did three lifts and planned to come back later, but what about the rest of us?

My heart was drumming about 200 beats a minute by the time I retreated to the dark, quiet classroom to do my stomach crunches. One, no kids, two, in my gym, three, this, four, is where, five, I don't have to deal, six, with that, seven, sh—!

I did 50 crunches without stopping. It still hurt two days later. Exercise done in anger is bad for the body.

I know this couple had a lousy choice. They could either give up exercise or bring the kids. I'm sure they believed that if they sat them in the lounge with a video and snacks, they'd stay there and let everyone work out in peace. What are you going to do when you're responsible for three young humans every minute of every day? I suspect this was the first time this couple had tried this maneuver. Now they know that all those shiny machines are like fishing lures. The children can't resist checking them out.

For that hour in the gym, I definitely sympathized with the childfree crowd. I wanted those brats out of my life. For all my pontificating about the glories of parenthood, I didn't actually want to be in the same room with actual children during my workout. Would it be different if they were mine? I'll never know.

Judging by the cross on the dad's shirt, they're Christians. So am I. What would Jesus do? He would do what I have seen parents do around little kids. He would have welcomed them, asked their names, explained the equipment and maybe even shown them how to do some exercises appropriate for their ages. He would have seen that these children were cute and that their mother looked great for having given birth three times. He would have applauded the couple for demonstrating to their children that exercise should be a lifelong activity.

189

Sue Fagalde Lick

In fact, the next workout day, I saw an older man, Pete, do exactly that with the new owners' children, a boy and a girl. He talked to them as if he were delighted to meet them. "Well, how old are you?" and "What do you like to do?"

These kids did go into the lounge and stay there, except for the daughter's brief foray to the ladies' room.

Sometimes I feel like such a bitch. But after all these childless years, I don't know how to do what Pete did. I just wanted the kids out of my gym. Are parents emotionally different from non-parents? Yes. If you don't have children, you never learn to share.

French author Corinne Maier caused a furor in France in 2007 with her best-selling book *No Kids: 40 Reasons for Not Having Children*. In an interview with Maier called "Enfants Terrible," Emma Tucker notes that Maier has created a new French word: *merdeuf*. It means "a woman who has children, so she no longer cares about anything else." It's a contraction of *me're de famile*, the traditional term for stay-at-home mom. But, says Tucker, "the contraction turns it into something that sounds like a combination of *merde* (shit) and *oeuf* (egg), carrying the implication that these patriotic mega-moms are "egg-shitters."

Some of Maier's reasons for not having children include the pain of childbirth, loss of time and freedom, and the likelihood of being disappointed by your children. "To open the nursery is to close the bedroom," she says, and "To be a mother, or to succeed: You must choose."

The decision to remain childfree is not a new one. Some of the greatest minds of the past two centuries have had their say on the subject. For example:

- "Having a first child is like throwing a hand grenade into a marriage."—Nora Ephron.
- If motherhood doesn't interest you, don't do it. It didn't interest me, so I didn't do it. Anyway, I would have made a terrible parent. The first time my child didn't do what I wanted, I'd kill him."—Katherine Hepburn

Childless by Marriage

- When you rescue a dog in bad straits and feed him, take care of him, and give him a home, the dog is grateful. This is the chief difference between a dog and a human being."—Mark Twain
- "My husband and I are either going to buy a dog or have a child. We can't decide whether to ruin our carpets or ruin our lives."–Rita Rudner.

My childfree friends, we hear you.

18
Can a Woman Be a Dog's Mother?

"Ursula's dog died," Mary announced at the beginning of rehearsal at the Episcopal church for our women's *a capella* octet. "She was sobbing over the phone. She's taking it real hard."

We swallowed, contemplating our own dogs, comparing their ages, thinking how we would feel.

After a moment of silence, we started singing. A large German shepherd mix with floppy ears trotted in. "Hey!" I exclaimed right in the middle of Brahms. Lydia, dog-daughter of church pastor Susan, came straight up to me and licked my face. I grabbed her in a big hug, then let her go on to greet the other women.

Where Susan went, Lydia went. Like Susan, we all had dogs instead of children. The week before, Jill had brought her shepherd Serena to rehearsal. We watched Serena and Lydia dance the playful-aggressive dance of two big dogs getting acquainted. We laughed, cheered them on and petted whichever dog came closest until Lydia went home with Susan and Serena had us all to herself. When she wasn't circling the room, rubbing legs, or getting full-body pets, she lay on Jill's bare feet, occasionally licking her toes. Jill held her sheet music in one hand, using the other to stroke, groom and inspect her dog's long silky fur. The dog was quiet and obedient, except for one time when Jill sang some unusually high notes. Serena poked her long nose right up against Jill's face and howled.

At home, my own dog, Sadie, sniffed me all over, jealous of the other dogs. "I'll take you next time," I told her. She raced to the bookshelf where I kept the box of Milk-Bones, then sat staring intently at me as she licked her lips.

"Okay, you can have a cookie," I said, reaching for the dog

treats. A minute later, she sat silently in front of the back door.

"Need to go out?" I opened the door and she flew into the darkness bounded by the $3,000 fence we had built for her. House-hunting, we would only consider places with yards big enough to suit our dog.

After a while, Sadie woofed at the door, and I let her in. She walked to her L.L. Bean dog bed, circled three times and lay down. Stretched full-length, completely relaxed, she closed her eyes and dozed. After a while, she started running in her sleep, her lips moving in silent conversation. Her feet finally slowed. She rolled onto her back and began to snore. Fred and I looked at each other and smiled.

We never set out to be a singing group made up of women who were raising dogs with human names, like Susan's Lydia, Mary's Charlie, Jill's Serena, and my sweet Sadie. We just wanted to sing together. But perhaps we were able to make the group a reality because we didn't have children to worry about. We were free to rehearse and perform days, nights, and weekends because dogs are so much more convenient. You can leave dogs in the back yard or the car. You can even bring them to rehearsal. Unlike children, dogs are totally trainable. You can hold them by a leash attached to a chain around their necks and order "Down!" They sink to the floor, eyes wide, tail wagging, awaiting your next command. Try that with young humans and you'll go to jail for child abuse.

Several members of our church choir had small children. When they brought them to practice, the little darlings pounded the piano, raced around the chapel, and badgered their parents for food, drink, help going to the bathroom, or toys to amuse them. If only we could have tied them to a leash and ordered them to lie quietly at our feet.

Two of us in the octet actually did have children, but they were grown up and lived far away. Mary and I were stepmothers, but we rarely saw our husbands' offspring.

A friend kept referring to me as Sadie's "mom," as in, "Aw, come on, Mom, she really wants to go for a walk." Or, "She just wants to hang out with Mom." Setting aside all issues of her being able to read Sadie's mind, Sadie was a dog, a beautiful

193

German Shepherd-yellow Lab mix with golden fur and natural black eyeliner. I loved this dog with all my heart, but I was not her mother. Her mother was a dog, a member of the canine species with four legs, a tail and a long nose.

I felt about as comfortable being called my dog's mother as I did years ago when Fred, Michael and I had a family portrait made and the photographer kept calling me "Mom." I suppose that's so he didn't have to remember my actual name, but by the time he finished shooting, I came very close to screaming at him. I certainly wasn't *his* mom, nor was I actually Michael's mom. In fact, I wasn't anybody's mom and in those days that fact was particularly painful. Besides, you don't just start calling a stranger "Mom." "Mrs. Lick" would have been more appropriate. "Sue" would have been acceptable. But Mom?

Jennifer Keene, co-owner of Beaverton, Oregon's Pup-A-Razzi dog training school, says she often calls her clients' owners Mom and Dad, even though not all consider themselves to be the dogs' parents; she just hasn't learned their names yet. So they're "Rover's Mommy" or "Buddy's Dad."

It's hard to define my relationship with Sadie because I did adopt her and I did feed her, take her to the vet, walk her, pick up her poop, and arrange for someone to take care of her when we traveled. That does sound a bit like mothering. Can one do what a mother does and not actually *be* a mother? Caretaker or caregiver sounds as if the dog is handicapped. She wasn't, although I helped her through four surgeries. She would have done the same for me if she had had hands, a checkbook, and a driver's license.

C an a woman be a dog's *mom*? A survey of 1,200 U.S. and Canadian pet owners by the American Veterinary Medical Association showed that *84 percent* refer to themselves as their pet's mom or dad. Seriously. They also reported that 63 percent celebrate their pet's birthdays, and 43 percent give their pet a wrapped gift. Similar numbers buy their pets Christmas presents, say the American Pet Products Manufacturers. And we're not talking about those cheesy plastic stockings full of dog biscuits. They give their pets Hawaiian shirts and sunglasses, days at doggy spas for massage and aromatherapy, and doggy cell phones. The latter, shaped like dog bones, attach to the dog's collar and let you call your dog and whisper loving words. They only accept incoming calls.

Back in 1955, when I was a toddler, only 55 percent admitted to calling themselves their pets' moms or dads. Dogs were just dogs. They certainly didn't spend all their time in the house and have their own L.L. Bean beds like mine did. (It was tan with faux paw prints all over it.)

Some pet stores put up signs that say "Dogs are just children with fur."

Well, yes, they're somebody's children, but not mine.

Are they?

I knew every inch and scar of my dog, but I didn't even know if any of my stepchildren had ever had the measles. If Sadie coughed or limped, I was on the phone with the vet. Any little sneeze or wheeze, and I was asking, "Are you sick? Are you okay?" I kept feeling her nose to see if she was hot. In her later years, when she started moaning, I kept asking her, "What's wrong?"

"She's just trying to talk," Fred said.

Perhaps telling me to let her be?

People may not be dogs' actual parents, but they certainly act like it sometimes. Honda in Japan is giving childless customers the option of installing doggy crates or Pekingese-sized glove compartment pet nooks instead of child car seats. With the childless rate nudging toward one-quarter of the population, the car manufacturer figures if they build it, people will buy it.

Intrigued, I researched car seats for dogs and found that Honda isn't alone. Doggy car seats are a big business, along with dog carriers, dog clothing, and dog strollers. They look a lot like baby strollers. You can even get a pink one for female dogs.

It gets worse. In August 2007, Reuters reporter Sophie Hardach wrote about Japanese eye surgeon Toshiko Horikoshi, who pushes around a pram containing her two dogs, Ginger, a teacup poodle, and Tinkerbell, a Chihuahua-Pomeranian mix. She dresses them up in tiny clothes and takes them everywhere she goes. She's too busy with her work to get married or have children, she says, but she gets lonely sometimes, hence the dogs.

She and her friends have parties with their dogs and even take them to hot spring resorts and spas offering dog massages and aromatherapy, reports Hardach, who adds that, "Dogs now outnumber children aged 10 and under in Japan—there were 13.1 million dogs in 2006. As the number of humans shrinks, the dog population is growing, research firm Euromonitor says, and so is the market for dog-related products."

For example, you can buy dog fashions at Fifi and Romeo, a Los Angeles-based boutique that has shops in both Japan and the USA.

It's crazy, right? It's little girls dressing up the family dog and pushing it around in a baby buggy, except these are grown women.

Gadgets with names like the Outward Hound fanny pack and the FidoRido car seat make us laugh, and yet, many of us who own dogs save the ads, thinking, maybe my little pupperdoodle should have one of those.

It's not just Japan. In an article about Asheville, NC, Susan Reinhardt describes doggy cocktail parties, daycare centers, bakeries and "pawdicures." She quotes the owner of a Schnoodle—a schnauzer-poodle mix—who prepared for her new dog just like she would prepare for a baby. She scoped out the vets and the shops, bought a Snugli front pack carrier and even asked a friend to be the dog's godmother. She signed her dog up for training long before she got her and spent oodles of money on toys, cages and carry-alls. I wouldn't be surprised if she had a puppy shower.

Google "Dog Mom" and you'll find 190 million entries, starting with tee shirts that say "Dog Mom" and "Dog Dad." Keep searching and you'll find everything from doggy couture to doggy orthodontia, not to mention diamond collars and acupuncture for cats. Is there a connection between the fact that nearly one-quarter of North American and European women are not having children and the fact that most of them have pets?

Where is the line between sweet and just plain nuts? I'm reassured that all of these dog accoutrements are designed for dogs 30 pounds and under, yappers we call them in my family. My Sadie was a real dog, all 60 pounds of her, and my other dogs have been even bigger. You can't put a dog like that in the glove compartment. I did consider getting a doggy seat belt, however, because Sadie liked to perch on the narrow armrest between the front seats, panting in my ear as we approached wherever it was we were going. She occasionally crashed into the dashboard when I hit the brake. But a pink stroller? Come on, she needed her exercise; she was always watching her weight.

Forgetting the logistics of trying to lift a 100-pound golden retriever into a car seat or stroller, consider that a small dog or, even better, a cat can be held against your breasts just like a baby. It feels good. Lying with a cat purring along one's sternum evokes a wonderfully contented feeling. That warm, small creature seems to fit perfectly. How different is that from holding a baby?

Is interspecies parenting possible? What about those stories you hear about a motherless lamb being smuggled into the goat pen and accepted as part of the family? Or a mother dog nursing a kitten? Or the true story of a Golden Retriever nursing tiger cubs at a Kansas zoo? A friend recently sent me a picture of a pigeon mothering an orphaned litter of rabbits. If animals can do it, why not people? Maybe I could be a dog mother. It's a puzzling question, which became more so when Sadie got so old that she was older than me in people years. Maybe she was *my* mother, and I only thought I was in charge.

I flash on my Grandma Rachel's dachshund, "Gretchie," whom she cuddled and coddled, much to the frustration of my grandfather. He preferred real dogs like the big mutts that used to keep him company on the ranch. They never set paw inside the house. Rachel's "baby" was a little rat to him—although when Gretchie's spine seized up, she dragged her back legs around for weeks before he could make himself take her to the vet for the fatal shot.

Grandma Rachel, my father's stepmother, never had children of her own, just two grown stepsons who resented the heck out of her and seven step-grandchildren who tolerated her many eccentricities because she was the only paternal grandmother we ever knew. She showered us with gifts and adored her nephew and nieces, but her dog was the only tiny being she could claim as her own.

197

Sue Fagalde Lick

Then there was that friend of my parents, also childless, who had a Chihuahua cuddled in blankets in a silk-lined Barbie bed when we visited. Ruby spent a lot of time alone while her husband Ray drove truck across the country and flirted with everything in skirts, including my 14-year-old self. Yes, that dog was Ruby's baby, always at her side as she sipped and smoked and waited for Ray to come home.

Now I remember others: the poet who used to bring her mange-riddled cocker-terrier to writers' group meetings. While we went over each other's poems, she would cuddle the smelly little dog, letting its paws get tangled in the fringes of her flowered scarves.

And the couple who used to live across the street. When they'd drive in, their tiny pug would be looking out over the steering wheel. He went to work with them every day at a local mini-storage place. Ron and Nita held him in the crooks of their arms—just like a baby.

Orpha, a retired Hollywood set designer, had Sergeant Pepper, a brindled Akita who accompanied her everywhere. Stretched full length, he was as tall and as heavy as a man. If you were sitting when he walked up to you, he looked you right in the face, eyeball to eyeball. When he died, Orpha went into a long slump. Then she adopted two incorrigible mid-sized dogs who curled up at her feet whenever she sat down. Children? She never wanted them. Dogs? Of course.

Lonely people do crazy things. Like adopting monkeys. The International Primate Protection League published samples of ads on its website as part of a warning about the vigorous underground trade for monkeys. People see them as cute pets and baby substitutes—until they mature and become ill-mannered, biting animals that nobody wants.

Typical ad: *Looking for a baby or young capuchin. My husband and I are unable to have children, and, after long and in-depth conversations concerning it, feel we are more than ready to make a monkey part of our loving family. Hoping not to exceed the price of $4,500. Please help us make our family complete!*

Says IPPL, "Owners of pet monkeys often dress their "babies" in human clothing, and sometimes call them 'monkids.' This is insulting

Childless by Marriage

to the natural identity of these animals, treating the unfortunate animals as human playthings."

People pay as much as $35,000 for baby monkeys, particularly favoring baby-faced capuchins, spider monkeys and marmosets. When the monkeys turn out to be worse than human teenagers, they desperately try to unload them for a tenth of that price.

Now here's a good question: What husband who didn't want children would agree to adopt a monkey?

One might understand treating a monkey, which looks somewhat human, as one's child, but what about a cow? In May 2007, an Indian newspaper reported that a childless couple held a Hindu wedding ceremony for their pet cow Sadhana and a groom bull they didn't name. The ceremony had all the Hindu traditions, including a procession and live music. Said Anusuiya Vishwakarma, "Sadhana's" owner, "I don't have kids of my own. I have brought up this cow as my own child, with lots of love and affection. One day I thought to marry it off just like I would have married my own daughter. So, I decided to hold this ceremony."

The wedding, which required two months preparation, cost almost 200,000 rupees, approximately $4,300. About 1,500 people attended the ceremony. They chanted Vedic hymns and enjoyed a feast afterward. As is the custom, the bride's family showered the groom's side with gifts.

My friend Carol lets her parrot Barney run her life. The other day when we met at the mailbox, she said she had to hurry back in because if she dallied outside, Barney would get angry and defecate on her. Weekends, Carol wears T-shirts torn by Barney's talons and teeth and stained by his droppings. Every day she plays music for him, takes him into the shower with her and shares her meals with him. She and her partner never go anywhere together overnight because they can't leave Barney alone.

Most children don't get the kind of spoiling that Barney gets. Nor will their parents put up with as much misbehavior. Recently, Barney bit Carol, leaving a deep red gouge in her finger. If it were me, I said, I'd smack him so hard there would be green feathers flying

199

Sue Fagalde Lick

all over the house. She smiled and shook her head. "I just told him not to do it again."

The name "Sadie" is the "Brittney" of doggiedom these days. I met four Sadies at the local kennel and another owner who gushed, "Oh, I have a Sadie, and she looks just like yours." I didn't name my dog. She was "Snapple" before the rescue agency decided it was the name that kept people from taking her home. Never mind that she couldn't get along with any other four-legged creature and would be in special ed if she were human, no matter what they called her.

I thought about claiming Sadiemom as my Internet monicker, but the name was taken ten times over. Also dogmom, poodlemom, pugmom, labmom, colliemom, etc. We might be creeping up to 25 percent of American women without children, but two-thirds of American families have pets, and nearly all of the childless women I have interviewed have at least one dog or cat. The American Pet Products Manufacturers Association reported in 2006 that an estimated 63 percent of American households have a pet AND that the majority of pet owners, 61 percent, either have no children or are parents whose children have left the nest.

At an Internet site for childless women, a new member wrote that she has no children, but she does have three dogs, a cat and a fish. The moderator responded that she has a dog, two cats, two frogs, and four rats. Nosing around the site, I found someone who had posted pictures of *16* felines, with their names and ages. I guess it beats all those grandchild pictures our friends insist on e-mailing to us and slipping into their Christmas cards.

With people treating their animals like children, it's no wonder that divorcing couples argue over pet custody with almost as much emotion as they feel about child custody. Although by law pets are considered "property," just like the refrigerator or Grandma's rocking chair, it's not as easy to settle who gets to keep the dogs, cats, rats, gerbils, or monkeys. Emotions run high, and logic runs away. The soon-to-be-exes present tearful testimony, photographic displays showing affection for one party

200

more than the other, and witnesses noting the attachment between pooch and pop. While judges roll their eyes, attorneys collect thousands of dollars in legal fees helping couples decide who gets to keep the kitty.

One couple mentioned on CBS's "The Early Show" agreed to shuttle their three dogs and three cats back and forth, but the cats didn't enjoy travel, so the wife ultimately was awarded full custody and "cat support" payments while the dogs continued alternating weeks with their "parents."

An article published in the *Anchorage Press* offered this scenario: take the dog away from both parties for three days, then put husband and wife at opposite ends of the same room. Have them call the dog and see which person it comes to. People have resorted to such tactics as smearing sausage on their hands, so impartial parties, such as veterinarians, are called in to make sure no one is cheating.

With our own dog Sadie, we wouldn't have needed a divorce court to know which of us she loved best. Every time we came home, she practically knocked me down to get to Fred. She liked me, but she adored my husband. After she had slathered kisses all over his face, she'd turn to me. "Oh, yeah, hi. Can I have a cookie?"

Jennifer Keene, whose own divorce inspired her to write *We Can't Stay Together for the Dogs: A Dog-Friendly Divorce and Break-Up Guide*, said she and her husband had never wanted children. While growing up, she had little exposure to small children. "My older sibling was an Old English Sheepdog." She laughs, but you get the impression she means it. She and her ex had adopted two rescue dogs, Moxxy, an Australian Cattle Dog, and Sixxy, a Pointer mix. When they ended their marriage, they each took the dog they felt closest to.

Not every couple settles the issue of pet custody so easily. "In the heat of the moment, the claws come out," Keene says. The main thrust of her book, she adds, is to "put your own issues aside and do what's best for the dog." Since pets matter no more to the courts than a couch or a soup tureen, "You have to be the bigger person so that you can make sure that your dog is taken care of."

Back when I got divorced from the first husband who didn't

Sue Fagalde Lick

want kids, he took both the dog and the cat. I took the VW bug that died a week later on the entrance to the 880 freeway. The pets were not listed in the divorce settlement, but that was 30 years ago. Besides, Jim had brought both pets into the marriage, so I was really just their stepmother. The cat didn't like me. He used to chase me around the house and corner me, his claws extended. The last time I saw him, he was sitting in a cage, his face pressed against the grill, yowling loudly enough to hear three blocks away. Bye, bye, Kitty. It was different with Heidi, our German shepherd. I still miss her more than the husband.

In addition to keeping Moxxy after the divorce, Keene adopted Buffy, a Cavalier King Charles Spaniel. She definitely does not call herself her dogs' mom. However, she and a group of other childfree dog owners recently held their first annual Dog Mothers Day celebration at a dog-friendly café called The Iron Mutt. They drew names and shopped for gifts to be given from their dogs to the owners, like a secret Santa exchange. Nobody knew who shopped for whom, so Keene says it really felt as if the gifts came from the dogs.

Jennifer Keene isn't the only one celebrating holidays with her dogs. Every year, says Sarah, an executive assistant from Virginia, her border collie, Mollie, buys her a Mother's Day gift--with a little help from the husband. And the dog always gives him a Father's Day card.

Another friend of mine named Carol has been married three times and never had children, but she has more pets than I can count. Every Christmas, sure as Santa Claus, we receive a newsletter written by the dogs and cats telling us what "Mom" and "Dad" have been up to during the year. "Mom lost her job this year, but she got really busy making quilts and now every surface seems to be covered with cloth. She gets really mad when we knead the fabric with our claws, but it feels so good," or "Dad is still singing with the barbershoppers. We hear him making the darndest sounds when he's warming up his voice."

I actually look forward to these newsletters. It beats all those cards full of tales about grandchildren and trips to Europe.

Childless by Marriage

Teary-eyed after watching a TV show about babies, I shut off the tube and headed for the back door where my "baby" was waiting.

"Come here, Lady," I whimpered, gathering my petite calico cat into my arms. I held her against my breast, and she felt just the right size and weight. I nuzzled her soft head and told her how pretty she was, how I loved her so. Without even thinking about it, I rocked back and forth, humming a lullaby. In response, the cat purred and dug her claws into my arm.

"You're my baby," I crooned. In a way, she was. But unlike real babies, she would never grow any bigger. We would never be able to talk. I couldn't teach her anything or tell her stories about her grandmother or great-grandmother. I couldn't watch her graduate from high school or get married. If she had babies, I would have to sell them or give them to the animal shelter. When I got old, she'd be dead because cats don't live as long as people.

In many ways, Lady was just an animal. She didn't eat with us, she lived outside, she prowled through the night, and sometimes I heard her yowling in a frenzy for love. If I went outside to save her, she'd narrow her eyes and walk away, her puffed tail twitching. It's none of your business, she'd let me know.

But when I came to her crying because I didn't have a baby and everyone else did—like the only girl in the neighborhood without a doll—she let me pick her up and hold her against my chest. She allowed me to talk baby talk and sing to her. For a few minutes, she let me pretend.

Alas, we lost Lady to a rare form of cancer after four years with her. By then Sadie had arrived. And no, we didn't pick rhyming names. Both animals were pre-owned and pre-named by other people. I wouldn't be one of those moms whose kids' names all rhyme or start with the same letter. Billy, Bobbie, Betty, Bridget, bleh.

One of the blessings of pets is that there's always another one that needs a home. The week after Ursula's dog died, we met Sophie, a just-weaned shepherd pup. We passed her around, laughed when she whined at our singing, and gave advice on how to train her. In other words, we acted like mothers, mothers of dogs.

Sue Fagalde Lick

Later, Mary's dog Charlie had to be put to sleep. She grieved. Only a few months earlier, her cat Hobbes had disappeared. She adopted two new kittens, Bach and Vivaldi. Instead of lingering at rehearsals, this never-wanted-to-be-a-mother maestro hurried home, saying, "My little kitties are waiting and they're *so cute.*"

N ot long ago, it was my turn to be the grieving dog mom. My beloved Sadie started panting and moaning. Then she refused to eat. I assumed the vet would tell me she was just getting old. It never occurred to me that she would have cancer. The vet found lymphosarcoma, stage four out of six.

Suddenly I was immersed in constant care. Sadie needed so many pills I had to put them in days-of-the-week boxes to keep them straight. First thing in the morning, I jumped out of bed to make her breakfast, including hot dog slices into which I inserted Prednisone and Lasix pills. At night, I hid her drugs in chicken breasts I bought and cooked for her. The drugs made her insanely hungry and so thirsty she would lick her bowl completely dry. Every time I sat down, she had to go out or wanted another Milk-Bone. How could I deny her? She was dying of cancer. It might be her last cookie.

We visited the vet weekly, usually early in the morning. My work schedule evaporated in a haze of dog care.

The weekend after the first chemo treatment, we thought Sadie was a goner. She woke up blind, with blood in her eyes. She had been vomiting for days and was so weak she kept running into things and falling down. It was Labor Day, but the vet agreed to see us. As we waited for our appointment, Fred and I sat on the laundry room floor with Sadie and cried. It looked like the end.

But it wasn't. Although she had lost 12 pounds, one-fifth of her weight, and we could feel her ribs and vertebrae, one magical shot stopped the nausea and Sadie was back to eating like crazy. Her vision cleared up that afternoon. By the next week, she had gained a few pounds back, her lymph nodes had shrunk back to normal, and the vet declared she was in complete remission.

Meanwhile, Susan, pastor of the church where our octet rehearsed, was going through the same thing. Her dog, Lydia, died. My heart ached for her, but I dared not contact her when my Sadie

204

was doing so well.

Three of Sadie's five chemo treatments were to be administered
orally at home. I was not to touch the pills, so I pulled on gloves, got
Fred to hold Sadie's rear while I pried open her cavern of a mouth,
stuffed the pill way back in, then closed her jaws until she swallowed.
It was horrible for me but didn't seem to bother the dog.

At one visit where she was doing better, the vet suddenly looked
at me and said, "And how are you doing?"

"I'm exhausted," said the "mother" of the cancer dog. All night,
I listened for her nails on the kitchen floor, her bark at the door, the
thump of her body collapsing in the bathroom.

I was wearing myself out providing food and pills, making sure
she peed and pooped, and writing checks that put us dangerously low
on cash, but so what? We were a family of three.

The rollercoaster went up and down until finally it just went
down. On a Thursday morning, Sadie was panting so hard I could
hear her from the opposite end of the house. It sounded as if she was
strangling. Her enlarged spleen made her gut so big she could barely
keep her balance. She'd get up, walk two feet, and lie down again. It
took hours to get her outside to pee. She glanced at her food and
rejected it. I spent all morning agonizing over whether to call the vet,
knowing what would probably happen. Was it time? Was it? As I
stood by the woodstove watching her, she suddenly looked straight at
me. Her eyes said, "Please do something."

The process was quick. Fred and I sat with her on the cool
linoleum floor of the examining room where we had spent so much
time lately. The doctor gave her a sedative first. As she began to
relax, her eyes starting to close, I said, "Good night, Sadie. I love you.
You're the best."

She fell into her first restful sleep in ages. Oh, if she could have
stayed like that. But Dr. F. quickly followed the sleep shot with the
injection that stopped her heart. Within seconds, she quit breathing, so
quietly, so easily. She looked peaceful there on the floor, like she was
still just sleeping. But we had to leave her behind. Ushered out the
back door, Fred and I held each other and sobbed.

Sue Fagalde Lick

F ive months later, my church choir gave me a puppy shower. I saw a singer bringing in the cake and assumed it was for one of our many spring birthdays. Then I read "Welcome puppies" in the frosting. Oh my gosh.

We hurried through rehearsal to get to the party. Everyone had brought gifts: toys, treats, baby blankets, balls, and puppy pee pads. I sat on the floor near the chapel altar and opened one present after another as the singers, male and female, showered me with advice.

It was just like a baby shower, only better because I was agile from yoga, not bloated and big-bellied. Plus I could put the tykes in the laundry room and sleep all night. I felt as if I had been waiting for this all my life.

I had seen a flyer at the post office. Puppies. Lab-terrier. I raced home and called the number. They lived on the next block. I hollered at my husband. "Put your shoes on. Let's go look at puppies."

Daniel and Gina, who was about to deliver their third child, had two litters from two mother dogs, a bunch of tiny black pups and a mixed group of slightly larger puppies. Suddenly we were surrounded by squeaking puppies. I'm not sure I even realized what we were doing until we were driving home, $100 poorer and committed to pick up two dogs, one black, one tan, the following Sunday. Fred, the man who didn't want human babies, agreed to bring home two canine babies. He chose the black one, whom we named Chico. I chose Annie, my little girl, tan with freckles on her nose. And yes, I bought them blue and pink blankets and toys.

When they came home, Annie weighed 8 pounds and Chico weighed 9. They were the same size as human infants and felt so right in my arms. Of course human babies don't lick your face. And they can't bite your fingers because they don't have any teeth.

However, I soon discovered many things puppies do have in common with human babies. They need expensive vaccinations, produce vast quantities of excrement, and are perpetually hungry. They're always crying or fighting. Once the puppies came home, I found myself skipping social activities to stay home with them. When we had to leave for a whole day, I took them to doggy daycare. I was always worried, always watching for fear something would happen to them. It seemed as if every time I looked out the window, they were

206

eating something that could kill them: wood, plastic, cloth, sheetrock. Fred, like most husbands, was oblivious. Some days I wanted to check into the Sheraton and stay there forever. What mother hasn't wanted to run away?

Cesar Millan, TV's "Dog Whisperer," would say we were doing it all wrong. In his book *Cesar's Way,* he writes that the trend to treat dogs as our babies is creating a population of spoiled, misbehaved dogs. Dogs are not little four-legged people, and we women who own them are not their mothers. We must ditch the baby talk and become their pack leaders if we want them be calm, healthy, obedient companions.

Dogs are dogs and people are people, Millan says. Treating them like substitute children might fill our needs, but it does not fill the needs of the dogs. The dogs need a leader they can depend on, and they need Millan's big three: exercise, unwavering discipline, and-- only after they have achieved the first two--affection.

Yeah, yeah, pack leader. But raising two at once is tough, and it does feel like having twins when they're going in two different directions, fighting over every toy and treat. You find that two hands are not enough.

When I told our dog trainer, Sue Giles, that we had gotten the puppies, she warned that I could not be lax with them because they were young. Every time I started to say, "But they're so small," she stopped me. Discipline has to start from day one. No excuses. We must not alter our lives to suit the dogs' desires. It has to be the other way around. Dogs are good friends, but they are not tiny people, not baby substitutes.

Are the puppies my children? No. But these are the first dogs (and the last) that I've had since just after they were born. I know their birth date, and I have met their biological mother, Roxie. Was she sorry to see them go? Nope, she was just tired of little dogs hanging off her teats.

When Chico and Annie were babies, we needed an extra trash can for all the used puppy pads. I fed them three times a day, checked on them hourly, cleaned up countless doggy doodles and wiped up endless puddles. Every time I filled their water bowl, they spilled it or fell in. We spent a fortune on vet bills and supplies. We even bought a bigger car, our version of the Mommy van. I didn't mind any of it because something had kicked in within my heart that allowed me to throw myself into their care while letting the house get messy and falling behind in my work.

Fortunately, dogs mature quickly. Both dogs turned out bigger than we expected, over 70 pounds. They're housetrained, the chewing has slowed down, and they did well at doggy school. They must have destroyed at least a thousand dollars worth of our possessions by now. But oh, the love and the laughs. My favorite thing is to sit on the floor between them, making myself the center of a dog sandwich. I'll be honest. This time, I do call myself Mom. Shamelessly.

A t a writers' meeting when the pups were small, I babbled on and on about them to my friend Bob, a tall, bald grandfather-poet. When I finally paused for breath, he said, "Sue, I think your maternal instinct is kicking in."

I responded, "Dear Bob, it's been there all along. But when I held those puppies in my arms, oh my God."

He beamed like the doting grandfather he is.

Part 4
For Better or Worse

19
Mothering Fred

I t started gradually, so gradually I can't even say when it really began. Fred had always been forgetful. At a restaurant or a show or the county fair, he'd see someone approaching and say, "Who is that? They look familiar." I'd supply the names just in time for him to greet them. He often introduced me to people I had already met. "This is my wife Sue." The other party would smile and nod. "Yes, hi, good to see you again."

When Fred would forget to take his calendar to work, he'd call in a panic, with no idea what his schedule was for that day. But I never thought he was sick; I just figured Fred didn't clutter up his brain with trivia the way I did.

The night his mother died, Fred and I went to dinner at a fish place on the Newport Bayfront. While we were waiting for our order, talking about his mother and her house, he said, "I can't remember anything anymore."

I reached across the table to hold his hand. "You're just upset," I said. "It's natural. Don't worry. I'll remember for you."

It was a crazy time, right before Christmas. I had just flown back to Oregon early from a residency in Los Angeles for my master's degree program at Antioch University. We had a million things to catch up on at home, Christmas was in two weeks, and Fred's kids were coming. Of course he had trouble remembering things. Who wouldn't?

After the holidays and a great visit with the kids that really felt like family, Fred went back to California to do his tax business. I finished cleaning out his mother's house. But our troubles weren't over yet. About the time I returned the keys to Helen's landlord, my own mother was diagnosed with cancer and I began traveling back and forth to California so often I didn't unpack for four months.

I began to notice things. Fred was more absent-minded and not his cheery self. He had switched from gin and tonic to just gin, and he had trouble functioning during sex.

He loved wine and had been working the tourist seasons in a tasting room on the Oregon coast, but now he complained that he wasn't getting along with his new supervisor, that she was taking away responsibilities and checking everything he did. When I visited at closing time one Sunday, I watched with alarm as he got so confused trying to count up the money at the end of his shift that I wound up taking over. There was nothing difficult about it, just sorting the bills, coins and checks, something a child could do, but it overwhelmed him.

Also, he had lost his sense of smell, a true handicap for a wine expert. Savoring the "nose" was an integral part of any tasting.

Fred had been a volunteer docent at the Oregon Coast Aquarium for years. He loved it so much he often hung out there on his days off, happy to share his knowledge with the tourists. He had been promoted to shift captain for the Tuesday afternoon crew, but now he had trouble making out the schedule and keeping track of his volunteers.

Meanwhile, our bills weren't getting paid on time and some of his tax clients were getting letters from the Internal Revenue Service about errors in their returns.

By the time my mother got sick, I suspected Fred was suffering from dementia. I had gone through it with Grandpa Fagalde, so I knew the signs. So did my brother. A few weeks before Mom died, we were taking a break in the sun-dappled courtyard outside Kaiser Hospital when I confided that Fred couldn't remember things. Mike looked at me. "Oh, shit." Nothing more needed to be said.

When my mother died, Fred was there for me. He stood sobbing in the corner while I comforted my dad, and held onto me when I broke down later.

His symptoms were getting worse. I kept pushing our doctor for help. In order to see a specialist, we needed a referral from him, but he kept dragging his feet. He believed Fred's problems, both sexual and cognitive, were simply the result of drinking too much.

Childless by Marriage

That summer, while I was away at college, Fred got arrested for drunk driving. He had been drinking wine at a friend's house. The police towed away his truck and took him to jail in handcuffs. He was terrified, but he wasn't drunk. Tests proved his blood alcohol was below the legal limit.

I was a thousand miles away. He had to wake up his friends at 2 a.m. to rescue him. Remembering the dark, windy street where those friends lived, I knew Fred was probably more confused than drunk. He found himself taking a wrong road, made an illegal U-turn and got stopped by a rookie cop with a reputation for overzealousness.

Things were definitely changing. My last term at Antioch, I was the graduation speaker for our class. It was a great honor, but I spent the whole residency with a stomachache. Fred planned to fly down to join me at the Marriott Hotel for graduation. Would he be able to negotiate the airport on his own? When I heard that LAX was shut down for a bomb scare right about the time he was scheduled to land, I was sure he'd be completely lost. He didn't want me to skip class to pick him up, but I no longer trusted him to take care of himself. I alternately paced, stared out the window, and debated whether to head for the airport. I was afraid I'd miss him, but he could be lost, and he didn't have a cell phone. Finally, he arrived at the Marriott in a taxi, an hour late.

The rest of my family couldn't come for one reason or another, but Fred sat proudly behind the graduates cheering me on. I handed him my camera and a tape recorder to document my speech, but it turned out he couldn't handle either device, so my big day went unrecorded except for the official photos. It was a long shot, expecting him to manage my camera and tape recorder when he couldn't operate my cell phone. But things got worse.

As we graduates were marching off the stage and down the aisle after the ceremony, Fred hailed me, all in a tizzy. "Sue, Sue, Sue, there's something there. Your chair. Sue!" What the hell, I thought. Tell me later. But he was in such a panic that I had to get out of line to see what was up.

Someone had placed commemorative tote bags under each of our seats. Nice, but why couldn't it wait?

Sue Fagalde Lick

In that moment, it all became clear. Fred was no longer able to pass for normal. It wasn't just absentmindedness anymore.

I peeled off my cap and gown in the hallway, along with the master's degree mantle I had craved for more than 20 years. Fred was waiting, and I was afraid he'd get lost, but I had to go to the restroom. While waiting for an empty stall, I leaned against the sink and stared at myself in the mirror. Would all this work be for nothing? Dear God, I thought, what am I going to do?

It took almost two years before we finally got an appointment with a neurologist, Dr. Gordon Banks, in McMinnville, Oregon, and learned that Fred had Alzheimer's Disease. The most common form of dementia, it's a progressive and fatal illness that eats the brain piece by piece. There is no cure.

As the elevator doors shut after that Nov. 4 appointment, Fred sighed and said, "Well, now what?"

I hugged him and said we'd take it one day at a time. At that point, he seemed as handsome, kind and capable as ever, even if he didn't know what day of the week it was or what city we were in. The mini-mental test that Dr. Banks administered would become all too familiar: Remember these three words. Count backward from 100 by sevens. Draw a picture of a clock. Spell "world" backwards. Fred only missed a few questions that first time, but it showed the direction things were going.

Over lunch at a posh restaurant near the hospital, we held hands across the table as I reassured him over and over that I would be there for him. He seemed to fear I'd dump him. A friend had suggested that if *her* husband ever got sick, she'd divorce him and put him in a nursing home immediately. But no, I couldn't do that. I loved Fred, and I would ride it out with him.

Now I had a new job: taking care of my husband.

Shortly after the Alzheimer's diagnosis, Fred sold his tax business. By then, his bosses at the winery had decided they no longer needed him. He had given the shift captain job at the aquarium to someone else, relieved to be just a docent. He had been singing with the Coastal-Aires men's barbershop chorus for years, but

214

now he complained every week about how much trouble he had reading the sheet music.

We bore the knowledge of Fred's illness alone for a long time. Perhaps if we had had children together, or if his children had been nearby, they would have seen the signs, too. He was diagnosed in November, 2004, but we didn't tell anyone that Thanksgiving, not until my brother telephoned afterward to ask why Fred wasn't drinking. Dr. Banks had told us that alcohol exacerbated the dementia symptoms, so he was trying to quit.

Mike knew Fred long before I did. He introduced us to each other. I had already told him that Fred was forgetting things. So now I told him that Fred had Alzheimer's and made him promise not to tell anyone else.

Eventually, strongly urged by my new support group, I did tell everyone. Some were devastated. Others couldn't believe it was anything to worry about. That's just Fred, they said. His kids stayed in denial for years. *It's not that bad. He won't forget us.*

But they weren't there to watch him first forget names, then his own phone number and address, then how to do tasks like make coffee, button his shirt or eat with silverware. They weren't there when he saw people in the bedroom at night or got lost on his way to the bathroom and urinated on the floor. They weren't there when he forgot who I was.

They weren't there years later when I was feeding him with a spoon, trying to get him to eat just one bite and trying not to hit his teeth because I didn't have a clue how to do it. They weren't there when I was trying to slide on an adult diaper, pull up his pants or tie his shoes, or when we sat in front of the TV while I trimmed his ragged fingernails.

Miles away, young and busy with their own lives, they sympathized over the phone but had long lists of reasons why they couldn't come all the way to Oregon.

If they were my own children, would they have come? I'll never know.

There's a stigma to AD. You don't want the world to know. Once they do, that's all they see, and they no longer trust the person who has it.

During Fred's last tax season, I helped him and eventually had to redo our own return when I discovered how many mistakes he had made. I made him do it again, but he forgot to save the completed forms on the computer, and it disappeared. I finally sat down at his computer with him looking over my shoulder, filled in the blanks as quickly as I could, and sent the return to the government myself. By then, I was ready to scream. I left Fred playing a computer game and hurried across the street to my friend's house to drink wine and let out my anger and frustration.

In summer 2005, we flew to Burbank, California to celebrate Fred's 50-year high school reunion. We had agreed not to tell anyone about his illness, but we gratefully let his friends Barry and Irene provide rides for us from one venue to another.

The whole scene was a revelation to me as we toured Fred's old neighborhood. Walking around John Burroughs High School, he and his classmates shared memories of those years in the 1950s when they played football, hung out at the malt shop and struggled through their classes. They talked about their children and grandchildren. Fifteen years younger, from a different generation, I felt like such an outsider. When they were at Burroughs, I wasn't even in kindergarten yet.

During the years when Fred lived in Burbank, he was with Annette. We drove by the Presbyterian church where they were married. They lived in the house next door and worked as caretakers for the church. Barry was best man at their wedding.

Fred had a whole life that I wasn't part of. They were living here when he went to college and when they adopted Ted. I was still in elementary school. But having heard his stories over the years, I was starting to remember more about his past than he did. He faked it, but I could tell he didn't remember as much as his friends did.

It was the banquet that really brought home Fred's illness. A live band played music from the 1950s. As Fred led me onto the dance floor, handsome in his blue suit, I put my head on his shoulder, thinking, "This is the last time we'll ever do this."

When had we danced last? It was New Year's Eve 1999, the turn of the millennium. While the world held its breath, wondering if the predicted Y2K computer crash would really happen, we joined a

Childless by Marriage

couple hundred other coastal residents at the Newport Performing Arts Center. We ate from a mountain of canapés and chocolates, sipped champagne from plastic glasses, and cheered as the clock struck 12. While the band played "Auld Lang Syne," we hugged and began to dance, holding each other tight, with no idea of what was coming.

Now, as we danced cheek to cheek, singing to each other, treasuring a moment that would never come again, I kept wiping tears from my eyes, telling myself not to ruin the moment by worrying about the future. We had agreed not to mention his illness, not to spoil the reunion for Fred or his friends, but God, how I wanted to confide in Irene. I longed for this motherly woman to hold me and tell me everything would be all right.

For a few years, we continued our trips back and forth to California, but travel became more and more difficult. On our way home from another Thanksgiving at my brother's house, we were driving north on I-5 when I made the mistake of deciding to drive on past Redding, even though I was getting tired and the car was low on gas.

We watched the sun set over the mountains, a ball of yellow fire that gradually flattened out to a long, slender cap and then disappeared just as we moved into the trees. For the next half hour, snow-covered Mount Shasta up ahead glowed pale pink, as did the mountains to the east.

By about 6, it was completely dark and I was seriously regretting my decision to keep going. Fred was sound asleep, his left leg jammed against the gearshift so I couldn't downshift out of fifth gear. Nor could I grab a sip of my tea because his arm was in the way. The headlights behind me and coming toward me made it hard to see, and I needed a bathroom badly.

Finally he woke up. "I can drive," he said.

"Really?" I said, gripping the wheel more firmly.

"I'm okay."

I thought maybe, having slept hard, he was. I knew I was not. Did we two fools never learn?

It was the longest 40 miles of my life. I literally watched the speedometer tick off every mile to Mt. Shasta City. Fred drove too fast and then too slow. Once I shouted as he almost went straight on a curve. He kept turning the high-beam lights off and on. Clearly he was having trouble seeing, or perhaps processing what he was seeing, but there was no place to turn off.

My heart thudded as I thought about how my father would react when he found out we died on the way home from Thanksgiving. Dry-mouthed, I couldn't think what to say that would sound positive yet help me determine whether Fred was as messed up as I suspected. The best I could come up with was, "How ya doin'?"

"Okay. Just trying to stay between the two white lines."

"I know."

"How are you?" he asked.

"Terrified," I said, going back to covering my mouth with my hand.

He did not reply.

Somehow God got us to Mt. Shasta City. I grabbed the keys and kept them with me for the rest of the trip.

F olks who assess Alzheimer's Disease patients should ditch the usual questionnaire and ask them to make waffles. It would tell them so much.

Two years after the diagnosis, Fred wanted to help with dinner. I was scrambling to make something out of nothing because I had written through my shopping time and hadn't bought groceries. "Make the waffles," I said, knowing he had made them many times in the past and used to be better at waffles than I was.

I would concentrate on what turned out to be a spaghetti omelet. It sounds bad, but it's in the *Poor Poet's Cookbook,* and I figured the tomato sauce from our leftover spaghetti would give the eggs a real spark. At that point, I didn't care that I was serving carbs on carbs.

Anyway, the waffles. Perhaps I shouldn't have recruited Fred. It had been a fuzzy-brained day. He sat at his computer playing basic solitaire in his bathrobe until after 2:00, then moved to the den to watch a video and couldn't work the remote control. He would have forgotten to eat lunch if I hadn't forced him into it. But now he really wanted to help. The day before, after he lost the debit card at the

Childless by Marriage

grocery store, he had declared, "I'm useless." Making the waffles would boost his self-esteem.

A little before 6 p.m., I set out the Bisquick mix, milk, vegetable oil, one egg, the big green bowl, a spoon and a measuring cup, trying to anticipate every complication. I had already plugged in the waffle iron.

Fred picked up the yellow box and stared at the recipe. It might as well have been written in Russian. He handed it to me and I read the first ingredient:

"Two cups of Bisquick."

"I only have one cup," he said.

"No," I said. "This holds two cups." I nudged the measuring cup closer.

He started spooning Bisquick in, a few grains at a time. "Is this enough?"

"No."

"There, that's it."

"No, honey. It's not full. You have to get it up to the line."

"Why?"

"So it'll come out right." I wanted to grab that box, shake in the Bisquick and move the process along, but I stuck to my own job, making my crazy omelet. I cracked five eggs into my bowl, watching the yolks float in an egg-white sea, then checked Fred's progress and decided *almost* two cups of Bisquick was close enough. I read the next waffle ingredient.

"Milk. One and one-third cups."

He stared at the measuring cup. "One third, two thirds, um . . ."

"One cup plus one third," I said.

"Oh." He poured. I think it said 1 1/3. Fifteen minutes had lapsed. I whipped my eggs into a yellow froth.

"Vegetable oil. Two tablespoons." I handed him the measuring spoon.

"I don't remember which hand I do this with," he said.

He had the bottle in his right hand, the spoon in his left. "Well, I'm left-handed, too, and that's how I do it," I said.

I just knew he was going to dump the whole bottle of oil in and then we'd have to scrap the waffles and figure out a way to pay to pay

219

for hamburgers down the road without debit card or cash. I hadn't gotten to the bank lately either.

Still working on my omelet, I stared at the leftover spaghetti a long minute, then emptied the plastic container into the eggs.

Although his hands were shaking, Fred got the oil in safely.

"One egg."

He remembered how to crack an egg. He started to stir the mixture. "It looks funny. Where's the milk?"

"Over there." Still in the measuring cup. "You have to put it in the bowl."

Twenty minutes after he had begun, he finally had batter. It looked a little runny, but I handed him a soup spoon to ladle it out.

"Where does it go?"

"On the griddle. It's hot."

He stared at the griddle, the batter and the spoon, then handed the spoon to me. "You do it."

I did, watching the white batter spread on the black squares. I shut the lid.

"Is dinner ready?" he asked two minutes later as I was peeling the first waffle off the griddle.

"No," I said, pouring the egg-spaghetti mixture into the omelet pan.

My spaghetti omelet took forever to solidify. I had piled up four cooked waffles and poured the last of the batter onto the griddle before I declared dinner ready at 7 p.m.

The waffles were limp but tasted good, and the omelet was . . . interesting. Somehow I couldn't believe I was eating spaghetti with maple syrup, especially when I was trying so hard to lose weight, but that's not what this is about—or maybe it is. You get desperate when you're trying to keep a brain-damaged man on an even keel by not upsetting the dinner schedule. All too often, the caregiver does not eat what she would like to eat.

Later that night my brother, the lawyer who at 52 had just figured out how to turn on the washing machine, would tell me on the phone that he couldn't follow a recipe either. He does not understand. Last year, Fred could make waffles. He could make French toast. He could even make beef stroganoff. Now he can't. It's only four

Childless by Marriage

ingredients. I remember when he used to coach me, telling me to watch for the steam coming out of the griddle.

Long after the dishes were done and I was falling asleep in front of the TV, Fred asked me if the last waffle was done yet. Oh my God. I had totally forgotten it. Dark brown and brittle, it dissolved into ashes as soon as I touched it. I threw the mess into the trash and unplugged the hot griddle.

For the first time that day, Fred smiled.

We had good days . . . Sometimes smart Fred came back. I had started teaching community college writing classes during my last year at Antioch University. One night I was racing around trying to prepare dinner, finish grading student homework, and get ready to leave for a meeting when he came home from his volunteer stint at the aquarium.

I called to him from the kitchen, "Do you by any chance know if we still have that big coffee pot, and if so, where it is?" I fully expected him to say, "What coffee pot?" or "I don't remember," then retreat to his chair, where on most Tuesdays he was asleep within 10 minutes.

"I know exactly where it is," he said. He went out to the laundry room, climbed the stepstool, moved a wine rack and a sleeping bag and produced the coffee pot. Then he volunteered to wash it, carefully, with lots of soap. He even put it in a bag for me, adding an extension cord just in case I needed one.

The next day, he was still with me, still sharp. We went to lunch, and he made his selection decisively, enjoyed his food and figured out the tip on his own. Afterward, we ran errands. We picked up a prescription, bought pellets for the stove that warms our house, and found the place he would be driving to that evening for a barbershop bass-section rehearsal. At the gym, where I usually had to direct every move, he had trouble starting the treadmill, but he lifted his weights easily, efficiently, adding more pounds to many of the exercises.

The following night, we both had rehearsals to go to. We piled our plates with leftovers, heated them in the microwave, ate quickly, and put the leftovers of the leftovers away.

221

Sue Fagalde Lick

If anyone was dim that night, it was me, feeding the same card into the ATM four or five times, being told each time that my transaction could not be processed. "Why?" I asked the machine, getting desperate. I had already paid bills with money that wasn't in my account yet. "I'm trying to make a deposit. I want to give you money not take any." But of course the machine just spit another piece of paper at me and offered my card back. I didn't realize until I was driving away that I had been stuffing Fred's credit union card in, rather than the card for my own bank account. Of course the PIN number didn't match and the bank didn't recognize the card. I went back, inserted the proper card and made my deposit, apologizing to the machine for being an idiot.

After our mutual rehearsals, Fred and I reunited in the spa, sighing as the hot water soothed away our aches from the gym, squeezing water out of the little rubber ducks as they bobbed past us. One side of the tub is set up like a bed. As I sometimes do, I slid down from a higher perch to the end of the bed. It was a perfect slide, fast and fun. "And she gets a 10!" Fred announced. "She wins the gold medal!"

We began to banter. I took on the persona of a 53-year-old Olympic gymnast who had been trying to place in the hot tub slide event since the 1960s. And now, my coach in his 90s, my closest opponents somehow disqualified, I had finally won. I credited it all to hard work and persistence.

Fred raised the bromine feeder, using it as his microphone. In a voice like that of TV sports commentators, he noted that there was a possible scandal arising, that perhaps I had poisoned my competitors. The autopsies would show the results . . .

"No, no. I earned that gold medal by my years of devotion to the sport," I insisted.

We dissolved into giggles and gave it up, not knowing where to take the game from there.

Yes, he couldn't remember what singing competition his group was practicing for, but here he was being smart, funny and cute. As I climbed into bed that night, I lay back on my pillow with a sigh. Beside me, Fred stirred, grabbed me and kissed me.

I slept so sweetly that night.

. . . and bad days

A few days later, Fred surrendered the checkbook. "I give up. I can't do it anymore."

"Do you want me to take it over?"

"Yeah." And he handed over the checkbook, the bank statement and his pages of figuring. He was angry, not at me, but at his disease. "I hate this!" he said.

"Me too."

As I added the bank papers to the never-ending stacks in my office, tears ran down my face. My father and the people in the Alzheimer's support group had suggested that one day Fred might give up the banking on his own, that I might not have to demand it from him. I didn't expect it to happen so soon.

The last time I had suggested it, Fred just looked at me and said, "You?" I expected to have to take it away from him, just like one day I'd have to help him dress himself, feed himself and clean himself, and finally one day I'd have to move this man I counted on for so much into a nursing home.

I went out to get the mail and stood by the mailboxes, crying over our bills, magazines and a new DVD. Nobody was home to see me, and I didn't want Fred to know I still hadn't stopped my tears.

Finally I wiped my face, went in, put on a smile and announced, "We got a movie!"

One by one, Fred let go of all the things he used to do, spending his days doing easy computer solitaire, watching TV, or going to the aquarium, where he became a "greeter" with no actual duties.

We met with a lawyer and drew up wills, made medical decisions and signed forms giving me power of attorney and putting the house in my name.

Two and a half years after his diagnosis, he handed over the car keys. He had driven us the 50 miles to Corvallis for his doctor's appointment, but after another mini-mental test, the doctor ordered him to quit driving. Now.

He complained but didn't argue. He would never be able to go

Sue Fagalde Lick

anywhere on his own again. No more errands, no more transporting himself to the aquarium, rehearsals or doctor appointments. From now on, I would always be in the driver's seat. I added chauffeur and ride coordinator to my other duties.

None of this was helping my career. At an age when I felt I needed to achieve my goals soon or give up, I had to pull back. I no longer felt free to travel, and I couldn't concentrate for very long at a time. Eventually I gave up my classes and stopped most of my freelance work, although I still tried to write a little every day and to keep selling my books.

On a typical morning, Fred came to my office door for the fifth or sixth time. He just stood there until I noticed him.

"I need your help. I can't uh--" and then he lost his words. I gathered something was wrong with his computer. "It won't—I can't--"

Impatient, trying to work, trying to listen to a CD, I snapped, "What!"

Finally I got up because he could no more tell me what was wrong than my dog Sadie could tell me why she was barking or whining. I had to leave my chair and look.

In a couple keystrokes, I had Fred's computer back on track.

Later that day, I heard the dog retch. She had slammed open the door to the laundry room and vomited just inside the door to the back yard. She couldn't yell, "I'm sick. Open the door!"

So it was with Fred.

I needed to hug him again. Hugs worked better than words.

It reminded me of the challenges faced by writers with small children who struggle to get a few words down between crises. In October 2007, I complained to my journal, "I never seem to get a meal in peace, can't read more than a paragraph at a time or write more than a half hour at a stretch. I find myself trying to finish bits of work in the car when I find I have arrived somewhere early."

In addition to my writing, I was also working at the church now, co-directing the choir and playing the piano. It got harder every week. Fred would see me getting dressed and ask where I was going. I hired aides to feed and entertain Fred when I couldn't be home. Although

224

they were usually too busy to help, Fred's sons managed to combine a beach vacation with care for their father that fall so I could teach at a conference to promote my new book about freelance writing for newspapers. I knew that I wouldn't be going far from home after that.

I was becoming afraid to leave Fred home without a caregiver. The agency I worked with sent out a constantly changing cast of barely qualified aides at $20 an hour. They did a little housework, gave Fred his meals, and took him out to shop, run errands or just go for a ride. Folks call them caregivers instead of babysitters, but it really amounted to the same thing. Fred didn't need medical attention; he needed someone to entertain him, feed him, and keep him out of trouble.

Some Alzheimer's patients go to "adult day care." It's a horrible term, but as with daycare for children, the idea is to keep them occupied for a few hours so their loved ones can work or just try to regain their sanity. We didn't have such a program here, but I'm sure Fred would have hated it.

As I assume it is with young children, anyone caring for someone with Alzheimer's finds her life becoming totally wrapped around his care. In both cases, friends who are not in the same situation or can't deal with what's happening drift away.

Shortly after Sadie died in 2007, I moved into the guest bedroom. Fred's nighttime hallucinations and occasional incontinence made it hard to sleep with him. Once he punched me, thinking I was attacking him. Another time, he tried to climb through the bedroom wall.

In my room down the hall, I lay awake, listening for him to get up. I installed a motion-sensitive light in the hallway. When it flashed on, I would spring awake, lying with my eyes open in the dark, ready to jump up to keep Fred from walking into the closet or out the front door. I didn't always make it. One morning he told me he had gotten up early, thinking he was still delivering newspapers like he did as a teenager. He went outside, got our own paper and brought it in without my hearing a thing. I was so exhausted I slept through it.

Some people use baby monitors to keep up with their demented loved ones. How different is it really from caring for a baby when

225

Sue Fagalde Lick

you're always listening for someone who is relatively helpless to get
into trouble, someone who doesn't understand things, who can't
communicate well? Unlike many of the spouses in our Alzheimer's
support group, I couldn't count on Fred's disabilities to hold him
down. Physically, he was as healthy as ever, bigger and stronger than
I was. Luckily, he never lost his sweet demeanor. I heard horror
stories of husbands who cursed, hit, and tore up the house. Fred just
wandered around, befuddled.

Coming home from our Thanksgiving trip that year, we checked
into a motel in Eureka, California. Fred went out to the car to get
something and didn't come back. I went looking for him but couldn't
find him. I stood on the balcony, not sure what to do. I knew it was
time to hook Fred up to the Lifeline service in which Alzheimer's
patients wear a medallion that states their name and a phone number
that will connect them to me and local police. I had already seen how
it saved a friend's wife who wandered away.

But for now, what should I do? The parking lot led to a busy
four-lane road. Fred had no idea what city we were in or what motel
we were staying at. He didn't know our home address or phone
number. I was just about to dial 911 when Fred returned with a motel
housekeeper. Unable to remember what room we were in, he had
asked her for help. She took him to the office, where she was able to
connect his name with a room number and guide him back. We were
lucky that time.

By then, I was handling all the bills, doing all the driving,
talking for Fred to doctors, lawyers, and anyone else who
called. I regretted my lack of parenting experience as I
became his spokesperson, nursemaid, and guide through the world.
Sometimes I felt more like his mother than his wife.

One week my clock got knocked down and broken. Then I found
Fred trying on my jackets. Another day, I found the satellite box
shoved almost off the TV and pictures knocked off the shelf, as if
vandals had attacked the den. Fred moved through the rooms of our
house like a blind man—or a toddler. I needed to Fred-proof the
house. It was loaded with things he could trip over or break: dog beds,
instruments, shoes. I had to put it all out of his way. He became more

226

childlike every day. He no longer remembered not to touch a hot stove or to take a key before locking the door.

One morning, a spark started a fire beneath the pellet stove. I kept smelling smoke but couldn't find the source. Fred couldn't smell anything, and I couldn't get him to understand that somewhere in our house a fire was burning where it wasn't supposed to. Finally, as the fire grew larger and the smoke alarm started wailing, I located the source. The pot inside the stove had cracked, letting the fire drop below. I managed to put it out with our fire extinguisher and disconnect the stove until the repairman could come. What if I had not been there?

As the disease ate into his memory, Fred would often start a sentence and suddenly stop, unable to finish. "I hate this," he would mutter. I tried to fill in the blanks for him, but I didn't always know what he was trying to say.

Until late in the disease, he had moments of blessed clarity. At those times, we would talk and talk. I remember sitting at the kitchen table, asking questions about his childhood, about his experiences in the Navy, about what his kids were like when they were young. We would talk about books, movies and music. We'd share memories of the many places we had traveled together, including Portugal, Costa Rica, Canada and Hawaii. We'd also talk about his illness. He was afraid for himself and worried about me. We'd end up holding hands. He would tell me again, "I love you so much."

"I love you, too."

Those times became more and more rare.

In spite of his illness, Fred continued to be the best date I'd ever had. On Valentine's Day in 2007, I assumed Fred wouldn't realize what day it was. I hadn't gotten him anything except a silly card. When I sat down to breakfast, I found a beautiful card with words of love that made me cry and a box of four jewel-like chocolate truffles from the candy factory near the Yaquina Bridge. Each the size and shape of an egg, they were decorated with sprinkles, one light chocolate, one dark, one green with mint inside, and one red with cherry filling.

He had written on the card "I love you so much." He once had

Sue Fagalde Lick

beautiful handwriting, but now the letters were shaky. It didn't matter. The gift had to have been his idea because his caregivers didn't know about the candy factory or that I loved those little boxes of truffles.

He came in and bent down to kiss me.

"I didn't get you a present," I said.

"You're my present," he replied.

Who could not love a man like this?

A few months after Sadie died, we added two baby dogs to the challenges we already had. It seems crazy now, but I know how much comfort they gave us with their energy and pure puppy love. Dogs have been proven to be effective therapy for people suffering from all kinds of woes. Something about dogs calms and comforts people. Chico and Annie made us laugh at a time when we really needed it. For that, they were invaluable, but they also caused a lot of stress, and ultimately they would prove Fred's undoing.

Fred loved the dogs but interacted with them like a timid child. They would jump on him or knock food out of his hand as he stood there, helpless. He couldn't handle them on the leash, couldn't help with training, and too often let them escape. Nor did he help with the endless cleanup tasks. If they wet on the floor, all he could do was point while I mopped at the warm urine sinking through the mauve carpet, creating yet another permanent stain.

For the first six months, the pups peed and pooped on everything. They could climb over or under anything and chewed up toys, clothes, shoes, sofas, walls and doors. At the same time, Fred wandered night and day. Sleep-deprived and depressed, I dreamed about my old job in San Jose, about being a star reporter again. Instead, I was picking up dog poop and telling Fred what day it was.

I had three beings counting on me as their caregiver now. What was I thinking? That puppies were soft and funny and loving and I needed something to think about besides doctors, drugs, and dementia. On the darkest days, Annie and Chico would come running in and jump all over me, kissing my face. It truly helped.

It was good for Fred, too. When they were four months old, we took the dogs to the beach for the first time. We each led a puppy as they stumbled around in the sand. "This is fun!" Fred shouted over

228

the wind and waves.
Those moments saved us both.

W e were both young to be dealing with Alzheimer's. Anything before 65 is considered "early onset." Fred was just turning 65 when the disease became fully apparent. I was 50. The other people in the Alzheimer's support group who were caring for their spouses were at least 20 years older than me. They were retired, not trying to build careers. Their adult children, my age, were helping them.

At the same time, my father was in his 80s and I worried about him. I complained to my friends that now I had two old men to take care of. I prayed that Dad would stay reasonably healthy for a while longer. Thank God, he did.

O ne difficult night, I heard Fred calling from the bathroom. "Mom!"
Crawling out of bed, I quietly corrected him. "No. I'm Sue." He eventually forgot my name, but he never called me "Mom" again. I have always wanted someone to call me "Mom," but not like that.

I spent my 50s doing what most women do in their 20s or 30s, taking care of someone else while letting go of their own needs and desires. When children leave the nest, their parents start life over, wondering what happened to the years in-between. I did the same, but I was caring for my husband, and we had no idea how long it would be.

20
Everything Changes

I was only gone for a few minutes. As I pulled into the driveway, Annie, the yellow dog, came running toward the car. When I opened the door, she jumped in. I heard her brother Chico barking from the back yard. Fred came limping toward me in tears, saying he was hurt. His left pant leg was torn and bloody and he couldn't straighten up.

I put him in the car and drove to Samaritan Pacific Communities Hospital in Newport. The ER doctor said Fred had strained his back. He patched up the bloody scrape on his knee, gave him Vicodin for pain and told him to rest. The next day, he was fine, in fact better than usual. I decided Vicodin was a miracle cure for Alzheimer's Disease.

I felt so guilty. These were my dogs, my babies, replacements for Sadie, who had died a little over a year earlier. Their mother was a Staffordshire bull terrier who lived down the street, their father a Lab who roamed the neighborhood. When we adopted them, they were tiny. Now approaching their first birthday, they totaled over 100 pounds of wild energy, and Fred couldn't handle them.

Not only were my dogs responsible for Fred's fall, but I had never gotten that raised, jagged piece of sidewalk fixed, even though I knew it was a death trap. Plus I had left Fred alone while I went to the post office, library and print shop. Bad mom, I'm thinking now. I wasn't his mother, but I needed to watch him every minute like a three-year-old.

Of course Fred could have fallen even if I had been home. And he had wanted these dogs as much as I had. He had picked out the male, Chico, and he was happy to adopt Annie, too. If I'd asked him, he would have told me to go run my errands. But maybe I should have known better.

Anybody can fall, but Alzheimer's patients are more at risk.

Messages between eyes, brain and feet get lost. When I asked Fred what happened, he said he fell out front, but I found blood on the back deck. He said he was "running like hell." A lifelong athlete, he was still fit and muscular despite his cognitive problems. We assumed he would be fine in a day or so.

But we were wrong.

Two days later, I awoke to the sound of Fred calling me from the bedroom. I found him on the floor at the foot of the bed, shivering and moaning in pain. I put my arms around him and tried to help him sit up.

"No!" he cried.

"Can you roll over, try to get up that way?"

"No, no, no."

I sat, stroking his soft hair. "What should we do?"

"I don't know."

I called 911, jumping into my clothes in the two minutes it took o hear sirens coming down our street. Neighbors gathered at the loor, asking questions as the paramedics carried him out. I had no answers.

We spent the morning at the hospital, mostly waiting. Fred kept rying to get off the gurney, and I kept reminding nurses, aides and loctors that he had Alzheimer's Disease, that he could not answer heir questions or understand what they were telling him.

The same doctor as before, a guy they called Dr. P., ordered a CT scan of Fred's back and announced that he had narrowing of the pine and bulging disks, common conditions for older people but dding to his pain. He ordered a stronger dosage of Vicodin.

After a few hours, Fred managed to get up and walk to the estroom on his own. Dr. P. sent him home. Take your pills, rest, and ou'll be okay, he said.

But he wasn't. At the pharmacy, Fred couldn't get out of the car. He opened the door, started to put a leg out, and hollered in pain. Just wait. I'll be right back," I said. I literally ran into Rite Aid to get is prescription, thinking that once he rested a while, he'd be fine.

We hadn't eaten all day. I suggested we get a meal at the nearby halet restaurant. But he couldn't get out of the car there either, so we opped at the Burger King drive-through instead. We ate in the car in

231

the parking lot. Fred had trouble with his hamburger, tearing it into pieces. I stuffed French fries into my mouth with one hand as I struggled to keep him from pouring his vanilla milkshake all over the dash.

At home, Fred still couldn't get out of the car. He put one leg out and began to shake. "No, I can't," he said.

"Yes, you can. Just ease your butt this way—wait. No."

He was over 200 pounds of dead weight. I held him half in and half out, unable to carry him, unable to get him to move the other leg. He hollered like a dog caught halfway through a barbed wire fence. Fortunately, our neighbor across the street heard our struggle and helped Fred into the house, placing him on the sofa. Fred slept awhile as I made phone calls, canceling things I was supposed to do over the next couple days. No way was I leaving him alone again.

As I turned away to start making dinner, Fred slipped to the floor with a soft whump. I couldn't get him up.

He lay between the ottoman and the piano shivering, speaking mostly gibberish, and trying to push his pants off. Whenever I tried to roll him back toward the sofa, he screamed. I sat beside him, stroking his arm and his hair. His skin felt hot and damp. "I can't, I can't," he kept saying, but he never finished the sentence. Only two words came out clear: "I'm sorry."

"Don't be sorry," I told him as we lay on the floor together 25 years after our first date when we made love on the floor of his house in Willow Glen. I brushed at the tears trickling into his beard and down around his ears. "It's okay." I leaned against the piano he had bought me for a wedding present, now scarred and out of tune.

A few months earlier, while we were staying at my aunt's house, Fred had gotten up in the middle of the night, scattered the contents of our suitcases around the living room, knocked her plants off the window sill, and torn a loaf of Portuguese sweet bread to bits. The next night, my aunt caught him in the back yard, naked from the waist down.

The week before he fell, I found him urinating on the carpet in the den. As I knelt at his feet mopping it up, he took off all his clothes.

Now he needed to pee. He was lying on his back, and couldn't roll over. We didn't own a urinal. I dashed to the kitchen and grabbed a plastic container, part of a set Fred had bought me at Costco. "Okay, you can go in this." As I supported his limp penis between my thumb and forefinger, ripe honey-colored urine splashed into the container that usually held leftover salad or rice. "Ah," he said. "Thank you."

I was about to dump the urine in the toilet when he began to shiver more violently. I set the container on the hearth. Assuming Fred was cold, I tried to pull his pants back on, but he cried out in pain. I grabbed a crocheted afghan from the back of the sofa and spread it over him. It was January, and the days were short. It was getting dark outside. The dogs were whining to come in. "I'm s-s-sorry," he stuttered, teeth chattering.

I remembered the stories told by others in the Alzheimer's support group about the crises that forced them to start looking at nursing homes.

Paul's wife wandered off, walking miles before a stranger found her dazed and confused at the Post Office and called the sheriff. That was bad enough, but then Paul fell and broke his hip. He lay on the floor for hours before he managed to drag himself close enough to a telephone to pull it down by the cord. He kept asking his wife to call 911, but she didn't remember how to use the phone. Fred didn't know how either.

Elsie had a similar story. Not having time to take care of herself while caring for her husband, she ignored her stomachaches until she collapsed one night with a bleeding ulcer, nearly dying before she was able to crawl to a phone.

Now Fred was on the floor.

I hated to send him back to the hospital, but I didn't know what else to do. I dialed 911. Again I heard the sirens coming down our street. In minutes, our living room was full of firefighters and paramedics. One of them had sung with Fred in the Coastal-Aires. Another went to my church. Newport was a small town. We had no secrets. Fred was lying on the floor, bare-assed, shaking and making noises that weren't words.

Bracing his head and neck, they eased Fred onto a gurney and carried him out to the ambulance. I fed the dogs and followed in the car.

233

Dr. P., still on duty in the ER, recognized us. He said he would admit Fred to the hospital, but it was almost midnight before the order came through. Meanwhile, pen poised over a form, he looked me at me and asked, "Do you feel that you can take of your husband at home?"

I wanted to weep. I had tried. I had done everything I could to keep Fred going with notes and lists, quietly taking over everything he used to do. I had hired nurses and aides. I had coerced friends and relatives to sit with him so I could teach a class or write a little bit. But now he couldn't walk. He couldn't stand on his own, and I couldn't lift him. We couldn't afford full-time help. We had no family nearby. No kids.

Dr. P. asked if we had railings, a handicap-accessible shower, and a wheelchair.

"No, we don't have any of that stuff," I said. "He was walking yesterday."

"Do you feel that you can take care of him at home?" he repeated.

Tears in my eyes, I shook my head. "Not like this."

Fred had begged me to keep him out of nursing homes. He had even asked me to use Oregon's assisted suicide law to end his life. I had told him I couldn't do that. Not only was I Catholic and pro-life, but the law required that the person who died be within a few months of death and able to understand what he was doing. He had to be able to take the deadly pills by himself. By the time an Alzheimer's patient is near death, he does not have the cognitive or physical ability to kill himself, legally or any other way. When Oregon voted on assisted suicide, Fred and I disagreed. He favored it while I voted no. Now I wondered about my choice, but in this situation, it didn't matter.

Over the next two days, I sat at Fred's hospital bedside, holding his hand, trying to make him understand why he couldn't get out of bed, covering up his genitals as he repeatedly threw off his gown and his blankets. The alarm on his bed kept going off as he banged against the railings. He insisted he had to go the bathroom, even as urine trickled steadily into his catheter bag. He also insisted that he saw a

234

door across from his bed. He wanted me to help him go through that door, but it was just a wall behind another bed. Meanwhile, doctors, nurses and social workers were putting together a plan to take Fred's care out of my hands. I kept thinking about women whose children are taken away. It felt as if they saw me as an unfit wife, and they wouldn't let me take my husband home. In truth, I was just a caring wife who had no one to help her.

One might wonder why a relatively minor back injury would have such an effect. As near as I can understand, it was the combination of the injury with Alzheimer's Disease. Not understanding or remembering what had happened to him, Fred only knew that it hurt. Panic and fear threw his confusion into overdrive. The medication he received didn't help. His neurologist later told us that Alzheimer's patients should never be given Vicodin. At the hospital that night, they also gave him morphine. I felt helpless as they kept asking him to rate his pain on a scale of one to 10. When he couldn't, they waved a diagram with happy and sad faces. He'd point at a number, but it didn't necessarily have any connection to his pain.

From the hospital, Fred was transferred to Newport Rehab—one day short of qualifying for Medicare coverage. They wanted $7,000 up front. From there, he went to an adult foster care home, where he would walk on his own but weep incessantly, begging me to get him out of there. Ultimately, after he tried several times to run away, I moved him to a nursing home where everyone had dementia. It took almost two hours to drive there, so I could only visit once or twice a week. By then, he didn't understand where he was and soon forgot that he had ever lived anywhere else. He forgot my name. On our 25th wedding anniversary, he didn't know who I was.

Alzheimer's Disease is the fifth leading cause of death for those 65 and older. It currently affects more than 5.3 million Americans. The number is rapidly increasing as the baby boomer generation reaches old age.

It starts with minor forgetfulness and confusion, eventually eating away the mind and the personality. Ultimately the body forgets how to function, and the patient dies. This process can take from five to 20 years. Residents at Fred's nursing home included former bankers, teachers, musicians, and CEOs. All were nearly helpless,

235

behaving like brain-damaged toddlers. Like children, they played with dolls, did simple crafts and watched mindless TV shows. Young workers in green scrubs changed their diapers every few hours and separated the residents when they started hitting and screaming at each other.

Some Alzheimer's patients are angry. Some become timid. Some weep, some scream, some hit. Some never stop talking nonsense while others, like Fred, lose their words. They can't read, follow a TV show or sign their names. All lose touch with reality. All become incontinent. All die.

Until he fell, Fred still sat every day in his home office, where he used to manage the family finances and prepare tax returns for extra money. Now he struggled through simple crossword puzzles on the computer. He still went to the aquarium, now as a "greeter" who was allowed to hang around for a few hours while the other volunteers kept track of him. He was still showering, shaving, and dressing himself. He couldn't work the TV remote, and he had forgotten how to make coffee, but I thought we still had at least another year together.

At home that first night without him, sitting alone on the living room floor picking pine needles out of the carpet, I kept seeing Fred lying, half naked, shaking and saying he was sorry. Behind me, the clock ticked away the night, and the pellet stove poured out yellow heat. The dogs snored in their crates. Outside, the trees rocked and bent in the wind.

Fred's face looked down from a photo on the wall. In the picture, he stood upright, clear-eyed, wearing his corduroy jacket, and smiling his crooked grin.

"It's okay," I said.

But it wasn't.

My husband was gone. Now it was just me and the dogs.

Part 5
Side-effects
of Childlessness

21
You Can't Tell from the Outside

I am bleeding profusely. My body built a nest for a baby, and no baby came. So now my body is throwing the nest away, just as it has every month for nearly 40 years.

I picture in my mind a woman sitting in her rocking chair in front of the television stitching a baby quilt by hand, squeezing one piece of thread after another into the tiny eye of the needle and pulling it up and down through the cloth. Occasionally as she pushes the needle through the thick layers of fabric and batting, the sharp end pierces her fingertip and it bleeds, leaving a spot of blood on the cloth. She wraps her finger in tissue and keeps sewing. She stitches every day for a month until the quilt is finished. It is warm and sturdy, with thousands of tiny, even stitches. It is perfect. But she has no use for it. There is no baby. She has more quilts than she will ever need. She tosses the quilt into the fire, all that pain and work wasted.

Sometimes I think that's what's happening in my womb. Every month, I build a nice cushy quilt, only to toss it into the fire. It's all a waste. Since I was 13, when my young energetic eggs sprang to life and my uterus started developing my first baby nest, my body has been fashioning a safe place inside and sloughing it away every month. It will probably be only a few more years before the last tired eggs ride the red tide onto a Maxi-pad, leaving my ovaries and my uterus empty and useless for the rest of my life.

Until I bleed, I can't see what's going on inside, but I can feel it. I feel my body growing softer and rounder, then suddenly going bony and empty. I feel the hormones working, the tension as they struggle to build the nest, the sudden sadness as their work is wasted, the hopeful joy as they start again. How will I feel when the cycle has ended forever? Bony and sad or soft and hopeful?

Sue Fagalde Lick

I wrote this before menopause occurred. Now I know how I will feel: soft and wistful. My body was designed to have babies. To have dozens of babies in the years between puberty and menopause. But I haven't. Nor have my childless sisters. Some have been hampered by illness or malfunction in their own bodies. But what about those of us who chose to ignore the monthly message of our mission, who decided no, we'll do something else? What about those women who decided as I did: *I choose this man who chooses not to be a father; therefore I will not be a mother?* What about us?

Did you know that childless women are more prone to osteoporosis and hip fractures? Worse, they have an increased risk of certain cancers. Why? Considering all the things that can happen to a woman's body during pregnancy, childbirth, and nursing, we should be healthier, right?

Not necessarily.

During pregnancy, the uterus changes from an almost-solid organ the size of a woman's fist into a large, thin-walled muscular sac capable of holding the baby, the placenta and a large quantity of fluid. Imagine the long-term effects of such a transformation.

Pregnant women experience a host of symptoms, including nausea, weight gain, swollen feet and ankles, dark or blotchy patches on their skin, varicose veins, frequent urination, hemorrhoids and backache. They may also suffer from gestational diabetes, anemia, high blood pressure and aggravation of whatever health problems they had before. Some of the less-known possible side effects include bleeding gums, yeast infections and hair loss. And yes, if you want to deliver a healthy baby, you must give up alcohol, caffeine and drugs for nine months.

The above risks don't even count the delivery, which can lead to death and certainly includes excruciating pain, a total loss of dignity and control, and permanent scarring from C-sections and episiotomies.

In North America, death from childbirth used to be fairly common. As recently as 1917, nearly one in 100 live births resulted in a mother's death, and it's still possible. The U.S. National Center for Health Statistics reported 17 deaths per 100,000 births in 2008. We

240

have it comparatively good. In other parts of the world, dying during childbirth is much more common. For example, in Tanzania, it is said that mothers commonly say their final goodbyes to their other children before giving birth, because they know they might not survive.

This is frightening, but most women deliver safely, and they say the end result is worth the risk.

Most of the bad effects are temporary, but some of the potential permanent effects of giving birth include stretch marks, loose skin, weight gain or redistribution, weakness of the abdominal and vaginal muscles, breasts that shrink and sag after breast-feeding ends, varicose veins, a loss of dental and bone calcium, and vaginal changes that can alter one's sex life and cause urinary or fecal incontinence.

Being in good health helps. Shelley Thompson, a physical fitness expert, says that her friends who were fit had shorter labors and easier deliveries. She sees a tendency for the hips to be wider in those who have had babies, but some of the hormonal changes actually seem to make the women more fit. "I think the body *is* different after a baby," she says.

We childless women might think we get off easy. Alison, a 28-year-old business consultant, brags, "My stomach is tight as a washboard . . . and my breasts are not sagging." Diane, 37, a childless-by-choice industrial maintenance technician, says she used to be jealous of her friend's perfect body, but after she had her first baby, her butt is shaped like a square now. My stomach looks great—no stretch marks, cute belly button."

We're not all that lucky. I've got my mother's well-padded body even though I've never been pregnant. But yes, those of us who have not given birth, the women whom scientists call *nulliparas,* do seem to get more sleep, more freedom, and less worry.

And yet, we are more at risk for osteoporosis, a weakening of the bones, and childless women seem to have higher rates of arthritis. Something about pregnancy seems to help prevent these ailments.

Then there's the cancer risk.

In "The Protective Effects of Childbirth," Amy R. Sobie writes about the important role that childbirth and lactation play in the overall health of a woman. "The failure of the body to experience these events appears to cause malfunctions which frequently result in health problems later in life, including possible increased risks from various types of cancer."

In simple terms, the rush of hormones that happens during pregnancy and the long break from ovulation appear to protect women from breast, ovarian and endometrial (uterine) cancer.

The Breast Cancer Prevention Institute explains that in women who carry babies to term, cancer-susceptible breast lobules mature into cancer-resistant ones. First-trimester abortions can actually make the risk higher than if one never was pregnant at all because a rush of estrogen has caused the breasts to start to grow and begin to add extra lobules that will allow them to produce milk. The process was stopped before they acquired the cancer protection that begins around the last eight weeks of pregnancy. This is frightening when you consider how many women have abortions, ranging from almost none in countries where it's illegal to 52 percent in Russia. The U.S. rate was last reported at 19.5 percent, or 1.2 million abortions a year. That's a lot of women courting an extra risk of breast cancer.

With spontaneous miscarriages, which occur in nearly a quarter of pregnancies, the breasts may not have begun the changes that increase their vulnerability to cancer. However, premature births after the first trimester and before 32 weeks gestation do increase cancer risks, because the breasts have begun to change and have created more places for cancer to grow. In other words, if you're going to get pregnant, you have to make it through the first two trimesters to get the cancer protection granted to biological mothers.

The longer you're exposed to estrogen, the greater your risk of cancer. The "window of susceptibility" extends from puberty to full-term delivery of a child. If you started your periods early, ended them late and didn't have a baby in the middle, you're at greater risk than your sisters who have children. Of course there are other factors, such as heredity, lifestyle and environment, but right off the top the risk is higher for childless women. In fact, the Breast Cancer Prevention Institute's "Breast Cancer Risks" brochure suggests that a woman's breasts never fully mature until she has given birth.

Sobie's article notes that while approximately one in eight

American women will have breast cancer in their lifetimes, a major study of 250,000 women from around the world found that "those who have their first child by age 18 have only about one-third the risk of breast cancer faced by women whose first birth occurs at age 35 or later." Or never.

Studies have shown that women who don't have children are also twice as likely to develop ovarian or endometrial cancer. The higher levels of progesterone during pregnancy help thin the lining of the uterus, reversing the buildup caused by estrogen and reducing the risk of cancers. In simple terms, it's all hormones, mostly estrogen, causing the trouble.

It's odd because estrogen is the stuff that makes us feel good when our periods come. Until 2002, when hormone-replacement therapy was shown to increase the risk of heart disease, doctors routinely gave it to menopausal women to cool their hot flashes and to help them feel young, sexy and happy. It was also said to decrease the risk of osteoporosis. We all knew hormone-replacement therapy increased the risk of breast cancer, but the benefits seemed to outweigh the risks. Now it's clear that too much of a good thing can kill us.

We are more at risk for the so-called "female" cancers, definitely concern, but Lacie Koppelman, a science analyst with the National Breast Cancer Coalition, assures us that "Before you start thinking you're a cancer magnet because you don't have kids, remember that your overall chances of developing these diseases are still quite low."

Some experts say we can mitigate the effects of childlessness by taking birth control pills to mimic pregnancy with the right combination of hormones.

The increased risks of not having children are not so high that we should panic over it. Yet it doesn't seem fair to have *any* physical consequences for not doing what most women do. Men, of course, have no known added physical risks for remaining childless.

I know women, mothers with husbands, who can't seem to do anything on their own. I've never had or wanted that privilege. Men have greater upper body strength, but otherwise I think women are a lot tougher than their male counterparts. One bout of

243

cramps, and a guy would be in the hospital hollering for narcotics. As our lady gym teachers ordered us back in high school, we just shut up and keep going. We don't have time to have the vapors.

Unlike some of the women in my survey, I can't brag about having a buffed body. My love of French fries shows. Except for the stretch marks and being about 50 pounds lighter, my body is an exact duplicate of my mother's, from the shelf her breasts became through the round belly to the size nine feet. My thighs aren't sexy, but I am strong.

If you had dropped by my house recently, you could have seen me scrape ice from the driveway and sidewalk, move 600 pounds of wood pellets (40 pounds at a time), assemble and transfer a dog crate almost as big as I am from garage to car and back again, shovel dirt for two hours in my back yard, walk one big dog for a mile and turn around and walk the other big dog for another mile, pretzelize my body in yoga class, plant eight cement stepping stones in my back yard, scoop a ton of dog poop, fix my own toilet, stand at the top of a ladder moving boxes, *and* take care of all the girl stuff one would expect, the cooking, cleaning, laundry, and mopping muddy floors. I'm not saying I wasn't crying, whining or groaning while I did these things, but I did them, all by myself.

When my mother, who died of cancer a week after her 75th birthday, was 57 or even 37, she could not do any of these things. She had no idea how, and she barely had the physical stamina to walk to the end of the block. My father and brother handled the "guy jobs." With all her needlework, Mom probably had the nimblest fingers in California, but she never exercised the rest of her body. She never took care of herself. She was too busy taking care of Dad and my brother and me. It was what women in her family did. If my father had died first, she would have called on my brother or other men to take care of the yard, the car and home repairs. She would have been the poor helpless widow.

I refuse to play that role. When the job is truly too big for one person, I will call for help, but I'm smart, and I have muscles. If I don't know how to do it, I can learn. I'm already eyeing Fred's tools in the garage and wondering where a woman my age can take a shop class.

Part of this comes from being my father's daughter. In his late 80s, he was still strong and stubborn. But part of it comes from being childless. I think we have to be more self-reliant.

My Aunt Edna lived to 100 years old. She had been widowed for 50 years and never had children. She was well into her 90s before she needed help from anyone. Likewise, her sister Virginia, also in her 90s, lived on her own until she fell and broke her neck. As of this writing, she's up and ornery as ever, even though she still has some health challenges to conquer. In Grandpa Fagalde's day, he would have called Edna and Virginia "tough old birds." Well, that's what I want to be, too. I want people to talk about how strong Aunt Sue was, not about how sad it was that she never had children.

On my birthday, I gaze at myself in the mirror. This is the body of a woman who has never been pregnant. How would it be different if I had given birth? Perhaps a scar would cross my abdomen from a C-section or I would have a tenderness down below from an episiotomy. Perhaps my breasts would be bigger or smaller, having swollen with pregnancy and shrunk after the baby was weaned. Perhaps I would be heavier than I am now, having gained weight for the baby and never taken it off. I still wear the same size my mother wore before she had children.

Most of my body is still smooth and, dare I say, juicy, like a well-baked turkey? I still enjoy sex and feel beautiful when the hormones are right. I feel like a babe, even if young guys see me as a mom. They don't know that I'm not a mom. My breasts are big and full of promise, a promise that my ovaries will never keep.

When I go to the gynecologist, the nurse asks how many pregnancies I've had, how many miscarriages, how many abortions. She can't tell by looking at me that I haven't left five children in the waiting room. I suppose when the doctor slips on the plastic gloves and starts feeling around, my cervix might feel a little like a new car that hasn't been broken in.

Years have gone by since I wrote the beginning of this chapter. Menopause has occurred. I have osteopenia, a weakening of the bones that isn't as bad as osteoporosis, but I worry and take my calcium faithfully. I'm also looking at a future hysterectomy for a prolapsed uterus, something I thought only occurred after multiple childbirths. My grandmother, who had two children, had the same problem.

But Grandma did not have cancer. Am I in danger because I never had children, never made her a great grandmother?

If you look closely at my eyes, they don't quite match, due to the after-effects of Graves' Disease, which returned with a vengeance in 1999 and required radiation to nuke it into remission. But you can't see any of this from the outside, any more than you can see that I have never given birth. What you can see are the signs of aging. My hair is streaked with gray now. The lines around my eyes follow the same pattern as my mother's wrinkles. We Souza ladies gray slowly but wrinkle overnight, like cheap cloth.

Most of my body is not aware that it isn't 13 anymore. I still get down on the grass to play with the dog. I follow her on my hands and knees, copying her walk. When I happen on a playground, I pull myself across the rings and bars and climb up the jungle gym. I run, and I dance when no one's looking. People often find me on the floor doing yoga postures. Would I stop doing these things if I were a mother? Would I have to stop playing? I hope not.

I'm a kid in an adult body, like Tom Hanks in the movie "Big." He didn't know what happened to him either.

I am glad to have this healthy, youthful frame. With luck, I can hand it back to God in another 40 years almost as good as I got it, just slightly used, like a library book that looks new except for a few toast crumbs where the pages come together.

Back in the days before modern medicine could fix most obstetrical problems, women often died giving birth. The babies got stuck inside them, their cervixes failed to open, their hearts couldn't take the strain, or they bled to death. They might contract an infection, with no antibiotics to counter it. Pregnancy and childbirth, while welcomed for bringing children, were also feared because they might bring death. Women who had one baby after another, with no contraceptives to stop the process, only a feeble "no" against the rush of hormones and eager husbands, found their bodies wearing out. Multiple pregnancies stretched their female organs, strained their muscles, and wearied their hearts.

My body is fresh and intact, safe. Cancer or heart disease might

246

Childless by Marriage

kill me from within, but not a baby. Yet if a baby should begin growing inside me today, terrifying as it would be at my age, I would thank God and do careful somersaults down the hall rug.

This is the body of a woman who has never had a baby. Although I have not given birth, when I look in the mirror at my naked body, it looks the same as my mother's did. Inside, however, it's not.

22
Do We Ever Grow Up?

Let me be the first childless baby boomer to just admit it. I'm spoiled. I want things my way and I want them now. When I have to get up early, I whine. When I don't get my lunch, I whine. When I have to clean the whole house by myself, I whine.

As a child, I didn't get everything I wanted. My parents were the ones with "rules," the ones who said "no" when everyone else was running off to somebody's backyard Doughboy swimming pool. My parents were the ones who would not drive us to sports activities or music lessons. They were the ones who laughed if we asked for an expensive toy.

And yet, if there was something I really, really wanted for Christmas or my birthday, I got it. In fact, on birthdays, I woke up with my bed covered with gifts. I was princess for the day, sent off to school in new clothes, presented with whatever I wanted for dinner—raviolis and potato salad—and feted in the evening by family members bringing more gifts and chocolate cake.

I have a feeling I got spoiled before I was old enough to know what was going on. I was the first grandchild and the first girl baby in ages. So I think that little tyke with wild black hair and big brown eyes was spoiled rotten. By the time my little brother came along and attention went his way, it was too late.

One day when I was working for the *Pacifica Tribune*, the editor sent me to report on a psychic fair. I had a bit of the flu and was ticked to be asked to work on a Saturday. The aura reader said my aura was calm and beautiful. Quack, I thought. But the palm reader got it right. He studied the lines in my hand and said, "I think Sue does what Sue wants."

Wow, I thought, this guy's for real.

I took my photos and my notes and got out before I fainted from all the incense and patchouli, filed my story, and went back to doing what I wanted.

The "me generation." That's what older folks call us boomers who came of age in the 1960s and early '70s. Rather than resent it, let's be truthful. They're right. Except for the threat of a bomb falling on us and all those useless red and yellow alert practices (as if duck-and-cover is going protect us from a nuclear attack), those of us born in the 1950s and early '60s in the suburbs had it pretty good. We had nice houses, great food, and Mom always around to take care of us. We had lots of friends our age to play with, and the world was safe enough that we could ride our bikes anywhere we wanted with no fear of kidnapping or rape. Besides, somebody's mother was always watching.

I feel for the Gen-X children who got shipped off to daycare until they were old enough to be latchkey kids. Although I never had children of my own, I still remember with guilt how my stepson Michael would get hungry and cook his own macaroni and cheese while I was off chasing newspaper articles. Even worse, when the epic 1989 Loma Prieta earthquake hit, Michael was home alone. Despite books and knick-knacks falling down around him, he ignored all previous instructions and sat under his bedroom window until the house stopped shaking. Then he ran to his friend's house, not next door to the daycare lady, but to John, whose parents would end up taking care of him more than I like to admit. Where were we? Fred was driving home from work, watching the power poles sway and the pavement move in waves, and I was at the downtown library reading microfilm for an article on urban anger.

Where did I go after that quake? First I hit the pay phone in the parking lot (no cell phones yet), eventually locating Michael and Fred. Then I thought about going home.

Big, knock-you-off-your feet aftershocks hit every couple minutes. The library was closed, the floors buried in fallen books and shelves. The power was out; we had no stoplights. I could see an endless stream of cars heading south, which was where I lived. So I didn't go south. I went west, back to my parents' house, sitting in the dark with them until bedtime, raiding their fridge when I got hungry.

Meanwhile, Fred had gotten home, collected Michael, and

Sue Fagalde Lick

started cleaning up. My office was the epicenter of fallen office supplies. Books, binders and that six-pound rock my father gave me years ago covered the carpet, but it was cleaned up before I got there. Likewise, the broken clock and the broken coffee mugs were gone. Fred, a parent, took care of things, while I reverted to the daughter role.

This wasn't the first time I had fled to Mom and Dad's house. When my first marriage broke up, where did I go? When the traveling show for which I had quit my newspaper job in 1983 went belly up before we even left the state, where did I go? I went home.

Thomas Lifson wrote in an article titled "Lost Posterity" that the idea of self-sacrifice is foreign to young Americans. Before the boomer generation, parents were willing to sacrifice everything for the good of their children. But things changed. With abortion, birth control and a new youth-oriented philosophy, self-sacrifice became totally uncool. We were advised to live in the moment.

"The arrival of children, which used to be the accepted course of things for the overwhelming majority of people everywhere and at all times, usually jerked people out of the narcissistic rapture of youth," Lifson said.

Backing Lifson, psychologist Sheila Rossan wrote, "Until you have a child, until you have looked after someone who cannot look after herself, you are not an adult."

But if you don't have children, are you doomed to perpetual self-centered child status? If I had children of my own waiting alone in South San Jose in the dark as aftershocks shook the area, wouldn't I have done whatever I had to do to rescue my babies, even if I had to walk or crawl the whole eight miles, rather than going to my parents' house? Does it count that if it happened now, I'd do it for my puppies, fearing those poor dogs would be crushed under a bookshelf?

Poet Molly Peacock, who is childless by choice, suggests in her memoir *Paradise, Piece by Piece* that becoming a parent instantly moves one into adulthood, but it's not the only way to get there. Dealing with the deaths of loved ones and other major life events ultimately evokes the same result. "So the childfree grow up, either by evolution or by the swift witchcraft of event—or both. Gradually the childhood world vanishes into its own reflection and we look back from the other side of the mirror."

Recent studies done on rats suggest that having babies causes permanent changes in the brain that actually make mothers smarter, more efficient and more dedicated to their young. A January 2006 *Scientific American* article titled "The Maternal Brain" explained that the dramatic hormonal fluctuations that occur during pregnancy, birth and breast-feeding increase the size of neurons in some regions of the brain, such as the hippocampus, which controls memory and learning. They also cause structural changes in other parts of the brain. In addition, other chemicals wrapped up with the mothering process seem to trigger motherly impulses. It's all designed to enhance the mother's ability to feed and protect her young.

If this is true, we childless women are missing out on a lot more than Mother's Day cards. But wait. The same report shows that after a while, the mere presence of the offspring can trigger maternal behavior. Researchers Andreas Bartels and Semir Zeki of University College London reportedly found that the pleasure centers of the human mother's brain were activated when they merely gazed at their children. Another study showed that childless rats given foster children did just as well in a maze as the mother rats. Aha. Maybe there's something to that warm squishy feeling I get when I look at my puppies when they're asleep and the fierce protectiveness that manifests when anything threatens to harm them.

Besides, any woman who takes care of a husband, stepchildren, dogs and everything in the house AND keeps a career going has to develop superpowers. That's not a mom thing; that's a woman thing.

When Fred and I moved from California to Oregon, I was 44 years old. I had never lived more than an hour away from my parents. I had no idea how hard it would be. I suffered homesickness and depression of the sort a kid ought to get over in junior high. I wanted to go home, but it was 700 miles and several hundred thousand dollars out of reach.

I've never cut the ties, the invisible umbilical cord. My mother has passed away, but more than a decade later, I still feel the need to go home, and I probably will some day. In my dreams, I always live in the house where I grew up.

Sue Fagalde Lick

Is this unusual? Never having become a mother, I'm the perpetual daughter. Most people's lives run in something of a circle. As each generation passes on, another one is born in its place, so there are always children, young adults, middle-aged adults and very old adults. As Elizabeth Gilbert wrote in *Eat Pray Love*, when people follow the usual pattern of marrying and having children, they always know where they fit at the family reunions, moving up the generations until they look back in their 90s at the dynasty they have created. However, when you don't have children, you're not sure where you fit, what table to sit at. Our lives seem to run in a straight line, with the older generations dropping off in front of us and no one coming up behind. Think of it as a dance where we reach back for a hand, and no one is there.

I married a much older man, a man who was not looking for a woman to be the mother of his children but for a companion in middle age and a caretaker in old age. As a younger woman, I would always be "cute" in his eyes. I would look up to him for his wisdom and life experience, and I would never outgrow him. I married a man who provided my financial support, my home, my car, my food, and my health insurance—just like Dad—freeing me to dabble in my writing, my music and my hobbies—just as I did when I was 12. I married a man who would allow me to remain the daughter. I make my writing students laugh by saying that I married a "sugar daddy," but it's true.

I don't know why it is shameful to admit marrying a father substitute, but it is. These days, we are supposed to be equal. I can have a career, and he has to help with the dishes.

Eventually I wound up mothering my older husband. In the Alzheimer's support group and at the nursing home, I found myself surrounded by much older people who assumed I was Fred's daughter. "No, no, I'm his wife," I would say, and they'd look at me as if they didn't believe me. And then when I said I didn't have children, they pitied me. How I envied those couples who could grow old together surrounded by children and grandchildren.

In the days of my Portuguese immigrant ancestors, middle-aged men routinely wed teenage girls who produced a dozen or more children. The man supported the family. In return, the wife and children obeyed his will in all things. When the wife became a widow, her children took care of her. By then she had matured into a mother and grandmother, taking her place in the chain of life. While not equipped to succeed in the outside world, she had learned to give herself over to others, to bear the burdens that must be borne for the good of the family. She had raised children, buried children, seen her sons and daughters through weddings and the birth of their own children, and shared their successes and their failures. She had grown up.

Or had she?

W hen I asked childless women if they felt they had missed a step in growing up, here's what some of them said:

Laura T., a 20-something writer from Southern Oregon: "I'm a perpetual adolescent."

Laura D., a 40-year-old massage therapist from Texas: "When people ask, 'Where did you grow up?' I answer, 'I haven't grown up yet!'"

Alison, a 28-year-old business consultant from Atlanta: "I do think there's some truth in this. I think that having children teaches you a whole new level of love and responsibility." Katreen, 36, a writer from Germany: "I find that most people I know who are parents are a lot less selfish and me-oriented than those who are childless. There is a glow, a particular warmth to people with children, a maturity, a sense of responsibility; they seem a lot more grounded."

Kathleen, a minister from Oregon: "I have noticed myself maintaining a childlike quality, a sense of hope, a sense of fun, a sense of youthfulness. Those are the positive sides. The other part of that is not so positive is an inbuilt lack of a sense of responsibility."

In the book *Wanting a baby*, a woman identified only as A. talks about her feelings when she was reunited with the child she gave up for adoption. "The truth was, thrust all at once into the costume of a mother, I was unsure how to act. I was the one who had always been the daughter—it had been my more enduring role; encountering her shook up my sense of myself. It made me aware of how mature, how

Sue Fagalde Lick

solid I was; not having children can keep you adrift in a perpetual late adolescence. But now I was confronted with the fact I had produced this complex creature, taller and more beautiful than I ever was, even if I hadn't raised her."

A lthough some childless women freely admit that they don't feel as grown up as their motherly peers, others aren't so sure. "Maybe, but that may be a good thing," says Martha, a writer from California. "I've had the luxury of being able to do things, like now, I've been able to do my power walks and I do yoga every morning after, but I'm also at the age where, if I had kids, they probably would be out of the home now anyway."

Tiffany, a Portland, Oregon performance artist, says, "We all have different experiences that enable us to grow in different ways. Most of the people who might, in a cruel mood, tell me I have missed out on an essential maturing experience, have never worked for a non-profit in Africa; traveled around Europe, Southeast Asia, Central America, North America, and the subcontinent; written and published a book; been intimately part of a technological and cultural revolution; edited a magazine; performed in numerous art and music festivals; lived in several 'world-class' cities, or curated exhibitions and performances. I suppose I could tell them that they are immature for not having had these global and cultural experiences which I've worked into my life. To anyone who's done all those things *and* had children, I'd say 'More power to ya!'"

Jane, a business consultant, writes from New Zealand, "My opinion is that 'grownupness' has more to do with personal attitudes and behaviors than having a child. However, many people don't acquire those attitudes and behaviors until forced into it by having a child. One particular aspect of being grown up, I believe, is taking full responsibility for yourself and your actions, which many people seem to never achieve! I guess the next step in that thought could be that taking full responsibility for someone else is one step up again in maturity. That's usually a child, but could be an aging or ill parent or partner. Many people have a child without actually properly taking on the responsibility though, leaving important aspects to chance or others. So maybe having a child gives you the *opportunity* to be more mature but that doesn't mean that people will take it. And you could get that opportunity elsewhere but you are less likely to."

Many women are adamant, angry even, at this question. It's the "breeders" who aren't mature, they say. Some feel that people without children have more time to develop themselves, to travel, study, go deep into spiritual practices and learn to be independent. Others go beyond that to say they are more mature because they had the sense to think before they got themselves pregnant, and furthermore, hanging out with kids all day seemed to turn some women into baby-talking idiots.

Robyn, an artist in New York, says, "I see children as a life experience we can choose to have or not have, rather than a 'stage' in growing up. If it were a stage in growing up that helps people mature, then every parent would be so much wiser than those of us who have no children, and this certainly is NOT the case, judging from some of the parents I have met."

Barbra, a writer from Illinois, says, "That's like saying if you don't go through a divorce you never mature, if you don't move out of your home state, you never mature. Some women go from their father's house to their husband's house to housewife. Are they any more mature than a woman who goes from her father's house to the White House? That doesn't make any sense. Think of the teenage pregnancy rate in this country. Are those people mature because their bodies are physically ready to procreate? I think that statement is backwards. I think a lot of people have kids too young and stunt their emotional growth. Then they have a midlife crisis to make up for it."

Then there's Susan Jeffers, author of *I'm Okay You're a Brat*. She maintains that parents are less likely to "grow up" than non-parents. Parents seem to sacrifice their adulthood when they have children. They can't talk about anything but kids for a while. They give up their sex lives and other adult activities. They have no time to read or socialize. She quotes one woman, "Not only do I lose my adult activities, I also lose my adult behavior. I can't remember ever behaving so badly."

This brings to mind those adults who can't seem to stop speaking that squeaky just-for-kids voice and call everyone honey or

255

sweetie. You know who I mean.

But then I think about how much fun I still have playing with kids, getting down on the floor to dress Barbie or build Lego houses. When I'm alone in a waiting room, I play with the toys. If I had children, I'd have a good excuse to play with the blocks and puzzles. I'm helping, right? To tell the truth, maybe I want to be the child again, not the mother.

Holidays, especially Christmas, bring the old feelings out. If you have children or grandchildren, the holiday seems to be all about the kids. With children, even adults start to believe a bit in Santa Claus as they take their offspring to sit in his lap and tell him their dreams. It's fun to buy gifts for children. Every doll, toy truck, plastic farm or video game is a gift of imagination, an addition to a fantasy world which only children and writers of fiction are allowed to inhabit. Sometimes, for a minute, they'll let you have a glimpse back into the imaginary worlds of childhood.

Jeffers would rather not go there. She writes about how stay-at-home parents lose their self-esteem and confidence. "I knew other adults were out there growing, learning, being, interacting, and doing what grown-ups do. I was at home shrinking: no time or energy to learn, grow, be, interact, and do what grownups do."

Unfortunately the same thing happens if one is home sick for a long time or caring for an elderly parent or spouse. Anything that keeps you out of circulation can have that effect.

Perhaps maturity is overrated. What's so great about growing up, ask many of my childless sisters. They prefer the free-spirited optimism of youth over what they perceive as the weary old-lady life-view of their contemporaries who choose to be parents.

I don't know. I think I ought to feel like one of the adults by now. Why do I want to hang out with my 30-something cousins? Why am I still building my career when other baby boomers are retiring? Why am I so self-centered?

If I had had children, would I truly be able to set aside my own ambitions to watch them pursue their goals? I don't see how that could be true. I could never be content to be "just a mom." And yet, what an accomplishment it would be to create a new human being and raise it from infant to child to adult. In comparison, all this writing and music-making is just goofing around.

Author Erica Jong, who has been both an author and a mother, writes in her memoir *Fear of Fifty* that she was terrified of having children, certain it would destroy her writing career. Then her daughter Molly was born.

"I know in my heart (as I know I will die) that Molly is more important than my writing. Any child is. That's why motherhood is so difficult for writing women. Its demands are so compelling, so clearly important, and also so profoundly satisfying.

"Who can explain this to the childless? You give up yourself, and finally you don't even mind. You become your child's guide to life at the expense of that swollen ego you thought so immutable. I wouldn't have missed this for anything. It humbled my ego and stretched my soul. It awakened me to eternity. It made me know my own humanity, my own mortality, my own limits. It gave me whatever crumbs of wisdom I possess today."

We missed all that. And someone to play Barbies with.

In *The Mask of Motherhood*, Susan Maushart says, "In traditional societies, the birth of a woman's first child marks her acceptance into full adulthood. It is the initiation rite par excellence, the portal through which, once having passed, one can never return."

I find this Maushart quote particularly interesting: "Motherhood is fearsome because it is so intensely powerful, entailing acts of creation before which all other human endeavor withers into shadow. In the creation stakes, motherhood is the big league, and everything else—art, science, technology—is a farm team."

Yes, growing a baby in your body and pushing it out your vagina does sound as if it would change a person, both physically and emotionally. It's a piece of yourself and now that it's not inside, where its care was automatic, you're responsible.

In other words, it's not about me anymore; it's about the kids. Perhaps that's why so many women today say nay to motherhood. They like their lives just the way they are. If they need something to parent, they get puppies.

Sue Fagalde Lick

Today's women of child-bearing age have grown up in a society in which women can choose any occupation. They can choose to be married or not, and they can choose to be mothers or not. In my mother's generation, the women who came of age during World War II, those who could not conceive were pitied. And if a woman chose not to be a mother, Lord help her, she must be deranged. To marry a man and find out later that he was impotent was tragic. To marry a man knowing that he was impotent or didn't want children—that was just plain bad judgment. And to marry a man who already had children from a previous marriage, well, that was asking for trouble.

Things have changed. Young women don't see children as essential. And second wives marry men with children.

So, back to the original question. Do childless women miss a stage in growing up? There's no one answer, but I do know this subject got the most heated responses when I asked childless women about it. In a way, I think we do miss an important step that in nature comes shortly after puberty. But I also think that if we live long enough, other life experiences will take us to the same place.

My experiences with Fred these last few years certainly forced me to grow up in many ways. Caring for a spouse with Alzheimer's is a lot like caring for a child, except that they never learn and become independent. As the disease progresses, you abandon much of your own life to manage their care. Like children, they cannot be left alone or handle their own affairs. In the wake of his illness, I suspect I'm getting closer to my own age.

I may not have given birth, but I'm starting to know that my needs can't always come first. That, as one of my favorite high school teachers said, is the definition of maturity.

You might say we miss the train most people are riding, but instead of being left behind at the station, childless women take a *different* train. Ultimately we all end up at the same place at the end of the line.

Have I grown up yet? I think I'm almost there.

23
I'm Going to be a Bag Lady!

When you're young, being child*free* may sound enticing. There's no question that children cramp your style. I admit that I didn't worry all that much about not having them when I was younger. I figured it would happen sooner or later.

Sure, and Santa Claus is going to come down the chimney.

At some point in the life of every woman who is committed to a man who doesn't want children, it's going to be too late to procreate. Menopause will seal the deal. Occasionally the big M starts early, and women are surprised. But Susan Sarandon and Geena Davis had babies in their 40s, and Maria Carey had twins, they say. They are exceptions to the rule. Those eggs are getting pretty tacky by your mid-40s and they're shot by 50, even if you're a late menopauser like me.

About that time, our parents are dying, and we may face serious health challenges of our own. We live longer than men, and some marriages don't last. If our husbands are not around, who will help us? What happens to childless women when we get old?

When I first started working on this chapter, it was all theoretical, but now it's my reality. When Fred moved to a nursing home, I joined the nearly 25 percent of Americans who live alone.

Just the other day, while I was selling books at an author's fair, my tablemate asked me where my kids and grandkids lived. I had to tell him I didn't have any. He was silent for a minute, then said, "Oh, you're one of those independent types."

"No," I said softly, "I wanted children."

"Oh." He changed the subject.

I'm living and working in the thick of the Grandma Club. It's worse than the Mom Club. My friends are constantly showing pictures of their grandchildren or taking off for visits. It's my grandson this and my granddaughter that. I still talk about my dogs.

I spend many afternoons at the dog park, where we dog parents sit on stumps and talk about our pets, watching Annie flirt with Frisco, Buddy romp with Scrappie or Shep trying to hump all the other dogs, regardless of gender. It's a relief hanging out where most people are focused on dogs instead of children.

Was Fred worth giving up children for? Most people don't get a love like we had. Even years into his dementia, the romance held steady. I have never met anybody as nice as Fred and never met anyone who could be so supportive of my crazy life of words and music.

But Fred is not here.

Most likely any other man I meet in the future will have children and grandchildren. It would be great if they welcomed me into the family I never had, but more likely I'd be Susie-come-way-too-late.

Meanwhile, there are no kids rallying around to take care of me, calling to see if I'm all right, taking me out to eat or stepping in when I need help around the house or a ride for a medical procedure. I do most things alone, and when I absolutely can't, I call on my friends.

I'm too young to be fully immersed in the senior citizen sisterhood and too childless to completely merge with friends my own age. I'm the spare wheel. Poor Aunt Sue.

When a mother becomes a widow, she still has her children. If they're young, she takes care of them. If they're grown, she spends her holidays with them and the grandchildren and eventually the great-grandchildren. Her husband is gone, but much of her life goes on because it revolves around the kids. Yes, I know there are parents who never hear from their offspring. But the women I know who have children wrap their whole lives around them.

With no children, my four-bedroom house feels like an empty stage set. In some ways, I find myself back where I was when I first met Fred. I often feel like that much-younger woman who moved to Pacifica alone after my first husband decided he preferred his girlfriend. Most of our savings has been spent on Fred's care, and now I'm on my own again. But I'm not that young woman. I'm forever changed. You make your choices. I chose Fred.

Childless by Marriage

Not so long ago, the reality of the situation hit home for me. Sitting in a tiny examining room in the ER at Samaritan Pacific Communities Hospital, I felt more and more sorry for myself. Everyone else had people with them, parents, children, siblings, friends, somebody.

"Who drove you here?" the first nurse asked.

"I did."

A look of concern passed over the nurse's face.

I had sat down to dinner but wasn't hungry. I had been sick for weeks, and now my right eye was scarlet, half closed with oozing puss. It was time to see a doctor. I called a friend who had always said to call her if I needed help. She wasn't home and doesn't have a cell phone. With no family nearby, I couldn't think of anyone else to call.

I put the food away, brushed my teeth, grabbed my purse and drove myself to the hospital. So there I was, alone, half blind, stuffed up, thirsty and wondering if I would be able to drive home. I kept thinking I should have had children or stayed in San Jose near my family.

I sat on the table, swinging my legs, waiting. I could hear a small dog barking. He had been barking for at least an hour.

Nothing else to do, I made notes about the room I was in: green plaid curtain, gray stool, plastic wall rack holding four boxes of blue plastic gloves marked small, medium, large and extra large, hazardous waste depository, paper towel holder, Corporate Service Excellence award posted for the third quarter of 2006. Tissues, swabs, sheets, pillow cases, blue hospital gowns, and vomit basins.

This room had fluorescent lights and a fire sprinkler. The floor was white linoleum with gray speckles. A rack outside the door held magazines. I was tempted to visit the bathroom across the hall, but what if the doctor came while I was in there? After two hours, I wasn't taking any chances. I had no one to save my place and say, "she went to the bathroom."

Finally the doctor, a short grouchy man with wiry hair, green scrubs, and white tennis shoes, hurried in. He swabbed the gunk in my eyes for lab tests, looked in my nose and mouth and listened to me breathe. Then he walked out.

Nearly four hours after I arrived, he returned with a diagnosis. I

Sue Fagalde Lick

had pharyngitis, an infection in the voice box, plus conjunctivitis, popularly known as pink eye. It was a viral infection, very contagious. I needed to use wet compresses and eye drops and keep my stuff away from everybody else's. For the throat, he advised salt-water gargles. "I'll send a nurse," he said on his way out.

A bit later, a nurse arrived with a pill bottle filled with the pain medication that I had told the first nurse I was allergic to. "No, I can't take that. I don't need it anyway," I grumbled. It was far too late for civility. The only pain I was feeling came from being stuck in that room.

"Suit yourself." She gave me my discharge form and said I could go home.

With the gunk wiped away, I could see a bit better. I drove home and prepared my own gargles and compresses. In a couple days, the first eye was clear. The infection had moved into the other eye, but I knew what to do, so it soon went away.

It was all minor, but I couldn't help thinking: What if this was something more serious where I could not drive, could not speak, could not tell anyone my name, date of birth, medications, insurance numbers and drug allergies?

A year later, I drove myself to the hospital again with a sprained wrist. A few months after that, I accepted the offer of a woman I barely knew to take me for my colonoscopy. More recently, a friend kept me company for cataract surgery. She dropped me off at home afterward to cope on my own with one good eye. It wasn't so hard, but it would have been nice to have someone offer me food and keep track of my eye drops.

Damn, I should have had kids. Those friends who are always there on TV shows are a myth. Childless, parentless, we're on our own. Remember that Tennessee Williams line from "A Streetcar Named Desire?" "Whoever you are—I have always depended on the kindness of strangers"? I'd rather not be that woman.

Yes, I know everyone says you can't count on your children to help you in your later years. But if you have them, at least it's a possibility.

262

Childless by Marriage

John Przybys wrote about "orphan boomers," aging folks who are alone and childless, in an article for the *Las Vegas Review-Journal*. He described a Reno resident who broke his leg and found himself trying to maneuver on crutches. All of us who have ever used crutches know that you can't even carry a glass of water from point A to point B. He worried about what would happen if he were more seriously injured and couldn't make decisions for himself.

Adult "orphans" need to develop some kind of support system among their friends, churchmates, co-workers or whoever is around. Many of us build families of friends who are not biologically connected but feel closer than our actual relatives.

Przybys warns that non-relatives cannot make medical decisions unless you have legally designated them to speak for you. If you have no immediate family, pick someone you trust and do the paperwork giving them your medical power of attorney.

Personally I never know who to put down as my emergency contact. Once, in frustration, I wrote down "God." How likely is my family in California to drop everything to come to my aide? Dubious. And the stepchildren? Not gonna happen. I thank God for my friends.

You know who's going to be standing by my hospital bed if I wake up hooked to machines and sutured from neck to navel? A nurse. Maybe not even a nurse, but a nurse's aide. If I'm back in California, she might not speak English very well; she might mispronounce my name. I might have to push a button to get her to come. And she will be busy, rushing off to help other patients. Who will be there just for me?

On the plus side, I won't have to feel smothered by people hovering over me. My mother couldn't take a breath those last months without my father or my brother and I commenting on it. People constantly told her what to do, what to feel, and what to think. They scolded her if she didn't eat, if she didn't sleep, if she didn't talk. I suspect she might have wanted to be alone a bit more. Maybe she even wanted to die alone, instead of surrounded by people. I don't know; at the end, she couldn't speak. As she breathed her last breath, I had my hand on her hot, bruised arm while my father held her hand.

There is a saying that a woman gives birth to a daughter who will be there to hold her hand when she dies.

263

Sue Fagalde Lick

If only.

In her book *Passages in Caregiving*, Gail Sheehy says people need to build a circle of friends and advocates to help. No one person can do it all alone. While caring for her husband through his long struggle with cancer, she organized most of his care, but she quickly learned that she needed help. That help doesn't have to come from your children. The team can include siblings, church members, doctors, hired aides, and friends.

Have I got any friends who love me enough to abandon their schedules and sit with me as I lie in bed looking awful, no longer telling jokes and smiling, not cooking for them or taking care of them, just being helpless, sick, and needy?

Yes, I do.

On a recent milestone birthday, I feared I'd be alone, but my friends surprised me with a party at a local restaurant. When I arrived for lunch, they were all sitting around the big table near the fireplace. They burst into a chorus of "Happy Birthday" as I moved a pile of gifts and cards off my chair. We laughed, talked and shared experiences that nobody in my family would ever understand. After stuffing myself with chocolate cake with mint green frosting, I came away feeling loved and knowing that I would never have to be alone unless I chose to. I live in a small town. Even people who didn't know me kept wishing me "happy birthday" that afternoon, having heard the commotion in the restaurant. I did not feel lonely at all.

A study by Professor Tanya Koropecky-Cox of the University of Florida on the well-being of parents and non-parents in their later years shows a lot depends on one's attitude: "Childless women who believed it was better to have a child were much more likely to report being lonely and depressed than their female counterparts who said it didn't make a difference." Some people throughout their lives held onto the idea that they were disadvantaged, she says. "They continued to feel left out of something that was important to them. But other infertile men and women adjusted to their childless status and voiced no regret."

Amy Pienta, a co-author of the Florida study, says childlessness might have an effect, but she found that childless women were as happy as other women. "But of course with today's complicated lives,

Childless by Marriage

children don't necessarily always live in the same place as their parents. So it might be idealistic to think adult children will always be the same type of caregivers to their elderly parents as they have been in the past. It's the untold story until we see how these things in society play out."

When I asked childless women whether they were worried about being alone in old age, their reactions ranged from not worried at all to "terrified."

Laura, 44, chuckled as she remembered talking about this with her dad. "My father, on my mother's deathbed, said, 'Laura, I don't want you to end up with no one visiting you when you're dying. Have some children with Bob. Do you want me to talk to him? I'll tell him he has to give you kids.'"

Ann, 45 and divorced, hoped she'd get married again and have someone to care for her. The oldest of seven, she had 17 nieces and nephews and three godchildren when we talked. "I'd better be nice to my nieces and nephews now," she said.

Sarah, who grew up in Scotland and moved to the U.S. for her American husband, said she always wanted a daughter, but her husband decided his two sons were enough for him. "I seriously do worry about old age. I can't see his kids caring whether I live or die. I don't think they'll be there making sure I'm not eating cat food."

A *New York Times* article by Jane Gross called "Single, Childless and Downright Terrified" says it all in the title. Gross acknowledges that her savings and long-term care insurance will take care of the necessities but says, "I'm haunted by the knowledge that there is no one who will care about me in the deepest and most loving sense of the word at the end of my life. No one who will advocate for me, not simply for adequate care but for the small and arguably inessential things that can make life worth living, even in compromised health."

Gross says that she has friends who have agreed to help, but they have their own families to worry about and won't be there for her in the way that she was there for her mother in her later years. And legally they can't. The rules need to change so that friends have the same legal status when it comes to helping in times of trouble.

265

Meanwhile, she's terrified.

Although some worry about the future, most of the women I interviewed don't think it would be different if they had children.

Barbra, 33, said, "I know many older people whose children never visit them, don't take care of them, and take advantage of them by sucking up every penny they have. So I don't think having children makes you any less vulnerable to life's inevitabilities."

A woman I sing with at church was worrying out loud the other day about how she will survive after her husband dies. As far as I know, he's in good health, and she does have adult children who might help, but it weighs on her mind. When he goes, so does his pension, and she won't have enough to live on. They blew their nest egg on a dream house at the beach.

Didn't we all? But for Fred's pension, I'd be a bag lady.

"You can live with me," I said. I didn't think about it first. She had just moved here, and I barely knew her. It just came out, but it makes sense. With my house and our combined incomes, we could make it work. In fact, a third woman would make it even better. I think people bonding together is the best solution, whether they're childless or simply have kids who are too far away or too busy to help. If we don't have an old-fashioned extended family to count on, let's create our own.

I daydream about a house full of people. We would share the cooking and other chores, take care of each other's pets, give each other birthday parties and hug each other as the clock strikes 12 on New Year's Eve.

If one of us were sick, the others would care for her, and when she recovered, oh, how we'd celebrate.

We'd be like TV's "Golden Girls." Kids, husbands? Who needs them?

Mindy, a childless-by-choice psychology professor, had this idea long before I did. When we talked, she said she had concerns about being alone in her elder years with no retirement fund and not enough savings.

"When I get old I will probably start a women's community, and we can take care of each other. I know a lot of other women who are

n the same position. They're really neat ladies, but they're afraid
they're going to wind up bag ladies and not have anybody to take care
of them."

I think we childless women, especially those who are single or
married to older men, ought to think about taking care of each other.
n fact, many already do.

I see women together, out to lunch, going to the doctor, or
playing bingo at the senior center. Yes, many daughters ferry their
ged mothers around, a look of martyrdom on their faces, but I also
see large, happy groups of older women who don't need kids to mess
up their fun. Not so long ago, we sat near a table of a dozen such
women celebrating a 90th birthday. They were laughing and talking
so loudly Fred and I couldn't hear each other. And that cake looked
so good.

That's where I want to be at 90, not being honored by offspring
doing it out of duty and not buying one of those little one-person-
ized cakes at Safeway to eat alone in front of the TV. I want to be
surrounded by peers who love me.

Martha, the writer from California, says she and her sister hope
to end up taking care of each other. "My older sister and I are like
est friends. I'm really close to her two girls and we have these
dreams that when we're really old, we're going to live together, so if
anybody's going take care of her, then they'll have to take care of me,
too."

Kathleen, a church pastor, says she sees friends having a special
rapport with their grownup daughters, and she misses that. But in old
ge, there are no guarantees. She knows a couple of elderly ladies
whose daughters have abandoned them. That is sadder than not
having children at all, she says.

For herself, she has cats and wonderful friends. "One of the
lovely things about being this age is that I have woman friends who
re mature, who are past so much stuff, have realized some real
important truths for ourselves and are living from that base. We are a
lot calmer, a lot more peaceful within ourselves, and I have those
delicious people to relate to in my life. I am just so glad to be here.
My women friends are like gold, just jewels."

267

Sue Fagalde Lick

To young women in their 20s and 30s considering a future without children, I say look at it from my perspective. I know that when you're 26, you don't want to be a matriarch. You're still pretty much a kid yourself. You think of children as needy little creatures who will keep you from developing your career and enjoying your social life. But you will get old, my friends.

I know I sound like an old biddy, but one day, you will see other women in the company of their adult children and grandchildren and feel a tug at your heart. You will, I promise. Even the most child-hating anti-breeding non-mommy will find herself sitting alone at Denny's at a tiny table near the kitchen sneaking glances at the big family seated at the round table in the center of the room. There's Grandma, who happens to be the same age as our childless woman, surrounded by her children and grandchildren, laughing, talking and hugging, all knowing that they belong together, right up to the day they stand beside her casket listening to the priest, minister or rabbi say the final good-bye. And who are you dining with? A dog-eared novel from the secondhand store. Maybe that's okay. Maybe you prefer your book to that noisy crowd. But know what's coming if you accept a childless life.

I'm 60 now. My grandparents are gone, my mother is gone, and my dad is too old to race up to Oregon if I get sick. Fred, the love of my life, is not here. Who will be there for me? Who will be there for you?

My parents took care of their parents when they were dying. Fred and I took care of his parents. When the doctor told his mother she had cancer, we were sitting there with her. We hurried to her house whenever she needed anything and arranged for hospice care when death drew near. I sat with her on the floor when she lost her balance and couldn't get up. I held her when she cried. My sister-in-law and I made Thanksgiving dinner when she was too sick to get dressed or eat. After she died, Fred and I sorted and distributed all of her possessions. We closed her accounts and informed everyone of her death. Who will do that for you and me?

God willing, your spouse or partner will be nearby when you need help. But if not, someone *will* be there, I promise. I don't have children, but I do have other people who love me. So do you. Worried about old age without children? Reach out to your friends and relatives. Promise to take care of each other. You don't have to be alone unless you want to be. Make sure somebody cares enough to drive you to the hospital when you get pink eye and to keep you from eating cat food when you run out of groceries.

24
Alone at the Kitchen Sink

Washing the Christmas dinner dishes in my own grownup kitchen, I think about my mother. She used to work awfully hard on the holidays. Having spent all day cooking and serving, now she had to tackle a ton of dishes, pots, and silverware, plus a greasy roasting pan, all without an electric dishwasher.

Then I remember that after Christmas dinner, she never did this task alone. I was always at her side, towel in hand. By age 10, I could dry as quickly as she could wash.

On Christmas and Thanksgiving, the big wooden silverware box lay on one side of the kitchen table. Pumpkin pies and cakes filled the other side. We stacked the green and white china in the center for Dad to put away later in the cupboard over the refrigerator.

On holidays, Grandma Anne and I would vie for the dishes. I can remember the powder-and-perfume smell, the soft feel of her fleshy skin, and the jersey fabric of the blue and black dresses she wore. Sometimes Grandma Rachel was there, too, not really working much but making that corner between Mom and the cupboards mighty crowded.

My grandmothers are gone. My mother is gone. I have no children. I have three stepchildren, but we rarely spend holidays together. On a recent typical Christmas, Fred's kids celebrated in California while we were snowed in here in Oregon. I cooked a 10-pound turkey for Fred and me. We'd be eating the leftovers all week. I forgot to use the good china, the blue and whites we inherited from Fred's mother. We ate in front of the TV, watching football. We filled our plates from pots on the stove. Fred clinked his coffee mug against my water glass, and that was it. Merry Christmas.

But what if I had a daughter? For a minute, I can almost feel her

Childless by Marriage

standing beside me. She'd be an adult now, perhaps with children of
her own. Maybe a granddaughter would be wielding a towel, too,
stacking dishes on the table. For a second, I can see them so clearly,
hear their voices, remember the wild unwrapping of toys, the
sneaking of olives and salami, the blessing I would say at the big
table the way my mother always did.

This daughter working beside me would be someone I could talk
to, share my concerns, find out what's new with her and the kids . . .
It rips my heart out to think *I could have had that.* I could be the
mother surrounded by family talking, doing dishes, making jokes,
watching TV, snacking on turkey sandwiches and fudge. I wouldn't
be doing all this alone, scrubbing the turkey pan, leaving the dishes to
air dry, going off to type a few words with the Beatles playing in my
headphones.

Dear God, why did you let me do this? Free will? Screw free
will. I want a family. I want to go back and change it all. I want
babies. I want to help my children grow up. I want to hold my
grandchildren in my arms.

Okay, breathe. My father, 700 miles away in San Jose, went out
to dinner by himself. His wife, my mother, died several years ago. His
kids and grandkids live far away.

Some people have cancer. Some folks are lying forgotten in
nursing home beds. Some people are huddling in the rain, hungry and
homeless. I have no right to complain. I took one road, which meant I
could not take the other.

Perhaps I could create an imaginary daughter, the way lonely
children create imaginary friends. I want to call her Amanda; I don't
know why. I had always planned to name my daughter Emily Elaine.
Maybe I'm still saving that name.

We would talk:

Me: The stuffing turned out well, didn't it?

: Yes, just like Grandma used to make.

Me: She always got up at dawn and had the turkey in the oven before
I woke up. Dinner was always ready at 2:00. I don't know how she
prepared that whole meal, especially on Christmas morning, when we
had to go to church, unwrap presents, and eat linguica, eggs and
pancakes before our company came. She was quietly amazing.

Sue Fagalde Lick

A: I really miss her.
Me: So do I.
(Note that my daughter is perfectly unselfish and loving.)
Silence. Amanda dries a handful of knives and places them in the red
velvet slots in the silverware box.
A: Mom, I'm thinking about getting a job.
Me, turning to stare at her: Oh? It seems like you already have
enough to do.
A: I know, but we really want to buy a house of our own. We just
can't afford it on one salary. I didn't want to work full-time until
Jessie and Charlie were both in school all day. But we can't seem to
save enough for a down payment. Jack is working so hard. We don't
waste any money, but our bills suck it all away. We don't want to rent
forever.
Me: Maybe we could help you out.
A: No, that wouldn't be right. But I love you for offering.
Me: Well, any boss would be lucky to have you. And I would be
happy to babysit while you work.
    She reaches over and gives me a hug. I get soapsuds on her arm
and nose. We laugh.
Fred (home and healthy in my fantasy): Hey, what's so funny in here?
Me: Just girl stuff.
Fred: Figures. Is the pie ready?
A: God, Dad, aren't you full? I'm ready to explode.
We hear the trample of tiny tennis shoes that light up in the dark.
Charlie: I don't like pie. I want chocolate cake.
Me: Don't worry. We've got cake for you. (When did I do all this
baking? What about my deadlines? Oh wait, maybe Amanda,
knowing Charlie wouldn't eat pie, brought the cake, or even better,
since I'm fantasizing, cupcakes with little green Christmas trees on
them.)
    Have I lost myself in fiction? How about a whole new genre: life
as you wish it were?
    What if I forgot these people were imaginary and talked about
them wherever I went? People wouldn't question it. The standard 50-
something woman has children and grandchildren.
    So, Amanda and I finish the dishes. We join the men and talk

272

awhile. Maybe we play a game. Do people still play board games anymore or do they gather around the computer?

Maybe I'd have some idea of games to play if I had kids. If we were still in California and a little Kennedyesque, we could play touch football or go for a walk. Maybe Amanda has a dog. No, it's the kids' dog, a terrier of indeterminate breed they rescued from the animal shelter and named "Dude." Yes. And Amanda's husband Jack really hates that dog. Little Jessie might be allergic to him.

Jack's a professional landscaper. Now he's standing at my door, rubbing the stubble on his shaved head. "You gotta get the weeds out of that lawn, Mom."

"I know, I know, but I don't know what to use that won't poison the birds or the dogs or wash out with the next rain."

He sighs. "You can buy stuff that works in any weather and isn't poisonous. I'll come over next week and spread it around. Otherwise the holes are just gonna get bigger."

"Thanks. I don't know what I'd do without you."

I hand Amanda the last pan, which she deftly grabs and dries. Then I open the drain and watch the soapy water disappear, sprinkle Comet cleanser and scrub the pot marks out, then rinse the sink clean. Amanda dries the dish rack and hands me the towel. I wipe my hands. She hangs the rack on the hook under the sink.

"Thanks, honey."

"I couldn't leave you alone with all these dishes."

"Good thing I had a girl, huh?"

We laugh again.

These are the best days of my life. . . .

Of course I could make up a sister or a friend, too, or even transform my husband into someone who did dishes with me instead of watching football. Ah, that's not nearly as much fun. I want the daughter and grandchildren fantasy.

What if I had more than one daughter? What if I had a whole mess of kids, maybe two girls and three boys? Wait, that's a TV show on Sunday nights.

To be honest, I like being able to sit here typing and listening to Beatles music while the last of the dishes soak. If I had company, I couldn't do that. I might be able to scratch a note on the phone pad and stick it in my pocket, but this long period of typing out my fantasy would be impossible.

Shoot, either I live my mother's life or my own. I can't do both.

All this Beatles music brings back memories. I was that teenager doing dishes next to Mom when these songs were new. When the dishpan hit the sink, I scurried to the kitchen and grabbed the dish towel, usually a white cotton one with a day of the week embroidered on it. Mom would be slinging the hot soapy glasses my way. If I didn't hurry, they'd fill the rack and there'd be no room for more.

As I dried, I put the dishes away. Glasses second shelf on the left, plates first shelf, bowls in the upper right cupboard, silverware in the left-hand drawer, frying pans and lids in the stove drawers. Seconds after Mom finished washing, I finished drying.

She would always thank me. Every time.

So, thank you, Amanda. Go relax. Go home? No, stay a while longer. I can't eat all this fudge alone.

And yes, if you're wondering, I do have a dishwasher, but it's not the same.

25
What Will I Leave Behind?

I'm dusting my grandmothers' teacups, carefully arranged on a shelf from Grandpa Fagalde's house. The cups have been in our family for almost a hundred years. I lift them up to admire a white cup with pink flowers, a black one with gold edges, a tall one painted with a picnic scene.

To the left of that shelf is my mother-in-law's china cabinet, which holds her blue and white dishes, my flowered serving platters, and a few special wine glasses.

To the right, under Grandma Anne's framed apple loaf cake recipe are my cookbooks, with comments and dates when I made the various dishes. I have collected so much history just in this one corner of my kitchen. There's more spread all over the house; it's beginning to look like a museum. What will happen to everything when I'm gone?

Dying can be like getting arrested (I hear). You're lucky if you get to put some clothes on before they haul you out empty-handed with nothing but the right to remain silent. So I'm not ready. I probably never will be.

Grandma Rachel wasn't ready to die either. She had stomach cancer, but it had never been diagnosed because she refused to go to a doctor. Finally she fainted in the bathroom. A neighbor found her there and called an ambulance. Grandma Rachel died a month later in the hospital. A writer, artist and collector, she left heaps of books, papers and paintings. She also left rubble from the 1989 Loma Prieta earthquake, which had hit the Bay Area almost two years earlier. She had never found the energy to clean up the broken dishes in the kitchen cupboards or put back the knickknacks that had fallen off the shelves. Her life, like most people's, was a work in progress. She left appointments on the calendar, notes of things to do later, gifts that hadn't been wrapped yet, clothing she had meant to mend or to wash, letters she hadn't finished--so many things she never had a chance to take care of.

Grandma Anne, a diabetic, left cupboards full of cake mixes, some of them starting to rot.

Dead people have no secrets. If you leave an incriminating journal, letters from an old boyfriend, hemorrhoid cream or a Weight Watchers form that shows how much you really weigh, someone will see it.

Most of us, given our druthers, would like to know exactly when we will die and have time to organize everything, put on our favorite outfit, get our hair and makeup done, lie down in a ladylike position and say, *Take me now.* But that's not how it works.

Grandma Rachel was a childless woman. Having outlived her siblings back in New Brunswick, she was fortunate to have her stepfamily and one sister close by in Los Gatos to take care of all the arrangements and clean out her house. I am certain they didn't do things the way she wanted them to be done. She had arranged for cremation by the Neptune Society, but everything else was left to others. Her stepchildren and step-grandchildren oversaw her care in the hospital, planned her memorial service after she died, and decided where to scatter her ashes.

They also decided what to do with Grandpa. Grandma Rachel had been caring for him and ignoring her own illness, so that none of the family realized how sick either one of them was. When she went to the hospital, my parents took Grandpa to a nursing home, and he never returned to that cottage in Seacliff again. My father sold the quaint yellow beach house with Grandpa's roses out front and Grandma Rachel's paintings on the wood-paneled walls to strangers. He assembled a team of family members who kept some of the things in the house, donated some to charity and sold some at a yard sale. What they couldn't sell or give away they tossed into a giant dumpster.

Busy working in Saratoga, I wasn't around for most of the process, but I did make one trip to the house with my parents. Sadness, guilt and excitement over found treasures mingled as I helped my mother empty the kitchen cupboards. I set aside Grandma

Rachel's teacups to add to my collection, along with Grandpa's big wooden cutting board. Did I want the little bookshelf? Sure, if nobody else did. How about the coat rack? Um, okay. I couldn't help remembering Grandma Rachel puttering around in this kitchen, stirring food in pots on the stove, washing dishes, and quizzing me about my boyfriends. Many a Sunday afternoon we all sat around the table, which now had been stripped of its plastic tablecloth and piled with boxes ready to go out to our cars.

Mom and Dad were anxious to get the job done. Sweating and cursing, my father didn't allow time for sentiment. "You want it? Take it. You don't? Throw it out."

My mother found a pile of Grandma Rachel's poems and set them on my pile. To Dad, they were just useless papers, but Mom knew I'd want them. I still have them in an envelope in my cedar chest.

Within a few hours, the kitchen was empty of everything but memories. I drove home with my car stuffed with my grandparents' things. They smelled of smoke and mildew. I felt guilty for taking them, but I also knew that I would love and treasure each thing, remembering where it came from.

At least Grandma Rachel's stepchildren and step-grandchildren made an effort to distribute things properly. Strangers could be the ones pawing through your stuff, taking what they want and destroying the rest.

After we claimed what we wanted for the family, we held an estate sale at Fred's mother's house. The dealers arrived first. They literally ran from room to room, claiming their purchases. Then more casual browsers followed, picking through her dishes, her jewelry, and her books. It was the holiday season, and people took Christmas decorations right off the shelves and walls. I flinched as a stranger carried her bathrobe out. Familiar objects that had been part of a life, part of a home, were now just cheap merchandise that people examined and rejected like crows picking at road-kill. It was snowing outside as a couple of men tied Helen's easy chair into the back of their pickup truck and drove away without bothering to cover it up.

I wasn't supposed to be there; I was just going to unlock the door

Sue Fagalde Lick

and skedaddle, but the organizer's assistant never showed up, so I was drafted to help customers and take their money. I pasted on a fake smile. I wanted to scream at everyone to get the hell out of Helen's house. I would want someone to do the same for me. But who would that be?

Everyone, but especially those of us who have no children, needs to make plans for what we want done with our bodies, our money and our possessions after we die. We need to do it right away and we need to do it officially in the form of a will or a trust to be carried out by someone we know will honor our wishes. If we don't have wills, the law will determine who gets our possessions. If your husband is no longer in the picture, your estate will go to your siblings and their children or your cousins if you're an only child. If you have no family left . . . I don't know.

As I write this, I keep stopping to make lists because I'm beginning to panic. I'm relatively young, but I could die today. I could be killed in a head-on collision on the way to the post office. I could have an aneurysm explode in my brain. So, let's see, the clothing goes to my niece if she wants it, the women's shelter if she doesn't; the crockery to whichever stepchild wants it or needs it; the guitars, my Lord, the guitars, all three of them and both mandolins, no one will love them like I do; and my quilted wall hangings, of which I am so proud, will they end up gathering dust with the doilies and tablecloths in an antique store? What about the teacups? They should go to my children, but I don't have any.

I reach an impasse. When my mother died, I brought home boxes of stitchery books and yarn, sheet music, and clothing, adding them to the things I'd already brought home from my mother-in-law's house. But where will my treasures go? My stepdaughter has no interest in the things that I cherish. We are opposites in every way. My sister-in-law and my niece are not sentimental. Get rid of it, they will say.

Many childless women have children or adults in their lives who are so close there is no question who will care for them in old age and who will dispose, lovingly, of their possessions. My Aunt Edna, at 100, depended on her 92-year-old sister, Virginia and my Aunt Suzanne, her nephew's wife, to take care of everything.

Some name stepchildren, nieces, nephews or friends as heirs.

278

Childless by Marriage

Others insist they really don't care. "Stuff is just stuff; it comes and goes," says Angie, a childless dog psychologist. She just wants somebody to take care of her dogs and preserve the redwoods on her property in the Santa Cruz Mountains. As for the house and what's in it, whatever happens is fine.

The wiser women among us are already making plans. Mary is cultivating her step-grandson's nascent musical talent and planning to leave him her instruments and sheet music. The rest she may donate to her alma mater. Another friend, a writer, has already arranged to leave her books and papers to her university.

Many simply don't know what to do. Joyce, who died of cancer while this book was in progress, said she hoped to leave some things, like her earrings, to her step-granddaughter, but she wasn't sure about "direct female stuff," such as antique quilts that had been passed down through the generations. "I do not want them to go to relatives who don't care, but relatives who don't care is a better choice than, say, a garage sale. If I could find a museum that would take them, that's where they would go."

In other cases, childless women look ahead, see no one coming after them and avoid saving things. Chris says she feels a pang when other women boast that they're putting together photo albums for their children. "I don't have to do that because who's going to want mine?" The thought that she has no one to give her pictures to, no one to care about her things, makes her sad. To protect herself, she tries not to collect things. "Heirlooms, I don't have them. I haven't concentrated on them because who do I give them to?" She's quick to note that if she had children, they might not have wanted her things anyway.

Karey is troubled by the same problem. "I wonder why I'm saving all my family photos, my wedding dress, and all the other sentimental things you collect throughout your life. I have no one to pass them to. I have no one to tell my family heritage and stories to. All these mementos will probably be tossed when I'm gone. It's very disheartening to think that no one will visit your grave, no one will weep at the loss of you. No one will remember you or care that you are gone. "

Jill looks at it from a more practical standpoint. "I'm a pack rat,

279

and I feel sorry for the people who are going to have to clean it up. So I'm actually trying to clean it up now." She has had dozens of friends die from AIDS and has distributed a lot of personal effects. "I know how much easier it is when you have a guideline, so it's very important to me to not be a problem when I'm shipping off."

Only one in four people complete a will before they die. We don't get around to it, we don't want to think about death, or we assume that things will automatically go to the right people. If you have children, they are the legal heirs, but those of us who don't have children need to think extra hard about it. In most states, stepchildren don't automatically inherit anything. Legally, they're not family. Think about that for a minute.

Gay couples have an especially difficult time because most states don't recognize their partnership as a legal entity. The only way to guarantee that one's beloved receives what you want him or her to receive is to take the legal steps to make it official with a will. Otherwise he or she has no legal connection to you. Even in states where domestic partnerships or same-sex marriages are recognized, put your wishes in writing. Gay rights are so volatile these days there's no guarantee the laws won't change before you die.

Making arrangements to distribute your possessions is not as morbid as it seems. In fact, it can be quite satisfying. My mother-in-law labeled everything for the future. We squirmed when, at dinner, she pointed to the tiny diamond earrings she always wore and asked, "Who should have these, Ashley or Harriet?" I wouldn't get them because I didn't have pierced ears. But putting your house in order is comforting, almost as good as cleaning the house, donning your favorite outfit, and saying, *Take me now.*

Besides that, as writer Yuwanda Black noted in an article she posted online about childlessness and wills, organizing your own stuff can really be an act of love. She describes how her stepfather made out a detailed document designating to whom everything should go. He got down to basics like photos and cookware. It made the process after his death much easier. Plus, as Black says, "It provided a sense of comfort to those of us left behind that we knew what he left us was what he wanted us to have. Certain photos went to my sisters, some came to me. Now, when I look at what he left me, it's less about the photo than knowing that he looked at it, took my personality, connection and feelings about it into consideration and said, "This should go to Wanda . . . she'd love that."

In her book *Marriage Without Children*, Diana Burgwyn writes: "Non-parents—if they value themselves and their possessions of a lifetime—look to others in the family, to friends, causes. One of the most treasured items I have is a small vase given me by a childless widower of eighty whose wife had recently died. They had been a devoted couple. He chose with care a number of remembrances from among her personal possessions and gave one to each of her friends, wanting to see their pleasure during his own lifetime."

Most of us don't have vast amounts of money, just keepsakes, clothing, household furnishings and whatever tools we use for our work or hobbies. But even if we have amassed substantial wealth, we need to take steps to make sure that whatever we have goes where we want it to go.

Some people start giving away things they don't need anymore. Grandma Rachel was always giving me books and trinkets. Years before she died, Helen gave me her old clip-on and screw-on earrings because she had gotten her ears pierced and wore only her diamond studs.

My friend Dorothy has followed a Native American tradition of giving things away on her major birthdays. Recently she celebrated her 75th, loading her friends with everything from Christmas ornaments and tiny bottles of shampoo to quilts and wool blankets.

I am the keeper of the family heirlooms. Besides my grandmothers' teacups and recipes, I have Grandma Anne's diamond-and-sapphire engagement ring, Grandma Rachel's poetry, and Aunt Edna's gold earrings. I'm wearing my mother's blue blouse right now. I have photos going back to my Kodak Brownie camera days and more ruby glass than most antique stores.

Many mornings I sit in Grandma Anne's wooden rocker softened with the pillows I crocheted for it and rock as I write in my journal. Occasionally I wonder what will happen to the many volumes of my journal after I die. Should I burn them to hide my secrets? At what point in my life should I do that? Or should I keep them for future biographers, in case I became famous? Do I want my secrets aired? Will anyone care? Maybe I should torch the early '80s when I did a few things I don't think I want to share.

What will happen to the sweaters I knitted, my slides from Portugal, the photos from my weddings? Who will sort them? Who will cherish them?

It's not just a childless thing. If you're lucky enough to have a son or daughter who understands and cares about the same things you care about, you might hope they treat everything with respect. But they might not.

The truth is everybody's stuff is up for grabs. Grandma Rachel never had kids of her own. Grandma Anne had two children and six grandchildren, but both ended up with young folks plowing through their possessions, throwing lots of things away and offering the rest to anyone who wanted them. That's how I got the china cups and a turquoise necklace that Grandma Anne probably never wore.

That's how I got Mom's clothes, too. After she died, I bagged and brought home the ones that fit. My father, distraught from his loss, just wanted them gone.

Nobody cares about your stuff as much as you do.

People do some pretty strange things with their wills. For example, singer Dusty Springfield wanted her cat to sleep on her nightgown and have someone play her records to it every night at bedtime.

Many childless people leave their estates to good causes, such as scholarships, charities, animal shelters, medical research, etc. A Washington couple who had been saving all their lives, left $1.1 million to the Doernbecher Children's Hospital in Portland, Oregon—after bequeathing $5,000 each to a nephew, three nieces and a couple of close friends.

Some folks go a little farther outside the norm. For example, an AOL web page on wacky wills notes that George Bernard Shaw bequeathed millions to anyone who could devise a new alphabet that made more sense than the one we have. It should have 40 letters, he specified. Imagine the size of computer keyboards!

Louis da Camara, a Portuguese man with no family, picked

strangers out of a Lisbon phone book to be his heirs. Ed Headrick, perfector of the Frisbee, asked that his ashes be molded into memorial discs to be sold, with profits to be used for a Frisbee museum. You're tossing it to the dogs wondering, are they chewing on Ed?

My favorite: Ruth Lilly, an amateur poet, left $100 million to a poetry magazine that had repeatedly rejected her work. Go, Ruth.

Here's a good one from the UK: A Mr. F. left several relatives each "one penny, as that is what they are worth as members of my family." Show of hands: how many of us have been tempted to do that?

Without children—and assuming the spouse goes first—we are free to bequeathe as we please.

W e also need to take some control as far as our death and disposition of our bodies. I have written my own obituary. It's in my office in an envelope labeled "If I die." I don't want one paragraph that says, "She was survived by one niece, one nephew and her dog Annie. No services are scheduled." No way. I want the long obituary, the full Catholic farewell package, and my maiden name included on the gravestone, preferably one of those shaped like a book. I'm telling you now in case I'm comatose when the time comes. Also, if there's no hope, for God's sake pull the plug.

Even if you have children, you need to make your wishes known. Sitting at the funeral home with my father and brother after my mother died, we didn't know what kind of funeral she would like. She never wanted to talk about it. We didn't even know what her favorite color was, so we used mine. But at least we were there and we cared.

To whom it may concern: I like red and yellow, and I hate carnations. I also despise organ music. I would prefer a bluegrass gospel quartet, but if that's impossible, tasteful piano music would be acceptable.

Oh, and don't bury me in a dress. I'm more the blazers and blue jeans type. Put my glasses on so I can see where I'm going.

Sue Fagalde Lick

I don't know if it's everyone or just me, but I have a great fear of being forgotten. I want to leave my mark on the world. If nothing else, those who have children will be remembered as their mother.

In her book *Committed*, Elizabeth Gilbert discusses her feelings about being a childless woman. She chose not to have children, having seen too many women sacrifice themselves for their families. In researching marriages all over the world, she found that a consistent minimum 10 percent of women in any society remain childless. These women play an important role in what she calls the "Auntie Brigade." Because their time and money are not tied up with raising their own children, they are free to help anyone who needs it. She lists many famous people who were raised by their aunts, from the Bronte sisters to John Lennon. The world would suffer greatly without these women, she insists.

Aunt or not, many childless people have left their mark in the world, among them Amelia Earheart, Emily Dickinson, Louisa May Alcott, Katherine Hepburn, Marilyn Monroe and Oprah Winfrey. Men who never became fathers include U.S. presidents James Madison, James Buchanan and James Polk, Truman Capote (raised by his aunt), Leonardo Da Vinci, Cole Porter and J. Edgar Hoover.

It is impossible to walk this earth without leaving footprints. Even those of us who are not famous make an impression. We work, we witness, we teach, we give, we love. Just being here makes us part of history.

My mother always said that her greatest accomplishment in life was raising my brother and me and helping to raise her brother's four children. I'm counting on my books and music as my legacy. And perhaps someone will remember me fondly when I'm gone.

When I asked other childless women what they felt their greatest accomplishment in life would be, the question raised hackles among many. Although some mourned that their lives were worthless without children, most said that they certainly didn't need children to make their lives count. "Children are people, not accomplishments," said one. In fact, many claimed that if they *did* have children, it would keep them from doing what they felt was most important in life.

Childless by Marriage

Alice, 37, an accountant, says, "My greatest accomplishment will be to live a life that was fulfilling. This is only possible for me without children."

Barbra, 33, a freelance writer, insists that whether or not one has children should not mark the value of a woman's life. "If everyone's greatest accomplishment was their children, where would that leave us? Would there have been no Rosie the Riveters? No Rosa Parks? No Eleanor Roosevelt? I think it [parenting] should be your most important job, not your greatest achievement."

In general, the women surveyed sought success in their careers and wanted to make the world a better place. If being childless helped them do that, they were satisfied.

So, we're coming to the end of the story. I thought I wanted children, but I got a great husband and a career instead. As so many mothers and non-mothers have told me, too many women give birth for the wrong reasons. They want a baby to cuddle, a child to teach and to show off. They want to fit in with the other mothers, and they want someone to keep them company in their old age. I wanted all that. I think I would have been a fabulous mother. But when you come down to it, isn't the real purpose of giving birth the same as it is with every other creature: to carry on our species, to have someone to take our places on earth when we die? Isn't that why we say we "reproduce?"

As I settle into menopause and graying hair, I'm finding it easier every day to deal with not having a baby, a toddler or a teenager. I know from experiences with my stepchildren that for every hour spent hugging a soft, sweet infant, a mother gets three hours lying awake wondering whether her son will make it home alive from the rock concert and wondering why her daughter is running around in ripped jeans with her derriere hanging out. Babies aren't always sweet. Sometimes they cry for hours. Toddlers will scream "I hate you!" in the cereal aisle at the supermarket. And then they turn into teenagers. I know that later they become adult people, but there are lots of other adult people in the world. They don't have to be mine. Do I wish they were? Yes, but I can't change that now.

A lot of the heartache other women experience, all that empty

285

Sue Fagalde Lick

womb angst, was eased by the instant family that came with my husband. And I don't have stretch marks from giving birth.

Yet it's not the same. A visitor who came to the house to talk about something completely unrelated to her offspring must have mentioned her grandchildren at least six times in 30 minutes. They're such an integral part of her life that she simply can't have a conversation without talking about them. With Fred gone, I rarely have any contact with his children and grandchildren. The connection is broken.

Sometimes I do feel alone. I'm the stump end of a limb of the family tree that will never branch out. Susan Fagalde Lick, it will say, married to Frederick Allan Lick. Period. Empty space with no names. Perhaps some unwitting genealogist will attach Fred's children to my family tree, but they belong on his first wife's tree, not mine.

"She was the one who didn't have any kids," some descendant of my brother or my cousins will say to their children about Aunt Sue. "Married twice and never got pregnant. But she was smart. A writer. She worked for the newspaper and wrote books. She was a good singer, too. Professional. She even performed at the Cow Palace once."

That kind of reputation wouldn't be bad. But what if they just said I was the strange one? They might, you know.

What about that black-haired, brown-eyed girl I could have produced? What about her chubby sisters and brothers? Perhaps we would have had kids with Fred's greenish-brown eyes, my brother Mike's dimples, the strong Fagalde chin, and the crooked Souza nose. They would surely have been nearsighted and needed braces, but we are good, strong people, kind-hearted, morally tough, bright, leaders in the community. I can picture myself sitting on a sofa with the photo albums, talking about Great Grandpa Fagalde, who lived to be 98, or Uncle Mike the lawyer, or Grandma Elaine, who baked the best cookies in the world.

I have not reproduced myself; I have not left a copy behind to carry on when I die.

Then I think of Grandma Rachel, who was not really my grandmother but played that role for most of my life as Grandpa F's second wife. She never had children either, yet she seems every bit as

286

much a part of the family history as any one of us.

I can be like Grandma Rachel. One of a kind. Without children of my own to occupy my days, I can spread my love to all the kids in my life, stepchildren, nieces and nephews, cousins, and friends.

There's a place for me on that family tree. Every branch reaches a stopping place, yielding the sun and rain to another branch destined to grow on. Perhaps that's what I am, the fulfillment of my particular branch. Instead of spending all my energy creating another branch out of myself, I can spread my light and warmth to the branches blooming all around me.

Epilogue

It's the 23rd anniversary of our first date. On this icy-cold December night, the houses and hotels of Nye Beach glitter with strands of red, white and green Christmas lights.

Fred has Alzheimer's Disease, and he doesn't like to go out much, but this is a special day, the day we fell in love. We dress up, drive to Georgie's Bistro, and sit at a table by the window. Outside, I can see the white edges of the surf and the lights of crab boats on the horizon. Inside, in the flickering candlelight, we quietly eat our salads. Fred's impaired memory makes it difficult to carry on a conversation. Whatever we begin, he soon loses the thread; his sentences trickle off into silence.

A young couple with a baby is seated at the next table. The dark-haired tot is probably about eight months, with pudgy cheeks and a killer smile. Sitting in his high chair gnawing on French bread, he sees me watching him. His face lights up, and something inside me melts. All those Christmas card pictures of my contemporaries with their children and grandchildren are getting to me. Our own cards just say "Merry Christmas" or "Have a Great Year." No pictures.

Suddenly the words pour out of my mouth. "I should have had one of those. Our family photos should show more than two people and a dog."

And then, my husband breaks my heart. He looks right at me with those green-flecked brown eyes. "Did you want children?"

He doesn't know? He doesn't remember all those years of angst, the book I'm writing about being childless, the misery of every Mother's Day? Has he forgotten the early talk about adoption and artificial insemination, followed by the conversation about how he just didn't want to have another baby? Does he not remember feeling guilty?

"Yes," I say. "I did."

"Then I was a fool!"

What? "You have made it clear all these years that you didn't want any more children."

Silence.

"I didn't push it because I didn't want to lose you," I say.

He doesn't remember any of it. He's looking at me like he doesn't know who I am. I feel tears welling up. I flee to the restroom. "What have I done?" I ask the wrinkled face in the mirror. Fred might finally be willing to make babies. I guess he forgot he didn't want them, but it's too late.

Back at our table, he's calmly eating his steak. My fish tastes like glue.

The baby waves at me and grins.

Fred passed away on April 23, 2011, after two years and three months living in nursing homes. By the time he left this world, he was more helpless than that baby, but I still loved him with all my heart. Perhaps, in the end, he gave me my parenting experience. All I know is that I chose Fred. Now I go on, mothering my dogs and anyone else who will let me.

Bibliography

Atwood, Margaret. *The Handmaid's Tale,* New York: Houghton Mifflin, 1986

Bialosky, Jill and Helen Schulman, editors. *Wanting a Child.* New York: Farrar, Straus and Giroux, 1999

Breast Cancer Prevention Institute, "Breast Cancer Risks" pamphlet, http://www.bcpinstitute.org

Brooke Medicine Eagle, *Childlessness Transformed.* Mount Shasta, Calif.: Earth Heart, 1989

Brown, Tiffany Lee. "The Bubble of Silence," *Oregon Humanities,* Fall/Winter 2008, pp. 33-35

Burgwyn, Diana. *Marriage Without children: Men & Women Tell What It is Like to be Childless by Choice or by Chance,* New York: Harper & Row Publishers, 1981

Burkett, Elinor. *The Baby Boon: How Family Friendly America Cheats the Childless,* New York: Free Press, 2000

Cain, Madelyn. *The Childless Revolution* Cambridge, Mass.: Perseus Publishing, 2001

Cannold, Leslie. *What, No Baby?* North Fremantle, Australia: Curtin University Books, 2005

Celizic, Mike. "Bogus Baby Boom: Women Who Collect Lifelike Dolls," Todayshow.com, Oct. 1, 2008, http://today.msnbc.msn.com /id/26970782

Childless by Marriage

Clinton, Hillary Rodham. *It takes a village to raise a child*, New York: Simon & Schuster, 1996

Cohen, Rabbi Uri. "Childless or Childfree?" Nishmat, The Jeanie Schottenstein Center for Advanced Torah Study for Women, http://www.nishmat.net/article.php?id=122

Dhaliwal, Nirpal. "The Men Who are Desperate for Kids," London's *Sunday Time,* April 19, 2009

Ehrlich, Paul R. *The Population Bomb,* New York: Ballantine Books, 1968

Furman, Beliza Ann. *Younger Women/Older Men.* New York: Barricade Books, Inc., 1995

Gilbert, Elizabeth Gilbert. *Committed*, New York: Viking Penguin, 2010

Gilbert, Elizabeth. *Eat, Pray, Love,* New York: Viking, 2006

Goodman, A. "Don't miss today." A. Goodman, aish.com, Sept. 24, 2005: www.aish.com/f/hotm/48956846.html

Gross, Jane. "Single, Childless and 'Downright Terrified,'" *New York Times,* July 29, 2008, http://newoldage.blogs.nytimes.com/2008/07 /29/single-childless-and-downright-terrified

Hochschild, Arlie and Anne Machung. *Second Shift*, New York: Avon Publishing, 1989

Jeffers, Susan. *I'm Okay, You're a Brat,* Los Angeles, Renaissance Books, 1999

Jong, Erica. *Fear of Fifty,* New York: HarperCollins Publishers, 1994

Sue Fagalde Lick

Kay, Jonathan. "Send in the Assmonkeys," Pinpricks and Pummelings blog, May 14, 2007, http://politicalmavens.com /index.php/2007/05/14/send-in-the-assmonkeys

Keene, Jennifer. *We Can't Stay Together for the Dogs: A Dog-Friendly Divorce and Break-up Guide*, Neptune, NJ: TFH Publications, Inc., 2010

Kinsley, Craig Howard and Kelly G. Lambert, "The Maternal Brain," *Scientific American*, Jan. 2006, http:// www.scientificamerican.com/article.cfm?id=the-maternal-brain

Lafayette, Leslie. *Why Don't You have Kids: Living a Full Life Without Parenthood*. New York:: Kensington Publishing Corp., 1995

Lifson, Thomas Lifson. "Lost Posterity," *American Thinker*, Aug. 2007, http: //www.americanthinker.com/2007/08/lost_ posterity_1.html

Lutz, Ericka. *The Complete Idiot's Guide to Stepparenting*, Indianapolis: Alpha Books, 1998

Maushart, Susan. *The Mask of Motherhood*, New York: Penguin Books, 1999

May, Elaine Tyler. *Barren in the Promised Land*, Cambridge, Mass.: Harvard University Press, 1995

Millan, Cesar. *Cesar's Way*, New York: Three Rivers Press, 2006

Mohammadi, Kamin. "First Person," *The Guardian*, Oct. 18, 2008, www.guardian.co.uk/lifeandstyle/2008/oct/18/family1

msnbc.com, "More U.S. Women Dying in Childbirth" (Aug. 24, 2007): http://www.msnbc.msn.com/id/20427256
O'Grady, Kathleen. "Contraception and Religion: A Short History," *The Encyclopedia of Women and World Religion*, New York:

Macmillan Reference Library, 1998, www.mum.org/contrace.htm.

Peacock, Molly. *Paradise, Piece by Piece,* New York: Riverhead Books, 1998

Pienta, Amy. "When to Have a Child, If Ever: The Impact in Later Life," University of Michigan News Service, May 1, 2007, http://deepblue.lib.umich.edu/html/2027.42/62014/children.html

Przybys, John Przybys. "Boomers Without Family Connections Must Plan for Future," *Las Vegas Review-Journal,* Oct. 19, 2008, http://www.lvrj.com/living/31247084.html

Rollins, Betty. "Baby Blues: How I Stopped Mourning the Child Who Never Was," *AARP Magazine,* July/August 2003, pp. 37-38

Sheehy, Gail. *Passages in Caregiving,* New York: William Morrow, 2010

Sobie, Amy R. Sobie. "The Protective Effects of Childbirth," *The Post-Abortion Review,* April-June 2001, http://www.afterabortion.org/PAR/V9/n2/childbirthprotection.html

Van Luven, Lynne, ed. *Nobody's Mother.* Toronto: Touchwood Editions, 2006

Welch, Bob. *My Oregon,* Eugene, Ore.: AO Creative, 2005

The Women Who Shared Their Stories

In gathering information for this book, I was blessed by many women who agreed to talk about their lives. In some cases, they shared information they had never told anyone before. Some names have been changed to protect people's privacy. The ages, occupations and hometowns are listed below as they were at the time of our interview. I thank them and the many other men and women who contributed bits and pieces to our shared story of childlessness.

Alice, 37, accountant, Gouldsboro, PA, childfree by choice.

Alison, 28, business consultant, Atlanta, GA. Her husband didn't want children, but she was also wrapped up in her life and her career. She was still thinking she might have children someday.

Angie, 33, dog trainer/psychologist, Los Gatos, CA. Chose not to have children. Later, her husband's illness made it impossible.

Ann, 53, writer, editor, teacher, Los Angeles, CA, childless by choice.

Ann O., 45, special ed teacher/resource specialist for grades K-5, San Mateo, CA. Her husband, who had children from a previous marriage, surprised her by not wanting any more children after they were married.

Barbara, 70, retired nurse, Ashland, OR. Never married, never had kids.

Barbra, 33, freelance writer, McHenry, IL, childless by choice.

Bela, 37, college professor, India. She was having fertility problems and husband wouldn't submit to medical intervention. His family ames her for not giving them children.

nnie, 57, financial analyst, childless by choice and later by cumstance.

eryl, 36, writer, Ray, MI, childless by choice.

ris, age not given, school bus driver, Toledo, OR. Her first husband n't want children. Her second husband had two children and a sectomy.

rissie, 55, writer, Nelson, New Zealand. She said she chose to be ildless because her husband would have been a terrible father.

ane, 37, industrial maintenance technician, Cumming, GA. Too sy with other things to have children.

ise, 49, high school teacher, Newport, OR. Had two abortions, rried later in life, agreed not to have children.

na, 42, court reporter, Fairfax, CA, childless by choice.

i, 57, retired teacher/freelance writer/editor, Grand Junction, CO. ildless due to "incompetent medical care." After suffering the ults of improperly treated infections that scarred her fallopian es, she had a hysterectomy at 45. Also, her first husband kept aying the decision, and her second had a low sperm count.

ie, age not given, business consultant from New Zealand.

, 51, music teacher, Newport, OR. Couldn't get husband to commit children, divorced, never remarried.

50+, yoga teacher, London, England. She dated a married man for rs. She wanted to have a child with him, but he said no. When he ke up with his wife, she thought maybe now they would have a ld, but he went back to his wife. They finally broke up on her 50th birthday. She says he used up all of her fertile years.

Joyce, 54, artist, Florence, OR. She married a man who had two children and didn't want any more. She decided she didn't need children either. She died before this book was published.

Joyce L., 54, court reporter, San Francisco, CA, childless by choice.

Karen M., 38, university director of student services/playwright, novelist, screenwriter, Gold Canyon, AZ, unable to have children and has chosen not to adopt, boasts of being childfree.

Karey, 35, corporate travel agent for Fortune 500 companies, Stratham, NH, childless by marriage. She desperately wants to have a child, but her husband has a child from his first marriage and doesn't want any more.

Kathleen, 55, Unity church pastor, Yachats, OR. Married twice, couldn't conceive, second husband had a vasectomy.

Katreen, 36, writer/actress, Luebeck, Germany. She wanted children, but her boyfriend didn't. When we talked, she was still hoping.

Laura D., 40, massage therapist/day spa owner studying for degree in aviation, Houston, TX. She wanted children, divorced husband over this, now struggling because her current partner doesn't want them either.

Laura T., mid-20s, writer, southern Oregon, never wanted children, was glad to find husband who felt the same way.

Lee Ann, 47, disabled by multiple sclerosis, Yachats, OR. First husband wanted to wait, second had two daughters and a vasectomy. Reversal surgery didn't work.

Linda, 49, writer, training workshop leader, Sidney, OH, childless by choice.

Lisa L., 40, accounting student, Schertz, TX, chose childlessness because her husband's daughters' problems took all of their energy.

Lisa M., 33, writer/craftswoman/customer service rep, Lewiston, ID. Childless by marriage: After a series of relationships with men who either didn't want children or didn't want to commit to marriage, she married an older man with two grown children and two grandchildren. He had had a vasectomy. At one point, she hoped a reversal would be possible, but then she became content to follow her own dreams and enjoy the grandchildren.

Marie, prefers to keep age and occupation private. Married twice, first husband didn't want children, second had two kids and a vasectomy.

Martha,, 48, speech teacher turned writer, Los Gatos, CA. Her husband had two sons from a previous marriage. She felt it was better to put all of their attention on them rather than have more children.

Mary, 56, music director/teacher, Waldport, OR. Never wanted children. Second husband had three adult offspring and a vasectomy.

Matilde, 44, paralegal/shop owner, Boston, MA. Childless because both husbands declined to have children.

Mindy, 54, psychology professor, Prescott, AZ. Childless by choice, reinforced by early menopause after chemotherapy treatment for breast cancer.

rpha, 66, retired Hollywood set designer, Newport, OR. Came from sfunctional family, never wanted children.

achel, 25, BA in modern European languages, freelance journalist, hellaston, Derby, Ireland, childless by choice.

Rebecca R., 42, business manager, City Beach, WA. First marriage, children. Second husband had been married twice before, with children. She still wanted to be a mother, but learned after she had left the country to live with him that he strongly opposed having more children. Ultimately she decided she wanted to be with him more than she wanted to have children.

Robyn, 40, artist/writer/public relations professional, Oyster Bay, NY, childless by both choice and circumstance. Art was always her priority, plus she had health problems and was living with a longtime boyfriend with no plans for marriage or children.

Sarah, 40, executive assistant for a nonprofit organization, Potomac Falls, VA. Her husband has two sons from a previous marriage. He declared after he married Sarah that he did not want any more children. She still hopes to change his mind, but is aware of time running short.

Shelly, 33, physical fitness expert/writer, Bozeman, MT. When we first talked, she said she hadn't wanted children but now had changed her mind and was hoping to be a mother. Three years later she was married and had a baby.

Talia, 34, journalist, Paris, France. She wanted children, but had had problems with a boyfriend and an ex-husband who didn't want to have children with her.

Tanya, 45, nursing home marketing director, Albany, OR. She has two sons from her first marriage, but makes it clear to men she dates that she does not plan to have any more children.

Tiffany, 38, writer/performance artist, Portland, OR, For years, she chose not to have children. When we talked, she really wanted a child, but her husband didn't. When last heard from, she had welcomed a baby girl.

About the Author

Sue Fagalde Lick spent many years as a newspaper reporter, photographer and editor before retiring to become a fulltime writer and musician. She has published books about Portuguese Americans, freelance writing, and life on the Oregon coast. A graduate of the MFA program at Antioch University Los Angeles, she has taught writing at Oregon Coast and Chemeketa community colleges and at conferences and workshops across the country. On weekends, she puts on her music hat as a Catholic music minister and singer-songwriter. She lives with her dog Annie in South Beach, Oregon.

Sue blogs about childlessness at www.childlessbymarriage.com. For more information about her work or to find out about talks, workshops and upcoming events, visit www.suelick.com.

Lightning Source UK Ltd.
Milton Keynes UK
UKHW020900250223
417646UK00009B/1057